I0819262

The Vegan Asian Kitchen

AVERY
an imprint of Penguin Random House
New York

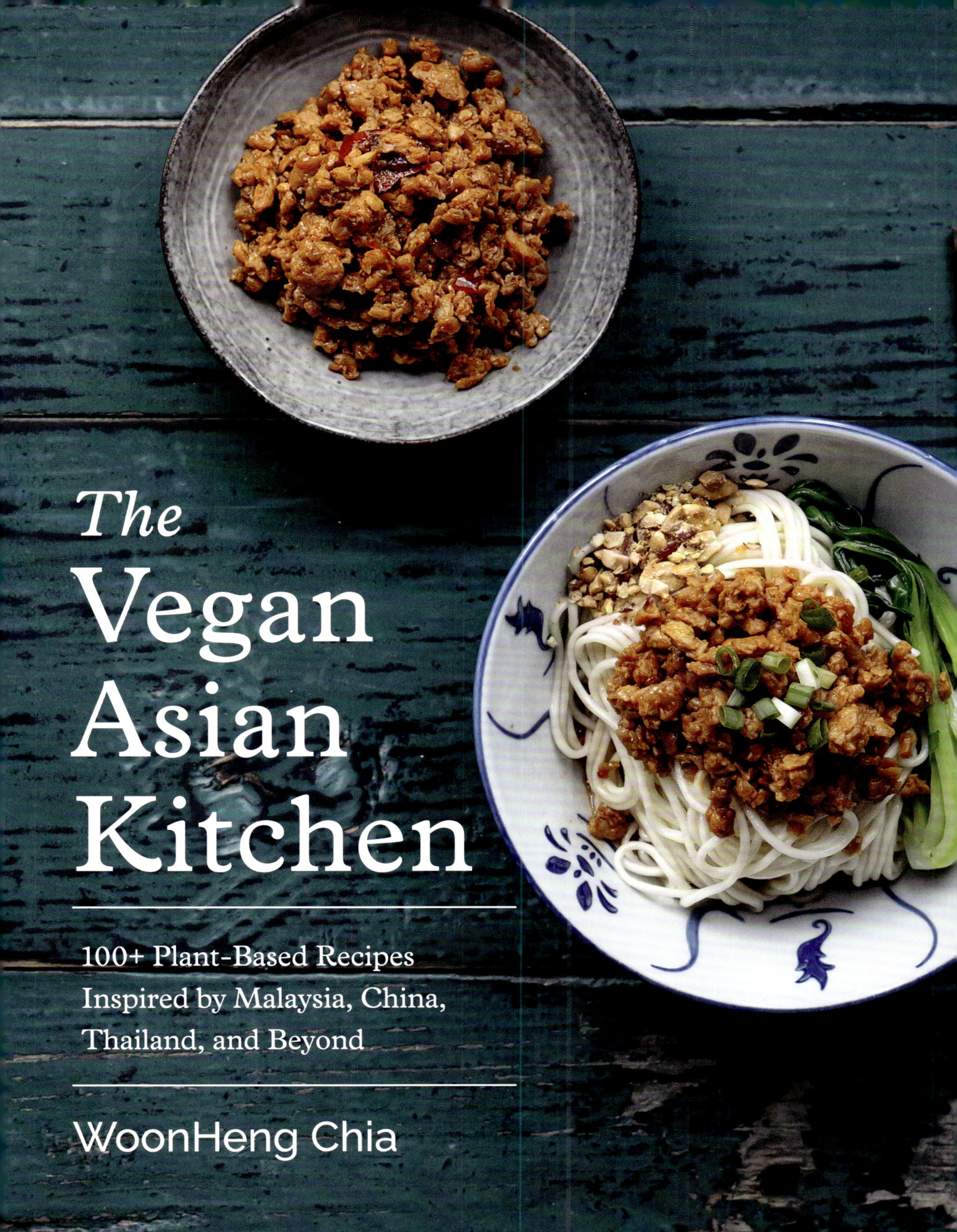

The Vegan Asian Kitchen
100+ Plant-Based Recipes Inspired by Malaysia, China, Thailand, and Beyond
WoonHeng Chia

AVERY
an imprint of Penguin Random House LLC
1745 Broadway, New York, NY 10019
penguinrandomhouse.com

Most Avery books are available at a discount when purchased in quantity for sales promotions or corporate use. Special editions, which include personalized covers, excerpts, and corporate imprints, can be created when purchased in large quantities. For more information, please email specialmarkets@penguinrandomhouse.com. Your local bookstore can also assist with discounted bulk purchases using the Penguin Random House corporate Business-to-Business program. For assistance in locating a participating retailer, email B2B@penguinrandomhouse.com.

Photographs by Shein Loong Yap

Book design by Ashley Tucker

Library of Congress Cataloging-in-Publication Data

Names: Chia, WoonHeng, author.
Title: The vegan Asian kitchen: 100+ plant-based recipes inspired by Malaysia, China, Thailand, and beyond / WoonHeng Chia.
Description: New York: Avery, an imprint of Penguin Random House, [2026] | Includes index. |
Identifiers: LCCN 2025027528 (print) | LCCN 2025027529 (ebook) | ISBN 9780593543290 hardcover | ISBN 9780593543306 ebook
Subjects: LCSH: Cooking, Asian | Vegan cooking | LCGFT: Cookbooks
Classification: LCC TX724.5.A1 C475 2026 (print) | LCC TX724.5.A1 (ebook) | DDC 641.5/6362095—dc23/eng/20250702
LC record available at https://lccn.loc.gov/2025027528
LC ebook record available at https://lccn.loc.gov/2025027529

Printed in China
10 9 8 7 6 5 4 3 2 1

The authorized representative in the EU for product safety and compliance is Penguin Random House Ireland, Morrison Chambers, 32 Nassau Street, Dublin D02 YH68, Ireland, https://eu-contact.penguin.ie.

To my dear
husband and
our two amazing
children

CONTENTS

Fresh vegetables and fragrant herbs fill stalls to the brim at a lively Malaysian pasar.

INTRODUCTION

Food has always been at the core of my life. I love to eat! Tasting and savoring new flavors, textures, and aromas—whether a tangy calamansi squeeze or a smoky chili paste—is as much a part of my creative process as cooking itself. My kitchen has evolved with me through every stage of life, from my childhood to the family I cook for today. I grew up in Malaysia, an ethnically diverse country where the warm air was always scented with the smells of sizzling food, of lemongrass, turmeric, and coconut spilling from hawker stalls and fragrant herbs piled high in wet markets. In Malaysia, food is life, and this shaped my earliest memories.

Little me with Mom and my brother, my food-loving buddy; we always bonded over meals during our younger years off-frame.

My heritage is a blend of Teochew and Cantonese, both groups from southern China's Guangdong province. Teochew cooking is characterized by light, fresh notes—steamed fish kissed with ginger, soothing rice porridge—while Cantonese food offers indulgence—rich dim sum and roasted meats dripping with savoriness. As a child, I lived with a Hakka family, whose rugged mountain roots introduced me to dishes like hearty stuffed tofu, and I later married into a Hokkien clan from Fujian province, masters of noodle stir-fries and umami-packed braises.

I was surrounded by incredible home cooks: my mother, aunts, and grandmothers, and my Hokkien mother-in-law, who I call Mama. Their kitchens were my classroom, and their pots clanged with lessons. Some of my aunts ran food stalls, where I'd perch amid the busy pasar malam. Watching the hustle of these markets instilled in me a deep respect for the art and craft of cooking. As the eldest in my family, I took to cooking for small celebrations, experimenting with pandan or tamarind to re-create childhood favorites. The kitchen became my playground and sanctuary, a place to connect with loved ones and pour myself into my food.

Papa and Mama, my beloved in-laws, fueled both my cookbook and life lessons with love and culinary magic.

Little me (far right) with my grandmother, a cherished cooking inspiration, surrounded by our loving family.

After moving to the United States—where I attended college in Oklahoma, then settled in Dallas—I faced a new challenge. Malaysian food was hard to find. As I learned to build the flavors from my roots, blended with local ingredients and multicultural twists, I crafted an East-meets-West cooking style that's now my signature. I have no formal culinary training—my skills grew from years of hands-on experience. Burnt rice and overseasoned dishes were my teachers, which over time helped me develop an intuitive understanding of cooking beyond recipes.

In 2002 I started volunteering at my Buddhist temple in Dallas, where I watched venerables craft plant-based meats like soy "chicken" and tofu "fish," sparking my passion to veganize traditional Asian classics. Many of my recipes reflect that shift—Eggplant "Unagi" (page 107), Roast Mushroom "Chicken" (page 105), Sweet and Sour "Fish" (page 117), and Lion's Mane Mushroom Rendang (page 95) reimagine dishes from my youth, while keeping their traditional names because they hold meaning for me. It's my way of showing that flavors can be enjoyed by everyone, without losing their essence.

My husband and me, diving into new flavors with endless love. He's my fearless food explorer and the talented photographer of this book.

I've also included a section in this book on everyday home cooking—in chapter 2, "From Mom's Roots to My Kitchen"—with dishes that might not be found in restaurants but are the soul of my home cooking. These are the meals I grew up with, like my mom's Lotus Root Soup (page 73), Spicy Tempeh Goreng (page 75), Onion Fried "Egg" (page 83), and Nai Yau Gu (page 93), the ones that bring a family together around the table. And there's a taste of Malaysian street food too, bringing the sizzling aromas of pasar malam and kopitiam (café-style) fare into your kitchen, like Char Kuey Teow (page 249), Apam Balik (page 327), and crispy Roti Empat Segi (page 333).

My husband and children, my true recipe testers and critics, savored every dish in this book with love.

One of the most exciting additions to this book is the Sichuan section, inspired by the past few years when my family and I moved to Chengdu, China. The bold and aromatic mala flavors of the local cuisine left a lasting impression on me, and I wanted to bring dishes like Lao Gan Ma Thousand-Layer Tofu (page 129), La Zi Ji (page 139), and Chao Shou (Wontons in Chili Oil, page 177) to your kitchen. These recipes are a tribute to the Sichuan dishes that have captivated me, and to the locals who I've shared these dishes with.

A market scene in Chengdu, my true inspiration for Sichuan food, where I've loved cooking and living.

My life has always revolved around food—not just as a necessity, but as a source of happiness, creativity, and connection. My hope is that this cookbook serves as a guide and a resource, a collection of recipes and techniques that inspires you to cook with confidence, try out new dishes and flavors, and create meals that bring joy and nourishment to your loved ones. *The Vegan Asian Kitchen* is the culmination of what I've learned and lived so far, but it's also an ongoing journey. I'm excited to see how it becomes a part of your own culinary adventures!

Terms You'll Find in This Book

What is kopitiam?

Kopitiam is Hokkien for "coffee shops." In the morning, these old-school cafés would be filled with people, their chatter loud over the humming fans and the rich aroma of kopi beans roasted with margarine and sugar, a Malaysian specialty that gives the coffee its deep flavor. My family loved to start our mornings together, sipping kopi-o (black coffee with sugar) from small ceramic cups and eating kaya butter toast (soft bread with coconut jam) alongside hawker classics like char kuey teow and nasi lemak. My late grandma would cool her coffee in the saucer—a quirky habit I adored. These kopitiam, with their casual environment, strong coffee, and good food, are still a cornerstone of the Malaysian culture and landscape to this day.

What is dai chow?

Dai chow (大炒), or "big stir-fry," is a Malaysian-Chinese tradition: casual, open-air stalls or eateries where chefs sling woks over roaring flames. Known for their lively, slightly chaotic atmosphere, these eateries serve up dishes made to order and shared family-style. Usually we'd order plates like chili crab, or stir-fries like sweet and sour pork or salt-and-pepper tofu—it was always a treat to dine out instead of cooking at home. Air-conditioning was rare back then, but the thrill of people-watching and sharing dishes with my family made these trips the highlight of my childhood. In this book, I've veganized some of my favorite dai chow classics.

What is pasar malam?

Pasar malam, Malay for "night market," is an open-air market that comes alive after dusk, streets with neon-lit stalls that sell street food, desserts, clothes, and trinkets. The air wafts with the sizzle of char kuey teow and the fragrance of steamed kuih. These markets draw in tourists and locals alike. My husband and I love wandering through the bustle, grabbing grilled skewers or sticky sweets to share, as a way to unwind at night and savor the local food scene.

What is pasar?

Pasar, Malay for "market," refers to the open-air daytime wet markets that Malaysians visit for produce and cheap eats. I'd go with my grandma in the mornings, walking around the lively stalls and hawkers selling fresh meat, seafood, dried goods, flowers, and vegetables, trying not to slip on floors slick with water or melted ice (thus the name *wet market*). While Grandma haggled for groceries, I'd hang out at the food stalls, munching on breakfast—maybe a steamed bun or a bowl of hot noodle soup. With its clatter of cleavers and abundance of food, this place could wake me up.

Kopitiam

Pasar malam

Dai chow

Pasar

ESSENTIAL PANTRY INGREDIENTS

Wet Seasonings

Soy Sauce

Growing up, I often heard "si yao lou fan" (Cantonese for a poor man's meal of soy sauce with rice) used to describe something basic, but to me, it was heaven. I'd happily dig into a bowl of rice with just soy sauce. Now, I use it both as a seasoning and for cooking, tossing it with noodles or adding a splash to build flavor in stir-fries. I stick with Chinese soy sauce—a dark, salty liquid made from fermented soybeans, wheat, and salt. Lee Kum Kee Premium is my go-to. For Thai stir-fries and noodle dishes, I reach for Golden Mountain brand seasoning sauce, a variant of soy sauce that's my secret weapon. It adds a depth of flavor that makes a Thai dish taste like a Thai dish, in my opinion.

Dark Caramel Soy Sauce

Dark caramel soy sauce, or lou chao in Cantonese, is thicker, less salty, and sweeter than regular soy sauce, with a caramel note that turns dishes a rich brown. My mama always reached for it when braising or stir-frying in the wok, thanks to its appetizing color and savory depth. It can taste bitter straight from the bottle, but heat transforms the flavor. I recommend Cheong Chan Dark Soy Sauce, also labeled Cheong Chan Cooking Caramel, for its thick, syrupy texture, perfect for the majority of recipes calling for dark caramel soy sauce. For a thinner, saltier variety (which I just call "dark soy sauce"), I love Lee Kum Kee Dark Soy Sauce, especially in Si Yao Wong Chao Min (King Soy Sauce Fried Noodles, page 155).

Some of my must-have sauces, brimming with flavor.

An artisan stirring a vat of rich chili bean paste at the Pixian doubanjiang museum in Pidu.

Vegetarian Oyster Sauce

Oyster sauce, traditionally a glossy brown reduction from oysters, brings intense umami and mild sweetness. It's thicker than soy sauce, with a velvety, briny note Chinese cooks call xian. In my kitchen, we use Lee Kum Kee's Vegetarian Oyster Flavoured Sauce, a mushroom-based version that matches the savory richness. Before vegan oyster sauce was common, I once re-created a similar sauce with mushrooms—now, it's easy to find at grocery stores or Asian markets.

Sesame Oil

Sesame oil, pressed from toasted sesame seeds, is a dark amber oil with a deep, nutty aroma, used throughout this cookbook whenever recipes call for it, like Ginger–Sesame Oil Fried Rice (page 275). I love its distinct scent and prefer Kadoya Toasted Sesame Oil for its roasted intensity. Use sesame oil as a finishing touch—it is potent when drizzled over stir-fries, soups, or chilled dishes.

Chili Paste

Chili paste, a thick mash of ground chiles, varies from raw to ready-to-eat. Boh Chili Paste, raw and lightly seasoned, is my shortcut for sambal when I'm short on time—just cook it down with other ingredients (check if it's vegan, as some may include shrimp paste). Fully cooked versions are handy condiments, ready to spoon onto dishes straight from the jar.

You Po La Zi (Chili Oil)

You po la zi is a spiced chili oil loaded with aromatics like garlic and star anise, delivering smoky, tingling heat. I was introduced to this magic condiment in Chengdu—it's basically chili oil on steroids. An effortless way to add irresistible flavor to dumplings, noodles, or rice, like in the sauce for Chao Shou (Wontons in Chili Oil, page 177).

Lao Gan Ma

Lao Gan Ma is another shortcut condiment that adds a savory punch to any dish. There are many kinds, but my favorite is the variation with fermented black beans. It's especially tasty with tofu (see Lao Gan Ma Thousand-Layer Tofu, page 129).

Bean Paste

Bean paste is a flavor powerhouse. Here's the breakdown of the main types:

- **Doubanjiang (Pixian/Sichuan):** Spicy, salty, and packed with umami, this dark red paste is made from fermented broad beans (fava beans) and essential for Sichuan dishes like Mapo Tofu (page 209). Its earthy savoriness delivers heat and a rich color.
- **Taucu (Yellow Bean Paste):** Milder and slightly sweet, this Malaysian favorite is made from fermented yellow soybeans, with whole beans for extra texture. Use it for stir-fries, sauces, and stews like Yong Tau Foo (page 79).

- **Tianmianjiang (Sweet Bean Paste):** This sweeter, northern Chinese cousin of bean paste is a fermented concoction of wheat flour, soybeans, sugar, salt, and water. It's rich and slightly sweet, and often used in spring rolls or to enhance marinades.

Chinese Black Vinegar

Chinese black vinegar, aged from fermented rice and grains, is dark and aromatic, with smoky, earthy notes and a subtle sweetness that makes my mouth water. It's less sharp than rice vinegar, cutting richness in braises or adding brightness to hot and sour soup and dumpling dips, especially paired with ginger. I recommend Chinkiang or Zhenjiang black vinegar, or Baoning vinegar (a wonderful Sichuan variety) if you can find it.

Coconut Milk

Creamy from pressed coconut flesh, coconut milk brings richness and a tropical fragrance to curries, nasi lemak (page 295), or kuih muih (see page 302). In the US, look for the canned or boxed version, not the thin sweetened drink in beverage cartons. In Malaysia, it's called santan, and the best coconut milk is thick and fresh from markets or pressed at home, with a nutty depth that clings to rice or simmers into gravy. My mama's mi hoon kuih wouldn't be as fragrant without it. Coconut cream is a thicker, richer version of coconut milk, but both serve the same purpose in most recipes. I use full-fat coconut milk like Nature's Charm or Thai Kitchen, and always simmer it gently in dishes. Never a hard boil, as my grandma taught, or the oil will split.

Shaoxing Cooking Wine

Shaoxing cooking wine, an amber fermented rice wine, has a nutty, caramel taste with a strong alcohol scent and savory depth. My mom splashes it into stir-fries to cut bitterness or boost savoriness, especially for vegetables like gai lan. I use it for marinades, sauces, and deglazing; dry sherry works as a sub.

Mijiu

A clear rice wine that's a staple in my pantry—lighter and milder than Shaoxing cooking wine, with a clean, sweeter note that lifts dishes without overpowering them. I reach for it in rich preparations like San Bei Tofu (page 191) to round out flavors and add subtle aroma.

Calamansi

Calamansi, a tiny citrus fruit with green skin and orange flesh, blends tart lime-lemon sourness with sweetness. I squeeze it over spicy Curry Laksa (page 263) to balance the heat. During Chinese New Year, my grandmother preserved calamansi from nursery trees—symbols of prosperity—to use in refreshing drinks we enjoyed long after.

Tamarind

Tamarind, or asam, is a sticky, sour fruit with a complex acidity. As a kid, I snacked on dried tamarind rolled in sugar, eating the membranous pulp and spitting out the seeds. For cooking, I use asam jawa blocks: soak the paste in hot water, mash, and strain the pulp for a juice to flavor sambal or curries. It's a sourness that citrus can't quite replicate.

Dry Seasonings and Spices

Kosher Salt

I stick with Morton kosher salt as the standard for my recipes, since it's the easiest to find in most stores. If you're using Diamond Crystal brand kosher salt, which is lighter and less dense, you'll need to bump up the volume a bit, roughly 1.5 times. So, for every 1 teaspoon of Morton, use 1½ teaspoons (or ½ tablespoon) of Diamond Crystal. Always start on the lighter side with salt, then adjust as needed to suit your taste.

Mushroom Seasoning

Mushroom seasoning or mushroom bouillon powder, derived from dried mushrooms, is my trick for succulent plant-based dishes. The fine granules are packed with natural glutamates, bringing concentrated umami to soups, stir-fries, and veggies. A little goes a long way; I use Po Lo Ku Mushroom Seasoning from Taiwan and bump down the salt.

White Pepper

White pepper makes frequent appearances throughout this book. It's paler and subtler than black pepper, and a dash or two delivers a cleaner, sharp pepperiness with a faint musky note, lending warmth to soups, stir-fries, and rice. Any brand works, but I personally love Sarawak White Pepper, a Malaysian brand.

Sichuan Peppercorns

Tiny husks with a citrusy, numbing buzz, used either whole or ground.

- **Red Sichuan Peppercorns** have a warm, earthy flavor with a citrusy tingle. I like to grind them into powder to sprinkle easily over dishes like Mapo Tofu (page 209).
- **Green Sichuan Peppercorns** are unripe and vibrant, with a fresh, floral aroma. They're more fragrant than red peppercorns and bring a strong numbing kick.
- **Teng Jiao:** A distinct green variety, found fresh or dried, they pop with a zesty, pungent sting that's less numbing than green.

To grind peppercorn powder, lightly toast the whole peppercorns in a dry pan and then blitz in a coffee grinder or blender until fine. Sift through a fine-

mesh sieve to remove any husks and store in an airtight container for maximum freshness. When buying dried peppercorns, look for bright red or green peppercorns that have cracked open—these are freshest and most potent in aroma.

Curry Leaves

These small, glossy leaves add a pungent, citrusy warmth: Just one sprig can transform a curry. Fresh or frozen is best, but dried works in a pinch. Store fresh leaves in the fridge and let them dry naturally to extend their life.

Pandan Leaves

Long, green blades that smell like tropical vanilla and infuse rice or desserts with a sweet, nutty fragrance. This flavor is the essence of many desserts and curries I grew up with (my neighbor had a potted pandan plant, a gift that kept giving!). *Tip:* When you find fresh pandan leaves at the market, buy them in bulk, wash them, and freeze them. This way, you'll always have pandan leaves on hand.

Chai Po (Preserved Radish)

Chai po, preserved radish (cai bu in Mandarin) or salted radish, is a crunchy pickle with a sharp bite, made by salting and drying daikon radishes. Store-bought varieties come in salty and sweet varieties, sold either whole or in preminced packets. It's eaten with porridge, or used to add a salty crunch to Chai Po "Egg" (page 85) or Chwee Kuih (page 313). Be sure to rinse it thoroughly to remove excess salt before using.

Suan Cai (Pickled Mustard Greens)

Mustard greens that are salt-preserved, pickled in brine, and sold in packets or jars, used widely in Chinese cuisine and a Teochew staple. Some include chiles for kick. Their refreshing acidity brightens rich dishes like Suan Cai Yu (page 141) or noodle soups. I like to rinse them first to reduce their saltiness.

Chinese Black Mushrooms

The first thing I packed when I moved to the US was two big bags of dried shiitake mushrooms! They are essential in my kitchen for flavor: The dark, meaty caps have a woodsy, umami depth. Soak them until plump for soups or braises, and save the flavorful soaking water for stock.

Wood Ear Mushrooms

A jet-black and crinkly fungus usually sold dried, these mushrooms are slippery and mild in flavor with a snappy crunch. I toss them in vegetable stir-fries and braised dishes once rehydrated. Just a heads-up: Don't overcook them in soups, as they can turn slimy when boiled.

Dried Chiles

Whole dried chiles pack smoky, sweet heat. Snip into pieces for stir-fries like La Zi Ji (page 139), or soak first for making sambal. The dark ones are milder, and the brighter ones generally hotter. Wear gloves when handling.

Chili Powder

Ground dried chiles like aromatic Sichuan chili powder or vibrant red Korean chili powder (gochugaru) are essential for making chili oil. As a seasoning, these have more flavor than the dried crushed red pepper flakes you might use on pizza.

Banana Leaves

Waxy and broad, banana leaves add a wonderful aroma to dishes as they steam. They're used to wrap rice dishes like Nasi Lemak Bungkus (page 295) or Kuih Seri Muka (page 307).

Butterfly Pea Flower (Bunga Telang)

Dried butterfly pea petals, which stain foods a vivid blue, are used in kuih muih (see page 307) and kerabu, an iconic Malaysian blue rice dish. To extract the natural coloring, simply boil the dried flowers in water and strain out the tea. Add a splash of lemon juice (or other acid) to turn the blue to purple. Find dried petals online at Amazon or at Asian groceries.

Types of Tofu

Tofu, pressed from coagulated soy milk, is a shape-shifter in the kitchen. It can be mild and creamy or firm and chewy, depending on the variety. I call soybeans the "mighty bean" for their versatility. Here are the kinds I like to use:

Soft/Silken Tofu

Silky and custard-like, it jiggles like pudding with a delicate, almost milky taste that melts on the tongue. It's fragile—handle it gently. Use for velvety soups or Mapo Tofu (page 209).

Medium-Firm Tofu

Soft yet sturdy, with a tender bite and subtle soy flavor that's faintly nutty. It holds its shape in San Bei Tofu (page 191), soaking up sauces without crumbling.

Firm Tofu

Dense and meaty, it's got a satisfying chew—pan-fry it golden for a crisp shell in Pad Kra Pao Tofu (page 187) or blend for stuffing in Yong Tau Foo (page 79).

Frozen Tofu

Frozen firm tofu turns spongy and porous when thawed—like a chewy honeycomb. It drinks up the sauce in Sweet and Sour Tofu "Pork" (page 203).

Semi-Fresh Tofu Skin
Pressed Tofu Sheets
Bai Ye
Smoked Tofu
Dou Bao

Smoked Tofu

Firm, smoked tofu with a dark, woody rind and a bacon-like savoriness that lingers. For dishes like Stir-Fried Celery with Carrot and Konnyaku (page 55), slice it thin for a chewy, meaty bite.

Tofu Puffs

Golden, deep-fried cubes, airy and spongy inside with a craggy, oil-kissed skin that crackles faintly. They soak up curry sauces like a dream (see page 71).

Tofu Skin

Thin sheets skimmed from the surface of boiling soy milk, they're nutty and chewy with a slight sweetness—like a soy crepe that bends to your will. They come in a few forms:

- **Dried Tofu Skin (Fu Zhu):** This is crisp and golden when dry, like fragile parchment, and softens into a chewy, wrinkled layer after soaking—great for braises or stir-fries.
- **Semi-Fresh Tofu Skin:** Found pliable and slick in the frozen section—not fully dried, with an oilcloth feel and a glossy sheen—it crisps at the edges when fried, or steams into a tender wrap for Sin Jyuk Guen (page 157).
- **Fresh Tofu Skin (Dou Bao):** Soft and velvety with a milky soy taste, this Chinese-style tofu skin is available in the US fresh or frozen, used for steaming in Dou Bao "Fish" (page 113).

Pressed Tofu Sheets (Gandoufu)

Leathery and compact, pressed between cloths—sometimes spiced or smoked as doufugan—they're dense with a firm, almost jerky-like bite and a concentrated soy taste. Slice them thin for salads after a blanch in hot water (see page 211) or stir-fries—they're tough enough to toss in the wok.

Bai Ye

"Thousand-layer tofu" isn't true tofu, but a soy protein with a bouncy, seafood-like snap and faint fishy tang. Pan-fry it oil-free—it puffs up, then shrinks—and it's perfect for mimicking fish cakes in thousand-layer tofu (page 129).

Fermented Tofu (Fu Yu)

Firm tofu cubes fermented with salt, rice wine, and sometimes red yeast rice that turn creamy, pungent, and funky—like a salty ripe cheese. It's the star in Fu Yu Ung Choy (page 69), lending a rich, savory depth.

Flours and Starches

Rice Flour

Refers to finely milled rice flour. It's powdery and light and turns sticky when you add water. I use it for dumpling skins, tender noodles, or Curry Chee Cheong Fun (page 259). Thai-style

Erawan Three Elephant is my pick—it's water-milled for a silkier feel than gritty Western brands.

Tapioca Starch

Made from cassava root, tapioca is a fine, starchy powder that gels into a stretchy, glossy consistency. It's magic for making bouncy doughs and chewy noodle strands, or for thickening sauces.

Wheat Starch

Cheng fen, a pale, airy starch sifted from wheat, gives dumpling wrappers their translucent, soft yet snappy skin, hugging around fillings. Store extra starch in the freezer to keep it fresh.

Noodles

Rice Vermicelli

These thin noodles made from rice flour arrive dried and pale—almost translucent—but turn soft and white once soaked. Rehydrate until they're pliable, and if stir-frying, add splashes of water to the pan since they absorb liquid quickly. Once cooked, they're tender and slurpable, with a light chew.

Yellow Oiled Noodles

These are wheat-based noodles, treated with alkaline water for a distinct flavor and yellow color—some brands sneak in eggs too, so check the ingredients. They are par-cooked and coated with oil. I recommend a quick blanch in hot water to wash off the oil. They star in dishes like Mee Goreng (page 253) or Mee Jawa (page 255).

Ramen Noodles

Stealing my heart with their alkaline tang and springy texture, ramen noodles are usually made with wheat flour, egg, and a touch of alkaline water. My favorite vegan brand is Sun Noodles—it nails that yellow color and chew and is found fresh in the refrigerated section in Asian supermarkets and major grocery stores. To cook, loosen the bundle, boil until just past al dente, shock in cold water, and then reboil in hot water. This cuts the bitterness and boosts that QQ (aka chewy, springy) bounce—try it in Malaysian-Style Wonton Mee (page 229).

Udon

Steps in for the thick yellow noodles I can't find in the US for KL-Style Hokkien Mee (page 231). Made simply from wheat flour, water, and salt, they can be found fresh or frozen in packs. I pick the thicker ones for their hefty chew—they're ideal for soaking up dark, rich sauces.

Mung Bean Vermicelli

Delicate threads made from mung bean starch, glassy and translucent when dry, softening into a slippery, chewy bite after soaking. I use them in Pad Woon Sen (page 241), where they absorb Thai flavors like a dream. Soak them in warm water until flexible—don't overdo it or they'll turn to mush—then stir-fry quickly for that perfect, slightly bouncy texture.

Asian Greens and Vegetables

Yu Choy (Choy Sum)

Yu choy, or choy sum in Malaysia, is a leafy green with tender, mild leaves and sometimes little yellow flowers. I love stir-frying it or pairing it with Malaysian-Style Wonton Mee (page 229) or Pan Mee (page 225) for a fresh, gentle bite.

Taiwanese Cabbage

Taiwanese cabbage, my pick over the standard kind, is usually flatter with a hollow core and leaves like a croissant's flaky layers. Sweeter and crunchier than green head cabbage, it holds up in the wok without turning soggy—great for stir-fries or as a crisp side.

Eggplant

Japanese eggplant, with its tender flesh, tiny seeds, and thin skin, is my go-to. Look for slender, light ones with smooth purple skin and a white brim. I also use round eggplants, diced small, in potstickers (page 167) with other vegetables.

Mung Bean Sprouts

Sprouted from mung beans, these crunchy delicate sprouts are crisp and mild, starring in noodle dishes or in a stir-fry (page 59). They are sold in prepackaged portions or in bulk at Asian supermarkets. (*Note:* These are smaller than soybean sprouts.)

Water Spinach

Known as kangkung in Malay and ung choy in Cantonese, water spinach has long, hollow stems and arrow- or heart-shaped leaves with a juicy, slightly earthy taste. I grew up eating it stir-fried with sambal at hawker stalls, but my Fu Yu Ung Choy (page 167) recipe pairs it with fermented bean curd for a funky, savory twist. It cooks fast, staying tender-crisp.

Chapter 1

The Basics

Sauces and Condiments

When I started sharing my recipes on Instagram back in 2018, I soon realized that the sauces I relied on at home weren't always easy to find in stores, making it tricky for people to re-create my dishes. I decided to take matters into my own hands and develop some recipes for basic sauces from scratch.

One of the first was a Vegan Fish Sauce (page 49), which I reverse engineered by studying the label on a bottle of Vietnamese vegetarian fish sauce. My husband, who's got an exceptional palate, was my go-to for taste testing. He can tell you exactly when something is missing or when a flavor is just a bit too much. While this fish sauce doesn't have the strong briny taste of seafood, it's the one I use for all my Thai dishes and more to amp up their umami.

Malaysian cuisine has always been at the heart of my cooking, and sambal is a staple in my fridge. Making it at home requires just a handful of ingredients, and it's wonderfully versatile. Use it in curries and rendang, to spice up tempeh and tofu, or mixed with tomato and onion to create a sambal base for Nasi Lemak Bungkus (page 295). If you're in the mood for something savory at breakfast, try slathering it on toast and topping it with cucumber slices for a quick bite.

My husband and I are also absolutely hooked on my homemade XO Sauce (page 45). Packed with umami from mushrooms and with just enough heat to keep things interesting, it's a condiment that begs to be eaten with fried rice and noodles. This section also contains elements that are found in the recipes for many other dishes in this book, like Basic Vegetable Stock (page 37), Chili Oil (page 41), and Pickled Green Chiles (page 39). Once you start using these building blocks, you'll wonder how you ever cooked without them!

Basic Sambal

1 cup (25 g) dried chiles

1 golf ball–sized clump (35 g) of tamarind paste

¾ cup (190 ml) hot water

8 ounces (225 g) fresh red chiles, such as Fresno or red jalapeños, stems removed, flesh roughly chopped

One 4 by 6-inch (10 by 15 cm) piece of dried kombu, soaked in warm water until soft (10 to 30 minutes, depending on the kombu's thickness)

5 large shallots, peeled, or 3 tablespoons (45 ml) store-bought shallot purée

¾ cup (180 ml) cooking oil

1 tablespoon palm sugar

1 teaspoon kosher salt

¼ teaspoon mushroom seasoning

Makes about 1 cup (240 ml)

Sambal is far more than just a chili paste in Malaysian cuisine—it's a flavor base and a finishing accent packed with heat and complexity. I stir it into rich curries, spoon it over fragrant nasi lemak, or spread this spicy condiment on toast. It's my go-to for adding depth of flavor to whatever I'm cooking. The foundation of a good sambal is all about the chiles: fresh chiles for vibrance and dried chiles for a smoky, layered depth. Traditionally, sambal leans on belacan, a pungent fermented shrimp paste, and plant-based alternatives were hard to track down in the past. So I turned to kombu instead, a dried seaweed with a slightly briny taste that gives the sambal just the right savory body.

Making sambal from scratch takes patience, but the payoff is worth it. You cook the chili paste low and slow, stirring constantly so it doesn't burn, until the oil separates and rises to the top—a stage called pecah minyak, or "breaking oil." That curdled look signals that the flavors have melded into a rich, beautiful texture. Keep it in an easy-to-find spot in the fridge; it's the kind of condiment you'll grab often.

1. **Soften the chiles:** Rinse the dried chiles, remove their tops, and shake out the seeds. Bring a large saucepan of water to a boil, then add the chiles and cook until they soften, 3 to 5 minutes.

2. **Make the tamarind juice:** In a small bowl, combine the tamarind paste with the hot water and let it soak for 5 to 10 minutes. Strain out the solids, reserving ½ cup (120 ml) of the tamarind juice.

3. **Make the sambal:** In a high-speed blender, blend the softened dried chiles, fresh chiles, softened kombu, shallots, and the reserved ½ cup (120 ml) tamarind juice until smooth, about 1 minute.

recipe continues

4. Heat the cooking oil in a large nonstick pan over medium-low heat. Carefully pour in the blended paste (it may sputter). Cook, stirring occasionally, until the oil begins to separate from the chili paste (a stage known as pecah minyak) and the mixture appears curdled, about 30 minutes.

5. Stir in the palm sugar, salt, and mushroom seasoning. Cook for another minute to fully incorporate the flavors, then remove from the heat and allow the sambal to cool.

6. Store: Transfer the sauce to a clean, sterilized jar, ensuring that the oil completely covers the solids—this will preserve the mixture and extend its shelf life. When using, always scoop out the sambal with a clean spoon to maintain its freshness. The sauce will keep for up to 2 weeks in the refrigerator, or frozen for up to 2 months.

"Chicken" Rice Chili Sauce

Makes about 2 cups (480 ml)

I call this "Chicken" Rice Chili Sauce—not because there's chicken in it, but because it was the very first chile sauce I came across as a kid, and it was always served with chicken rice. So now, whenever someone in my family asks for red chile sauce, they know exactly which one they're getting.

What sets this sauce apart is its simplicity. It's just fresh red chiles blended with aromatics and tart lime juice and vinegar—no cooking required. The result is a condiment with a bright burst of lime and vinegar that cuts through the richness of dim sum and carbs, adding a little heat to just about anything. You can serve it with stir-fried noodles, drizzle it on Ginger-Garlic Butter Rice (page 289), or use it as a dipping sauce for taro cake (page 321) or pan-fried daikon cake (page 163). The original recipe calls for calamansi, a slightly sweeter citrus available at Asian groceries, but if you can't find it, lime works as well, with its more straightforward acidity.

7 ounces (200 g) fresh red chiles, such as red jalapeños

One 2-inch (5 cm) piece (15 g) fresh ginger, peeled and roughly chopped

3 garlic cloves, roughly chopped

¼ cup (60 ml) calamansi lime juice (see Note)

3 tablespoons (45 ml) rice vinegar or distilled white vinegar

2 tablespoons maple syrup

2 teaspoons kosher salt

½ teaspoon mushroom seasoning

1. Prepare the chiles: Trim off the tops of the chiles, and if you prefer a milder sauce, remove the seeds and cores. Roughly chop the chiles and place them in a high-speed blender.

2. Blend the sauce: Add the ginger, garlic, calamansi lime juice, vinegar, maple syrup, salt, mushroom seasoning, and ½ cup (120 ml) water to the blender. Blend the mixture on high speed until it becomes a smooth paste, about 1 minute. Stop and scrape down the sides of the blender with a spatula if necessary to ensure everything is well incorporated.

3. Store: Pour the blended chile sauce into a clean, sterilized jar, sealing it tightly. Store in the refrigerator until ready to use. When using, always scoop out the sauce with a clean spoon to maintain its freshness. The sauce will keep for up to 2 weeks if unopened or scooped with a clean spoon.

Note:

Calamansi is less acidic than lime and the juice is slightly sweet, almost like a cross between a lime and a tangerine. If you can't find calamansi, you can substitute 3 tablespoons (45 ml) fresh lime juice (from about one large lime).

Basic Vegetable Stock

½ cup (90 g) dried soybeans

2 pounds (900 g) daikon radish, peeled and cut into 1½-inch (4 cm) cubes (see Note)

5 dried shiitake mushrooms, rinsed and dried

1 teaspoon kosher salt, plus more as needed

½ teaspoon mushroom seasoning, plus more as needed

Note:

Feel free to toss in any old vegetables you have lying around, such as carrots, cabbage, napa cabbage, cilantro stems, leeks, pea pods, turnips, corn cobs, etc. They will add a slight sweetness and mild flavors to the broth.

Makes about 8 cups (2 L)

This is my go-to stock recipe, as easy as it is versatile. I love this golden broth because it adds depth to just about anything, especially when it comes to noodle soups that feature Asian flavors. Daikon radish brings a subtle sweetness, mushrooms add that deep umami hit, and soybeans round it out with complexity. The longer you let the stock simmer, the more the flavors concentrate. It's on the lighter side, which makes it perfect as a base for my hand-torn noodle soup, Pan Mee (page 225), or other soups and stews that call for a light but flavorful broth.

1. **Soak the soybeans:** In a large bowl, rinse the dried soybeans a few times under cold water. Drain, then cover the soybeans with 2 inches (5 cm) of cool water and let soak and absorb the water for at least 4 hours, or until the beans are plump and swollen.

2. **Make the stock:** In a large pot, bring 1 gallon (4 L) water to a boil. Add the soaked soybeans, radish, and mushrooms. Stir in ½ teaspoon of the salt. Once the water returns to a boil, reduce the heat to a medium simmer, cover the pot, and allow it to simmer for about 1½ hours. The slow simmer allows the flavors to concentrate and develop.

3. Strain out the solids. Season the broth with an additional ½ teaspoon salt and the mushroom seasoning. Taste the broth and adjust the seasonings if necessary.

4. **Store:** Allow the broth to cool to room temperature and then transfer it to a clean, sterilized jar or container. Store in the refrigerator until ready to use. When using the broth in recipes, you can dilute it with more water if needed.

Pickled Green Chiles

Makes about 1 cup (240 ml)

Pickled green chiles are a familiar sight at noodle stalls, dai chow restaurants, and pretty much any place selling hot food in Malaysia. You'll find them in jars sitting alongside other condiments, waiting to be spooned over your meal. Whether you're diving into Wat Dan Hor (page 235), Malaysian-Style Wonton Mee (page 229), or Economy Bihun (page 221), this condiment is indispensable.

I find that green jalapeños work best for this recipe. They've got a good balance of peppery warmth and flavor. The pickling process is straightforward: Remove most of the seeds first, if desired to keep the heat in check, then a quick blanch in hot water softens the chiles just enough to soak up the brine.

7 ounces (200 g) fresh green chiles

Boiling water, for blanching

¾ cup (180 ml) hot water, plus more as needed

½ cup (120 ml) distilled white vinegar (see Note)

3 tablespoons (40 g) sugar (see Note)

1 teaspoon kosher salt

Note:

Feel free to adjust the vinegar and sugar quantities to suit your taste. For a tarter pickle, increase the vinegar; for a sweeter balance to the heat, add more sugar.

1. Blanch the chiles: Wash the chiles thoroughly and dry them with a clean towel. Trim the ends and slice the chiles crosswise into ⅛-inch (3 mm) rounds. Place the slices in a large, heatproof bowl and cover with boiling water. Let the chiles sit for about 10 minutes to loosen most of the seeds, which will start to sink to the bottom of the bowl.

2. Using a sieve, scoop up the chile slices, leaving the seeds behind. Shake the slices well to remove any excess water.

3. Pickle the chiles: In a clean, sterilized jar, combine the hot water, vinegar, sugar, and salt. Stir until the sugar dissolves completely.

4. Add the chile slices to the pickling liquid, ensuring they are fully submerged (add more hot water if not). Let the jar of chiles cool completely and then cover tightly with the lid and refrigerate for 1 to 2 hours.

5. Store: The pickled chiles can be consumed after the initial 1- to 2-hour refrigeration period, or they can be stored in the fridge for up to 3 weeks, unopened, to use as a condiment or in other recipes as needed.

Chili Oil

Makes about 2½ cups (600 ml)

Chili oil was something I didn't come across until I moved to the States. I was eating at a dim sum restaurant when it was served alongside a plate of steamed cheong fun, and I remember digging to the bottom of the jar for the richest, crunchiest bits of sediment. My appreciation deepened further when I visited Chengdu and locals showed me how authentic Sichuan chili oil was made from freshly ground dried chiles and cai zi you, a roasted rapeseed oil that gives it a distinct flavor. When you make your own, you can customize the heat level by choosing your own peppers.

In my recipe, you start by heating up ginger, star anise, and some other aromatics in the oil to build a foundation of flavor. (If you're into that numbing sensation, add some Sichuan peppercorns.) Then comes the fun part: pouring the hot, infused oil over the chili powder. The second it hits, it sizzles, releasing an incredible aroma. The scent of black vinegar mingling with the oil is enough to make your mouth water. This chili oil continues to develop flavor as it sits, so I recommend tasting it after 24 hours.

1 cup (100 g) chili powder (I used Sichuan ground chiles)

2 teaspoons sugar

½ teaspoon kosher salt

1 tablespoon black Chinkiang vinegar

1½ tablespoons toasted sesame seeds

2 cups (480 ml) high-smoke-point cooking oil, plus more as needed

1 small onion, thinly sliced

3 garlic cloves, lightly pounded

5 slices peeled fresh ginger

2 scallions, tied into knots

2 star anise

1 cinnamon stick

5 bay leaves

1. Prepare the chili mixture: In a large, heatproof bowl, combine the chili powder, sugar, salt, vinegar, and sesame seeds.

2. Infuse the oil: In a large, deep saucepan over medium-low heat, heat the oil with the onion, garlic, ginger, scallions, star anise, cinnamon stick, and bay leaves. The oil will start to form small bubbles, sizzling around the ingredients. Keep it at that sizzling temperature, around 360 to 370°F (182 to 187°C), stirring frequently to prevent burning. Cook until the onion and scallions start to brown, about 10 minutes. Turn off the heat and strain and discard the aromatics, reserving the oil and allowing it to cool for about 3 minutes (see Note on page 42).

recipe continues

Note:

Slightly cooling the oil before adding it to the chili powder mixture will prevent the chili powder from scorching. Adding the oil in batches also prevents burning, and allows the chiles to gradually release their aromas.

3. Combine the infused oil and chili powder mixture: Using a large, heatproof ladle, carefully add a scoop of warm oil to the bowl containing the dry chili mixture, stirring with a pair of chopsticks or spoon to combine. Continue adding the oil in batches, stirring between each addition until all the oil is incorporated.

4. Store: Allow the chili oil to cool completely. Transfer to a clean, sterilized jar, ensuring that the oil completely covers the sediment (you can add more oil if needed)—this will preserve the mixture and extend its shelf life. Store your chili oil in the fridge for up to 4 weeks and use it to enhance dishes like Sichuan-Style Dan Dan Noodles (page 265), Mapo Tofu (page 209), and more.

Shallot Oil and Fried Shallots

Makes ⅓ to ½ cup (80 to 120 ml) shallot oil and 2 to 3 tablespoons (15 to 30 g) fried shallots

This aromatic golden oil infuses vegetable dishes (such as Easy Soy Sauce Blanched Lettuce, page 63), steamed sticky rice (Loh Mai Gai, page 149), and noodle sauces (Malaysian-Style Wonton Mee, page 229) with a deep umami kick, making it a go-to for flavor enhancement. Save the crispy fried shallots to use as a topping—they add a nice oniony crunch.

½ cup (120 ml) cooking oil

2 large shallots, sliced crosswise into ⅛-inch-thick (3 mm) rings and blotted as dry as possible

1. Heat and fry: Heat the oil in a small saucepan over medium heat. To test the oil temperature, drop in a shallot ring. The oil should bubble gently around its edges.

2. Add the remainder of the shallot rings and fry over low heat, stirring frequently, until they turn lightly golden, 13 to 15 minutes.

3. The shallots will continue to darken after cooking, so remove from the heat as soon as they begin to color. Using a fine-mesh sieve, transfer the shallots to a paper towel–lined plate to drain. They will become crispy as they cool. Reserve the oil.

4. Store: Store the shallot oil in a clean, sterilized airtight glass jar in the refrigerator for up to 2 weeks. Heads-up: In the fridge, the shallot oil might solidify a bit, depending on the oil used—that's normal. Just let it sit at room temperature for a few minutes to make it pourable before using. Use the fried shallots immediately as a garnish, or store them in an airtight container with a paper towel or desiccant pack in a cool, dry place for up to 2 weeks. Alternatively, store the oil and shallots together, as my mama does; the shallots will remain crispy in the oil if all the water content has been removed and the oil is completely cooled before storage.

Vegan XO Sauce

1½ cups (150 g) dried mushroom stems, rehydrated

1 cup (240 ml) cooking oil

1 cup (150 g) finely chopped shallots

½ cup (75 g) finely chopped garlic

1 tablespoon red pepper flakes

½ teaspoon mushroom seasoning

½ teaspoon kelp powder (optional)

2 tablespoons soy sauce

1 teaspoon sugar

¼ teaspoon kosher salt

1 fresh Thai bird's eye chile, seeded and chopped

Makes 1½ cups (360 ml)

Traditionally XO sauce is made with dried scallops, shrimp, and even cured ham. Years ago, my mama brought home a vegan version that floored me—the sauce had the umami depth of dried shrimp and a texture that was almost like scallops. The secret? Mushroom stems!

Mushroom stems are often discarded, but they have that perfect chewiness that can stand in for meat in all the right ways. Once seasoned, this sauce will be your new best friend, and making a large batch is never a bad idea, as it keeps well and makes a great gift.

1. **Prepare the mushroom stems:** Using a food processor, pulse the rehydrated mushroom stems until they are finely chopped. Be careful not to overprocess. You want a coarse texture, not a paste. In a large wok over medium-low heat, add the oil and chopped mushroom stems and cook for 8 to 10 minutes, stirring occasionally, until the stems turn golden brown and start to smell delicious.

2. **Add shallots and garlic:** Stir in the shallots and garlic. Continue to cook over medium-low heat, stirring frequently to prevent burning, until the shallots and garlic lose their raw smell and start to color, about 10 minutes. Add the red pepper flakes to the wok, stirring them into the mixture until the oil begins to infuse with the chili and turn red. Stir in the mushroom seasoning, kelp powder (if using), soy sauce, sugar, and salt. Remove the pan from the heat and fold in the chopped chili.

3. **Store:** Allow the XO sauce to cool completely. (The flavor will continue to develop as the mushrooms and aromatics infuse the oil.) Transfer the sauce to a clean, sterilized jar, ensuring that the oil completely covers the solids—this will preserve the mixture. Store in the fridge for up to 3 weeks.

Ginger Scallion Sauce

9 ounces (250 g) fresh ginger, peeled

3 large (50 g) scallions

¾ cup (180 ml) neutral-flavored cooking oil

½ teaspoon sugar

¼ teaspoon mushroom seasoning

¾ to 1 teaspoon kosher salt, or to taste

Makes about 1 cup (240 ml)

A big perk of making this sauce is that your kitchen will smell wonderful. You start by finely mincing the ginger and then slowly cooking it in oil. This gentle frying draws out the ginger's starches and infuses the oil with lasting fragrance.

While I've included this sauce in the book to accompany Hainanese Mushroom "Chicken" Rice (page 291), it's versatile for many dishes. I've used it to make fried rice and stir-fries, tossed it with noodles, and used it as a dipping sauce for dumplings.

1. **Prepare the aromatics:** Pulse the ginger in a food processor to a coarse mince, for more of a bite, or a fine mince, depending on your preference. Remove the processed ginger and press into a mesh strainer to squeeze out the juice. Set the liquid aside (this juice can be reserved for making tea).

2. Keeping the white and green parts separate, trim and finely chop the scallions, mincing the white part more finely for better integration into the sauce. You should have about ½ cup chopped scallions total.

3. **Cook the aromatics:** In a skillet or nonstick pan, combine the oil, ginger, and white parts of the scallions. Heat over low heat until the oil sizzles around the aromatics. Continue to cook the mixture for about 5 minutes, stirring frequently, until very fragrant but the ginger is not yet browned.

4. Stir in the sugar, mushroom seasoning, and salt, mixing well to evenly distribute the flavors. Fold in the green parts of the scallions, stirring until they are well incorporated. Remove the sauce from the heat.

5. **Serve and store:** Serve the sauce immediately with Hainanese mushroom "chicken" rice, or allow the sauce to cool and then transfer it to a clean, sterilized jar. Store in the refrigerator for up to 1 week.

Vegan Fish Sauce

Makes about 1 cup (240 ml)

When I first started sharing recipes online, nailing down this "fish" sauce was my top priority. Inspired by the ingredients on a favorite bottle of Vietnamese vegetarian fish sauce, I set out to re-create that elusive balance of sweetness and depth, minus the seafood. Getting it right took a fair bit of trial and error, but with my husband's keen taste buds and some honest feedback from friends, I finally landed on a version that hits all the right notes. The ingredients are readily available, and the process requires very little effort: Just combine a few key ingredients, pour some boiling water over them, and let the aromatics steep. One of the best things about this sauce is that it ages exceptionally well—the flavors deepen and grow more complex as it sits in the fridge.

1 tablespoon minced garlic (about 3 cloves)

1 tablespoon red pepper flakes (see Notes)

1 teaspoon kosher salt

1 cup (240 ml) boiling water

3½ tablespoons (70 g) maple syrup

2 tablespoons fresh lime juice

1. Combine the sauce ingredients: In a medium heatproof bowl, combine the garlic, red pepper flakes, and salt.

2. Carefully pour in the boiling water. Stir in the maple syrup and lime juice until well mixed.

3. Store: Transfer the mixture to a clean, sterilized jar and let it cool before sealing. Store in the fridge for up to 2 weeks.

Notes:

- *The heat level of your sauce will vary depending on the type of red pepper flakes you use. For a spicier version, you can substitute a finely chopped fresh Thai chile.*
- *My homemade vegan fish sauce is on the sweeter side. If you use store-bought vegan fish sauce, which tends to be saltier, for the recipes in this book, you may want to reduce the amount of fish sauce and add a pinch of sugar.*

Textured Vegetable Protein Meat Sauce

2 pounds (900 g) tomatoes, preferably a mix of two types, stems removed (see Notes)

¾ cup (70 g) textured vegetable protein (TVP), rehydrated and squeezed to drain

2 to 3 tablespoons (30 to 45 ml) cooking oil

2 tablespoons soy sauce

Ground white pepper

Mushroom seasoning

Kosher salt

Notes:

- *To enhance the flavor of your sauce, try using a variety of tomatoes, especially when they are in season. If some tomatoes are on the sour side, balance them with sweeter varieties.*
- *I find it convenient to freeze the sauce in smaller portions, which makes it easier to thaw just the amount I need when cooking later.*

Makes about 4½ cups (1 L)

Made from soybeans, textured vegetable protein (TVP) is cheap and versatile and only needs a soak in water to come to life. One of my earliest TVP recipes came from volunteering in a temple kitchen. There, we made a hearty "meat" sauce that was served over steamed rice or stirred into noodles. This sauce was magic: It could turn the most unassuming ingredients into something so delicious. The trick to its depth lies in the tomatoes. As they simmer, they infuse the TVP with an umami-rich brightness!

1. **Prepare the tomatoes:** Chop the tomatoes into large chunks and add them to a high-speed blender. Blend until smooth (makes about 4 cups / 960 ml purée).

2. **Brown the TVP:** In a deep nonstick pan over medium-low heat, stir-fry the soaked and drained TVP without any oil until all the liquid has evaporated. Add 2 tablespoons of the oil and continue to stir-fry until the TVP begins to crisp up and turn golden brown, about 5 minutes. Add an additional 1 tablespoon oil if needed to keep the mixture moist.

3. **Combine the sauce:** Slowly pour in the blended tomatoes and mix well to incorporate. Bring the mixture to a simmer and continue to cook, stirring often, until the sauce turns a darker red and the TVP has absorbed the flavors, 15 to 20 minutes.

4. Continue cooking to reduce the sauce. When it has reached your preferred thickness (I like mine with a bit of extra sauce), stir in the soy sauce, white pepper, mushroom seasoning, and salt to taste.

5. **Serve and store:** Serve the meat sauce warm with noodles or over rice. Store any leftovers in a clean, sterilized jar in the fridge for up to 1 week or freeze for up to 1 month (see Notes).

Chapter 2

From Mom's Roots to My Kitchen

When I set out to write this cookbook, I wanted to invite you into my kitchen and share not just the popular recipes, but the everyday dishes at the heart of my cooking. These are the humble, comforting staples I lean on daily—recipes that might fly under the radar outside Malaysia but have brought nourishment to my family's table over the years.

Inspired by two incredible women, my mom and my mother-in-law, who I call Mama, this chapter blends no-fuss meals with the wisdom they've passed down. My cooking often follows the Cantonese "three dishes, one soup" philosophy—saam soong yat tong—a balance of flavors that I learned from watching them feed their families. In this concept, vegetables aren't just sides—they're central to the meal and meant to shine. On busier days, it might shrink to two dishes (usually something braised or saucy, like tofu, with some crisp stir-fried greens)—this plus a light soup feels like a complete meal for me.

My mama's kitchen is a marvel of speed and heart—her hands dance through tasks with efficiency and somehow also meditative grace. She can whip up feasts effortlessly. She cooks agak-agak, with a Malaysian knack for eyeballing ingredients, trusting instinct over measuring spoons—a lesson in feeling over rules. Her secrets sprinkle magic into these recipes. By contrast, my mom doesn't cook the same way Mama does—her kitchen thrives on effort, not finesse, but her bold creativity turns simple and often humble ingredients into something special. She is never afraid to add her own twist, and her resourceful style is at the core of my cooking today.

My mom (right) and Mama, my mother-in-law, radiant guides who shaped this chapter and lit my culinary path through adulthood.

This chapter is a tribute to these two remarkable women who've shaped my culinary journey. Most importantly, their kitchens weren't just about food; they were spaces of learning, sharing, and memory-making, and I've tried to channel that same spirit in this book. Though I may never quite match their gifts, I hope these recipes, from everyday stir-fries to soul-warming soups, carry forward their lessons.

Stir-Fried Celery with Carrot and Konnyaku

Serves 2 or 3

Ever tried celery in a stir-fry? I first tasted it when my husband and I were still dating at a dinner with his family—a restaurant dish with scored squid and celery, blending texture and flavor beautifully. Back then, I wasn't vegan, and that dish left such an impression that I later recreated it by swapping squid for konnyaku—mimicking that squid-like bite (see sidebar, page 57). Slicing the celery stalks on a bias makes the dish visually appealing, but it also increases the surface area of the celery, allowing the slices to cook more evenly and giving you that perfect crunch in every bite.

1 pound (450 g) celery, trimmed and tough strings peeled, cut diagonally into ½-inch (12 mm) slices (about 4 cups)

1 small (80 g) carrot, shredded

½ teaspoon cornstarch

1 tablespoon cooking oil

2 garlic cloves, minced

3 ounces (85 g) smoked tofu (doufu gan), cut into ½-inch (12 mm) strips

2½ ounces (70 g) konnyaku, cut into ½-inch (12 mm) strips (optional)

½ tablespoon vegetarian oyster sauce

¼ teaspoon mushroom seasoning

½ teaspoon kosher salt, plus more as needed

Cooked rice, for serving

1. Blanch the celery: Bring a large pot of water (4 to 5 cups / 960 ml to 1.2 L) to a rolling boil. Add the celery and blanch until it turns a vibrant green, about 1 minute. In the last 20 seconds of blanching, add the carrot. Drain the vegetables well, either by scooping them out with a sieve or by pouring the contents into a heatproof colander. Rinse the ingredients with cold water to halt the cooking process.

2. Prepare the slurry: In a small bowl, mix the cornstarch with ¼ cup (60 ml) water to create a thin slurry. Set aside.

3. Cook: In a large wok or nonstick pan over medium heat, heat the oil until shimmering. Add the garlic and sauté until fragrant, about 30 seconds.

4. Add the smoked tofu strips and konnyaku (if using) to the pan, stir-frying for 30 to 45 seconds until piping hot. Then add the blanched celery and carrots to the pan, tossing everything together.

5. Stir in the vegetarian oyster sauce, mushroom seasoning, and salt. Increase the heat to medium-high

recipe continues

and stir-fry for 1 minute, until the vegetables are tender-crisp. Then drizzle the cornstarch slurry into the pan, quickly tossing the ingredients until the liquid thickens into a glossy sauce that coats the vegetables and tofu.

6. **Serve:** Taste and adjust the seasoning with more salt if needed. Serve warm with rice.

Konnyaku is a unique jelly made from the root starch of the konjac plant, cherished in Chinese cuisine for its bouncy, almost gelatinous texture and satisfying chew. Packed with fiber and naturally low in calories, it's a versatile ingredient with a neutral, slightly fishy taste that makes it a popular seafood stand-in for plant-based dishes. You'll find it served up like sashimi, simmered in soups, stir-fried, or added to hot pots. It comes in fresh balls or blocks, knotted into ribbons, or even dried to mimic tripe. You can slice it thinly and score each piece with crosshatch lines, giving it that squid-like appeal.

Prepping Bean Sprouts

Even though it's not necessary, I prefer to pluck off the scraggly ends of my sprouts before cooking. It's something my mom taught me, an extra step that keeps them fresher for longer and makes them look just a bit nicer on the plate. I remember sitting around the table with her, newspaper spread out, as we'd help her prepare the sprouts together. It's something I still do when I have time, and now my two lovely kids help with it as well.

Stir-Fried Mung Bean Sprouts

Serves 2 or 3

I started learning to cook at a young age and often had to work within a budget. Mung bean sprouts quickly became one of my go-to ingredients. A small bag cost only 30 or 50 cents but could stretch into a simple, nutritious meal for my whole family.

The best way to cook mung bean sprouts is to stir-fry them quickly over high heat with some aromatics to intensify their flavor and preserve their satisfying crunch. It's all about letting the sprouts shine on their own, and if you're preparing multiple dishes, I would recommend stir-frying this one last, so it's still crisp when it hits the table.

One (8 by 8-inch / 20 by 20 cm) sheet fried tofu skin, or ½ cup (35 g) fried tofu puffs

1 tablespoon cooking oil

1 fresh red chile, thinly sliced (optional)

8 ounces (225 g) mung bean sprouts (about 3 cups), rinsed and shaken as dry as possible (see sidebar, opposite)

½ teaspoon soy sauce

¼ teaspoon mushroom seasoning

Kosher salt

Dash of ground white pepper

1 scallion, white and green parts, julienned

1. **Prepare the tofu:** Rinse the tofu skin or puffs with hot water to remove any excess oil. Cut the tofu skin into strips, or if using tofu puffs, halve them.

2. **Cook:** In a large skillet or nonstick pan, heat the oil over medium heat until shimmering. Sauté the tofu skin or puffs until the edges are lightly browned, about 1 minute. If you prefer a spicier dish, add the chile at this stage (see Note).

3. Add the mung bean sprouts and immediately increase the heat to high. Stir-fry the sprouts until they're piping hot and fragrant but still crisp, about 1 minute. Be careful not to overcook them, or they can become soggy.

4. **Serve:** Stir in the soy sauce, mushroom seasoning, salt to taste, and the white pepper. Fold in the scallion and toss for a few seconds, just long enough for the scallion to wilt. Serve immediately.

Note:

Sautéing the fresh chile with the fried tofu skin will result in a spicier dish. For a milder heat, add the chile at the very end, folding it in with the scallion.

Soy Sauce Okra

Serves 2 or 3

In Malaysia, okra is dubbed "lady's fingers"—a nod to its slender, tapered shape. As a kid, I wasn't fond of its slime, but by high school, I grew to love the crisp green pod. Now, it's one of my favorite vegetables to use in curries or Yong Tau Foo (page 79), and I especially love this elegant preparation my aunt taught me, inspired by a restaurant dish in Kuala Lumpur. To keep the okra vibrant and crisp, you blanch it and pat it dry, then toss it in a light, flavorful sauce, topped with sautéed preserved radish for crunch. It's simple yet sophisticated—my daughter, Tiffany, now cooking for herself at college, has added this dish to her rotation. It's a recipe we'll keep passing down!

2 tablespoons chopped preserved radish

12 ounces (340 g) okra, rinsed but kept whole (see Notes)

3 teaspoons cooking oil

1 teaspoon kosher salt

1 small fresh red chile, thinly sliced

2 teaspoons soy sauce

Ground white pepper

½ teaspoon toasted sesame oil

1 teaspoon crispy fried garlic (store-bought or homemade; see page 75, step 2), for garnish (optional)

Cooked rice, for serving

1. Soak the preserved radish in water for 5 to 10 minutes to soften. Rinse thoroughly to remove excess saltiness, drain well, and chop finely.

2. Blanch the okra: In a large pot, bring about 1 quart (1 L) water to a rolling boil. Add 1 teaspoon of the oil and the salt. Blanch the okra in the boiling water until crisp-tender and dark green, 30 seconds to 1 minute (see Notes). Use a colander to drain the okra and then pat them as dry as possible with a clean kitchen towel. Arrange the okra neatly on a serving plate.

3. Make the sauce: In a small saucepan, heat the remaining 2 teaspoons oil until shimmering. Stir-fry the chopped preserved radish over medium heat until fragrant, about 30 seconds. Stir in the chile, soy sauce, white pepper to taste, and sesame oil.

4. Serve: Pour the sauce over the blanched okra. Top with crispy fried garlic (if using) and serve warm with rice.

Notes:

- *I prefer to blanch the okra whole with their ends intact, as this prevents water from being trapped inside, which could dilute the soy sauce mixture. They're also easier to eat this way—you can pick them up by their heads with chopsticks.*
- *Okra cooks rapidly in boiling water, so 30 to 45 seconds of blanching time is enough, unless you prefer a softer interior.*

Easy Soy Sauce Blanched Lettuce

1 teaspoon kosher salt

Drizzle of cooking oil

1 small head (about 200 g) iceberg or green leaf lettuce, core removed and leaves separated

1 tablespoon Fried Shallots tossed with ½ tablespoon Shallot Oil (page 43)

1½ tablespoons soy sauce, plus more as needed

Serves 2 or 3

As my mama always says, vegetables are best served hot, so if you're making a larger meal, plan to cook this dish last so it's at its crispiest when served. And don't worry, this is a no-brainer recipe, turning a head of lettuce into something much more than just a salad base. Blanching the lettuce preserves the crunch of each leaf, keeps its color vibrant, and lets the natural sweetness of the lettuce shine through.

Here are a few simple tricks to getting it just right: Add a splash of vinegar to the boiling water to help lock in that bright green color, and use a large, open pot to encourage even cooking and prevent overcrowding. After blanching, drain the lettuce thoroughly before tossing it in the soy sauce mixture so you don't dilute the flavor. I promise this one is easy but impactful!

1. **Blanch the lettuce:** In a large pot, bring about 3 quarts (3 L) water to a boil. Add the salt and oil. Blanch the lettuce leaves for about 30 seconds, until they are just wilted but still crisp. Remove the lettuce with a sieve and shake a few times to remove any excess water. Set aside to drain.

2. **Make the sauce:** In a small bowl, combine the fried shallots in shallot oil and soy sauce.

3. **Serve:** Arrange the drained lettuce leaves on a serving plate. Drizzle the sauce over the lettuce. Taste and add additional soy sauce if needed. Enjoy as a side dish or a refreshing appetizer.

Stir-Fried French Beans with Tofu

Serves 2 to 4

When I need a quick way to bring tofu and greens together, a simple stir-fry like this one is my go-to. It's a family favorite: crisp French beans that hold their crunch against tender tofu, with a salty, doubanjiang-based sauce. I love the spicy Pixian variety of doubanjiang, though a milder taucu (yellow bean paste) works nicely too. To streamline the prep, I like to blanch the beans and pan-fry the tofu ahead of time, with a starch slurry ready in the fridge.

1 tablespoon plus 1 teaspoon cooking oil

8 ounces (225 g) firm tofu, drained and cut into ½-inch (12 mm) strips

Kosher salt

1 teaspoon distilled white vinegar

11 ounces (300 g) French green beans, ends trimmed and cut into 2-inch (5 cm) pieces (about 3 cups)

1 tablespoon cornstarch

1 tablespoon minced fresh ginger

½ tablespoon doubanjiang

½ tablespoon vegetarian oyster sauce

Cooked rice, for serving

1. **Pan-fry the tofu:** Heat 1 teaspoon of the oil in a large wok or nonstick pan over medium heat. Arrange the tofu in a single layer and pan-fry until golden brown on both sides, 5 to 8 minutes. Season with a pinch of salt and set aside.

2. **Blanch the beans:** Fill a pan or wok with water and bring it to a boil. Add the vinegar and a pinch of salt. Blanch the green beans for about 3 minutes, until they turn a vibrant green. Drain and rinse the beans with cold water to halt the cooking process.

3. **Prepare the slurry:** In a small bowl, mix the cornstarch with 5 tablespoons (75 ml) water.

4. **Cook:** Clean the pan and heat the remaining 1 tablespoon oil over medium-high heat. Sauté the ginger until fragrant, about 30 seconds.

5. Add the doubanjiang, vegetarian oyster sauce, and tofu. Stir-fry briskly to combine, then fold in the green beans. Stir-fry for about 1 minute, until the flavors meld. Then slowly drizzle the cornstarch slurry into the pan, stirring continuously until the sauce thickens and coats the ingredients in a glossy finish.

6. **Serve:** Taste and adjust the seasoning with additional salt, if needed. Serve warm with rice.

Mama's Braised Potatoes

Serves 3 or 4

Every family has a dish that warms the soul, and for us, it's Mama's Braised Potatoes—her own recipe, a treasure from my mother-in-law's kitchen. When Tiffany and Justin were toddlers, she'd make it during her US visits; the kids would devour it with rice. She'd peel the potatoes, chop them into hearty chunks, and soak them to rinse excess starch and prevent browning, ensuring a creamy braise. I'd watch her simmer the potatoes slowly, her patient hands turning each humble spud into starchy comfort—no frills, just love. Over the years, I've added carrots for crispness and subtle sweetness, balancing the potatoes' richness while sneaking in veggies. Mama would approve, I think, with her knowing smile. It's a taste of home I've tweaked to remember those early days and her steady wisdom.

2 tablespoons cooking oil

3 garlic cloves, lightly smashed

2 large fresh shiitake mushrooms, thinly sliced

1½ pounds (675 g) potatoes (I used russet), peeled, cut into 2-inch (5 cm) chunks, soaked for 15 minutes, and drained

1 small (80 g) carrot, roll-cut into 2-inch (5 cm) chunks

1 tablespoon soy sauce

2 tablespoons vegetarian oyster sauce

¼ teaspoon mushroom seasoning

Kosher salt

Cooked rice, for serving

1. Cook the vegetables: Set a deep pot over medium heat and heat the oil until shimmering. Sauté the garlic cloves until they're fragrant and starting to brown, about 30 seconds.

2. Add the mushrooms, potatoes, and carrot and stir-fry to combine. Continue to cook, stirring occasionally to prevent sticking, until the centers of the potato chunks appear translucent, 4 to 5 minutes.

3. Add the soy sauce, vegetarian oyster sauce, mushroom seasoning, and enough water to cover the potatoes, about 1½ cups (360 ml). Bring the mixture to a boil. Cover, lower the heat to medium-low, and simmer until the potatoes are fork-tender but not yet mushy, about 20 minutes.

4. Finish and serve: Uncover the pot and continue to cook until the sauce is reduced by half and slightly thickened. Taste and add salt if needed. Serve warm with rice.

Fu Yu Ung Choy

(Stir-Fried Water Spinach with Fermented Bean Curd)

Serves 2 or 3

In my fridge, there's always a jar of fermented bean curd ready to be eaten as a condiment with porridge (how my grandma liked it) or mashed into a rich paste to season a stir-fry like fu yu ung choy. Think of fermented bean curd as "tofu cheese," aged until it develops a pungent, salty flavor and creamy texture, like a cross between soft Camembert and miso.

Fu yu ung choy, as this dish is known in Cantonese, is a popular stir-fry using water spinach. Each household tweaks it, but the essence remains: The crisp, slightly sweet taste of the water spinach is paired with umami-rich fermented bean curd. It's the kind of dish that makes you want to scoop up every bit of sauce with your rice.

12 ounces (330 g) water spinach

3 cubes (about 30 g) fermented bean curd (see Note) plus 1 tablespoon liquid from the jar

2 tablespoons cooking oil

1 garlic clove, sliced

1 small fresh Thai chile, chopped

Kosher salt

Cooked rice, for serving

1. **Prep the water spinach:** Soak and rinse the water spinach thoroughly to remove any grit, discarding any discolored leaves. Snap or cut the stems and leaves into 2-inch (5 cm) sections. After draining, you should have about 10 ounces (280 g) of prepared greens.

2. **Make the sauce:** In a small bowl, mash the fermented bean curd with its liquid using a fork until well combined. If the mixture is too thick, add a little water to loosen it.

3. **Cook:** Heat the oil in a wok over medium heat until shimmering. Add the garlic and sauté until fragrant, about 15 seconds. Carefully add the fermented bean curd mixture and the chile.

4. Stir the sauce until it begins to bubble, then add the water spinach all at once. Increase the heat to high and stir-fry quickly, tossing the spinach until the stems are softened and the leaves are wilted, about 1 minute. If the wok becomes too dry, add 2 tablespoons of water and continue stir-frying until the liquid evaporates.

5. **Serve:** Taste and season with a pinch of salt if necessary. Serve the dish warm with rice.

Note:

Some brands of fermented bean curd are sweeter and/or saltier than others. If you are unsure about the saltiness, start with 2 cubes, and add more as needed.

Kari Jap Choy

(Mixed Vegetable Curry)

Serves 2 or 3

At eateries offering economy rice, or chap fan, a beloved hawker classic in Malaysia, you point to whatever calls to you from a colorful array of curries to stir-fries, served over rice for a wallet-friendly meal. My eyes always go straight to the kari jap choy, a mixed vegetable curry with juicy tomatoes, silky eggplant, cabbage, and tender okra. At home, kari jap choy is my go-to one-pot wonder, where I toss in whatever veggies and proteins I've got—like carrots, beans, or mock meats—letting everything simmer in the coconut milk. The tofu puffs soak up the curry like sponges, and homemade sambal lets me dial the heat just right, from mild to fiery. For a bit of sharp kick, I like to add a splash of tamarind juice at the end.

1 cup (240 ml) cooking oil

1 small eggplant, cut into 2-inch (5 cm) batons (about 2 cups)

2½ tablespoons Basic Sambal (page 31) with its red oil, or store-bought Malaysian sambal (if it looks dry, add 1 tablespoon cooking oil)

2 or 3 fresh curry leaves

1 cup (65 g) fried tofu puffs, cut in half

2 small tomatoes, cut into wedges

8 ounces (225 g) cabbage, cut or torn into 2-inch (5 cm) pieces

5 okra (3½ ounces / 100 g), tops trimmed, cut into 1½-inch (4 cm) pieces

Scant 1 cup (200 ml) full-fat coconut milk

½ teaspoon mushroom seasoning

Kosher salt

Cooked rice, for serving

1. Fry the eggplant: In a small saucepan, heat the oil to 375°F (190°C). Flash-fry the eggplant until bright purple, about 1 minute. Transfer the fried eggplant to a paper towel–lined plate to drain. Discard or reserve the remaining oil for another use. (Frying the eggplant will help preserve its color.)

2. Stir-fry the aromatics: Heat a large, deep pot over medium heat. Stir-fry the sambal with the curry leaves until the paste is fragrant and slightly darkened, about 30 seconds. Add 2 cups (480 ml) water and bring to a boil.

3. Add the tofu puffs and simmer until they soften, about 2 minutes. Add the tomatoes, cabbage, fried eggplant, and okra. (To minimize the okra's slippery mouthfeel, you can wait to add it until the last few minutes of cooking instead.) Simmer the curry for an additional 10 to 15 minutes, or until the cabbage reaches your desired crispness.

4. Finish and serve: Add the coconut milk and stir to incorporate. Season with the mushroom seasoning and salt to taste. Serve warm with rice.

Lotus Root Soup

Serves 4 to 6

I loved soup so much as a kid that my nanny gave me the nickname Soon Wong in Hakka, or "Soup King." When I was growing up, it was always on our dinner table—my mom liked incorporating nourishing soups like this one into our diet for its nutritional benefits. It's all about balance: Corn and dried jujube add sweetness, mushrooms bring umami, goji berries and cordyceps flowers offer color, and the lotus root itself is crisp, tender, and full of moistening texture.

After going meat-free, I missed so many of these soups. Most traditional recipes rely on bone broth or meat. But during my time volunteering at a temple, I picked up techniques for building rich, flavorful soups, thanks largely to nuts. In lotus root soup, you'd traditionally use peanuts, but cashews also work beautifully to thicken the broth, giving it a richness that mimics a meat-based stock.

1⅓ pounds (540 g) fresh lotus root

5 dried shiitake mushrooms

¼ cup (40 g) raw cashews

¼ cup (40 g) raw peanuts, preferably red-skinned

Boiling water, for soaking

½ tablespoon cooking oil

1 small (80 g) carrot, roll-cut into 1-inch (2.5 cm) chunks

1 ear corn, cut crosswise into 3 or 4 sections

3 or 4 (28 g) dried jujube (Chinese red dates)

½ teaspoon kosher salt, plus more as needed

1 tablespoon dried goji berries

Handful of fresh cordyceps flowers (optional; see Notes, page 74)

1 teaspoon mushroom seasoning

Cooked rice, for serving (optional)

1. **Prepare and soak the ingredients:** Trim the ends of the lotus root, then peel, rinse, and cut crosswise into ¼-inch (6 mm) slices (see Notes and sidebar, page 74). Place the slices in a bowl of cold water to soak for 20 minutes to prevent oxidation. In separate small bowls, soak the shiitake mushrooms, cashews, and peanuts in boiling water for at least 20 minutes. Drain the cashews and peanuts. Gently squeeze the rehydrated mushrooms to remove excess water.

2. **Cook the mushrooms and vegetables:** Heat the oil in a large, heavy-bottomed stockpot (I use a pot with an 8-quart / 8 L capacity) over medium heat. Sauté the mushrooms until aromatic and starting to brown on the edges, about 2 minutes.

3. Add the carrot and the peanuts and stir-fry to evaporate moisture, until the peanuts release their fragrance, about 2 minutes. Add the lotus root, corn,

recipe continues

Notes:

- *If you prefer, you can cut the lotus root lengthwise into quarters and then into 2-inch (5 cm) chunks, for fewer visible holes.*
- *Cordyceps flowers are not actual flowers but cultured mushrooms* (Cordyceps militaris), *with a bright orange color, slightly nutty flavor, and chewy, noodle-like texture that I love in this soup. You can often find them dried at Asian markets. Soak them in cold water for 10 to 15 minutes to rehydrate, then drain, rinse lightly, and trim off any tough ends before adding to the soup. If you are lucky enough to find fresh cordyceps flowers at specialty grocers, simply rinse and use directly. If they're unavailable, just omit or substitute with extra shiitake mushrooms for that umami kick.*

jujube, and cashews and stir-fry for 1 minute to combine.

4. **Boil the soup:** Add 12 to 13 cups (2.5 to 3 L) water, enough to fully submerge the ingredients. Season with the salt, cover, and bring the mixture to a rolling boil over medium heat. Uncover and cook at a full boil for 20 minutes, then lower the heat to medium and simmer for another 30 to 45 minutes. Occasionally use a fine-mesh strainer to skim off any scum that floats to the top.

5. Around the 45-minute mark, the soup will turn from clear to cloudy, and you may see a thin layer of oil floating on top. The carrots, cashews, and corn should be tender at this point. Add the goji berries and cordyceps (if using) and simmer for another 10 to 15 minutes (the soup will continue to build in flavor as it cooks).

6. **Finish and serve:** Season to taste with mushroom seasoning and salt. Enjoy the soup with rice, or on its own.

7. **Store:** Allow the soup to cool completely before transferring it to an airtight container and refrigerating for up to 3 days. Reheat on the stovetop or in the microwave. The flavors will deepen as it sits overnight.

Preparing Lotus Root

When prepping lotus root, it's essential to clean out any mud from its holes. After peeling, you can slice it thin for a more flavorful broth or cut it into chunks for heartier bites. A fresh lotus root reveals fine fibrous threads when sliced—these vascular bundles indicate freshness and quality and contribute to its unique crunch.

Spicy Tempeh Goreng

½ cup (70 g) red-skinned peanuts, raw (see step 1) or use pre-roasted and skip to step 2

3 tablespoons (45 ml) cooking oil, plus more as needed

2 garlic cloves, thinly sliced

10 ounces (280 g) tempeh, cut into ¼-inch (6 mm) slices

1½ tablespoons sugar

1 tablespoon soy sauce

¼ cup (60 ml) warm water

2 small fresh Thai chiles, thinly sliced

Kosher salt

Cooked rice, for serving (optional)

Serves 2 or 3

I first stumbled upon this dish with my husband when we were teenagers exploring the menu at a Malay eatery. Goreng translates to "fried," and at restaurants, the tempeh and peanuts are usually deep-fried until golden and crispy. But I prefer to pan-fry the tempeh for ease. My husband, who makes the best tempeh dishes, has the technique down—the trick is to slice the tempeh ultrathin, to develop those coveted edges that stay crispy even after saucing. And thanks to the sweet, spicy, sticky sauce on those crunchy tempeh slices, it's hard to resist snacking on this before you serve it.

1. **Roast the peanuts:** If using raw peanuts, spread them on a baking sheet and roast in a preheated 350°F (175°C) oven or toast them in a skillet over low heat until they are golden inside and fragrant, 15 to 20 minutes. Shake the pan frequently to prevent burning. Once roasted, transfer the peanuts to a plate to cool completely. You can rub them between your hands to remove the skins, if desired.

2. **Fry the garlic:** Heat the oil in a large skillet or nonstick pan over medium heat. Add the garlic and fry until aromatic and just starting to color, about 30 seconds. Remove the garlic with a slotted spoon and place it on a paper towel–lined plate to keep it crispy.

3. **Sear the tempeh:** Using the remaining oil in the pan, sear the tempeh slices in a single layer over medium heat until both sides are golden brown, adding more oil as needed. Transfer the seared slices to a paper towel–lined plate to drain.

4. **Prepare the sauce:** In a small bowl, mix the sugar, soy sauce, and warm water, whisking until the sugar dissolves completely.

recipe continues

5. Pour the sauce mixture into the same pan and bring it to a boil over medium-high heat. Once the sauce is bubbling vigorously, add the tempeh, peanuts, and chiles. Toss everything together briskly until the tempeh is fully coated and continue cooking until the liquid reduces to a glaze-like consistency, about 3 minutes.

6. Serve: Fold in the fried garlic slices and season with salt to taste. Enjoy as a snack at room temperature or serve warm with rice.

Yong Tau Foo

(Hakka-Style Stuffed Tofu and Vegetables)

For the tofu and vegetables:

1 small (160 g) bitter gourd (bitter melon; see Note, page 81)

5 small chile peppers, such as jalapeños or serranos

5 okra (3½ ounces / 100 g)

Kosher salt

5 long beans (choose the longest beans available)

One 14- to 16-ounce (390 to 450 g) package firm tofu, drained

5 flexible tofu skin sheets (about 4-inch / 10 cm squares), thawed if using frozen or rehydrated if dried

½ cup (120 ml) cooking oil

For the filling and frying:

2 teaspoons cooking oil, plus more for frying

1 medium king oyster mushroom, torn or cut into ½-inch (12 mm) strips

One 14- to 16-ounce (390 to 450 g) package firm tofu, drained and pressed

¾ teaspoon kosher salt, plus more as needed

Dash of ground white pepper

Cornstarch, for dusting

Serves 3 or 4

Yong tau foo is a cherished Hakka dish in Malaysia; the name means "stuffed tofu," though the technique extends beyond tofu to chile peppers, okra, eggplant, bitter gourd, tofu skins, and even knotted long beans. It's traditionally stuffed with fish or meat paste, but I learned a vegan version from Venerable Song during a cooking class while volunteering at my temple in Dallas. Her secret? Draining and blending firm tofu into a smooth, sticky paste, and then adding sautéed mushrooms for depth and savoriness. To keep each stuffed piece intact, be sure to pan-fry with enough oil to develop a savory browned crust. For extra flavor, I like to braise them with yellow bean paste, but they're just as delicious served with a dip of hoisin or chile sauce.

1. Prepare the gourd, chiles, and okra: Slice the bitter gourd into ½-inch-thick (12 mm) rings. Using a small, pointed spoon, scrape the core and seeds from each slice, removing as much of the white pith as desired (it's the most bitter part). With a sharp knife, cut the chile peppers in half lengthwise and scrape out the seeds. While keeping the ends intact, make a lengthwise slit down the center of each okra and remove enough seeds to make a hollow for the filling.

2. Blanch the beans: Bring a pot of salted water to a rolling boil. Prepare a bowl of ice water in the sink. Blanch the long beans until they darken to a vibrant green, about 30 seconds, then transfer to the bowl of ice water to stop the cooking. When cooled, the beans should be flexible enough to twist without breaking. Take one end of each bean and cross it over itself to form a ring. Weave the long end through the ring, wrapping it all the way around itself to form a 2-inch (5 cm) diameter wreath.

recipe and ingredients continue

For braising:

1 tablespoon minced fresh ginger

1 tablespoon minced garlic

1 tablespoon yellow bean paste (taucu)

1 teaspoon sugar

½ teaspoon soy sauce

For serving:

Cooked rice, or hoisin or chile sauce

3. Prepare the tofu: Cut the block of tofu lengthwise into 4 equal rectangles. Using a tablespoon, carefully scoop out a hollow from the top of each rectangle. Set the tofu rectangles aside and place the scooped portions in a food processor.

4. Prepare the filling: Heat the oil in a small saucepan over medium heat. Stir-fry the mushroom strips until they release their moisture and start to color, 4 to 5 minutes, then transfer them to the food processor. Break the tofu block into large pieces and add them to the food processor. Pulse the mixture into a smooth paste. Season with salt to taste and the white pepper, until the paste is very flavorful.

5. Stuff the vegetables and tofu: Prepare a sieve or small sifter for dusting the cornstarch. Working with one type of ingredient at a time, lay out the hollowed bitter gourd rings, chiles, okra, tofu rectangles, and long beans and dust them lightly with cornstarch by tapping the sieve or sprinkling the starch with your fingers. The starch coating will help the filling stick.

6. With your fingers, scoop a small amount of the mushroom-tofu paste into the opening of each vegetable-and-tofu rectangle and press to adhere. Add enough paste to gently pack each hollowed space. Dust the top of the filled surfaces with another layer of cornstarch—this will help the paste form a crust when pan-frying.

7. For the tofu skin parcels, place a spoonful of the filling in the center of each square. Dust the edges with cornstarch, then fold in the four sides to enclose the filling in a rectangular packet or roll it like a spring roll. Place seam side down.

Note:

Bitter gourd, also called bitter melon, is a bumpy vegetable, usually green but sometimes white (which is less bitter), with a sharp, bitter flavor that adds bold contrast to yong tau foo. Soak bitter gourd slices in cold water for 10 to 15 minutes to mellow the bitterness before stuffing. You can find this vegetable fresh at Asian markets, but it can be swapped with more okra if unavailable.

8. Pan-fry the vegetables and tofu: In a large nonstick pan or skillet over medium-low heat, heat enough of the oil to fill the base of the pan. Working in batches, pan-fry the stuffed veggies and tofu, placing them filling side down in the hot oil. Do not move the vegetables or tofu until the bottoms form a golden-brown crust, 3 to 5 minutes. Flip to brown the other sides, about 3 minutes more. Add additional oil as needed. Transfer to a paper towel–lined plate.

9. Make the sauce for braising: Reserve 2 teaspoons of oil in the pan. Over medium heat, sauté the ginger and garlic until fragrant, about 30 seconds. Add the yellow bean paste and stir-fry for a few seconds to release its flavor. Add the sugar, soy sauce, and 1 cup (240 ml) water and bring to a boil.

10. Carefully slide the stuffed ingredients back into the pan and let them simmer to absorb the flavors of the sauce. When the sauce is reduced to half of its volume, 2 to 3 minutes, taste and adjust the seasoning accordingly.

11. Serve: Transfer everything to a serving dish. Serve warm with rice as a meal or as a snack with hoisin or chile sauce.

Onion Fried "Egg"

Serves 1 or 2

When I was growing up, lunch often meant a bowl of simple but comforting porridge, prepared by my grandma and accompanied by an array of side dishes. Among them were two types of eggs she'd fry up: onion fried egg and chai po egg (page 85). Onion fried egg was simple and my personal favorite, but when I first made it for my kids, they didn't enjoy it as much as I hoped. It wasn't until my mama cooked the same dish, which the kids devoured, that I realized where I'd gone wrong. My onion had been too raw when I added the eggs, causing the eggs to set before the onion had a chance to release its sweetness.

What you need is patience and some technique: Slice the onion evenly to ensure the slices cook at the same rate, then sweat them out in the pan and let them turn translucent. From there, pour in the eggs and cook them slowly, so they can meld fully with the onion. The balance of sweet, meltingly soft onion with savory eggs reminds me of the simple comfort of my grandma's home cooking.

½ tablespoon cooking oil, plus more if needed

1 small onion, thinly sliced

¾ cup (180 ml) plant-based egg liquid

Soy sauce

Cooked rice or porridge, for serving

1. Cook the onion and egg: Heat a nonstick pan over medium heat and add the oil. Sauté the onion until it sweats and releases its natural sugars, becoming soft and translucent, 8 to 10 minutes. The slices will start to caramelize a little in the pan. If needed, add a bit more oil during the cooking process. Use a spatula to spread the onion evenly across the pan.

2. Pour the plant-based egg liquid into the pan over the onion, covering it evenly. Allow the egg mixture to cook until the bottom side sets, then carefully flip it to cook the other side, 1 to 2 minutes.

3. Serve: Once both sides of the omelet are golden brown, transfer it to a plate and season with soy sauce to taste. Serve warm with rice or porridge.

Chai Po (Preserved Radish) "Egg"

3½ ounces (100 g) preserved radish, rinsed thoroughly and drained

½ tablespoon cooking oil

¾ cup (180 ml) plant-based egg liquid

Light soy sauce or a pinch of sugar or kosher salt, for seasoning

Chopped scallion, for garnish (optional)

Thinly sliced red chile, for garnish (optional)

Cooked porridge or rice, for serving

Serves 1 or 2

Chai po egg is a staple in some Malaysian eateries, particularly at dai chow joints. The radish here—known as chai po or "preserved daikon"—is made by salt-preserving daikon radishes during the peak of the season, and in its whole form it looks a bit like a wizened carrot. Growing up, I'd watch my grandma enjoy a bite of chai po, often in large chunks or cut into pieces with plain porridge—little bursts of crunchy, salty savoriness. Ideally, you'd get the preserved radish whole, sold as cai bu or "dried radish" in Asian supermarkets. But many brands conveniently sell it pre-chopped as mince. Just make sure to look for the salty version for this recipe, and make sure to rinse the radish before using—it's salt-cured, after all! This combination pairs extremely well with a bowl of plain rice or porridge.

1. Cook the radish: Heat a dry nonstick pan over medium-low heat. Stir-fry the preserved radish until it becomes fragrant and starts to dry out, 1 to 2 minutes. Add the oil and continue to stir-fry for another 30 seconds, until the radish is evenly coated in the oil and starting to brown. Spread the radish into a single layer in the pan.

2. Pour the plant-based egg liquid over the radish, covering it evenly. Cook until the bottom side sets, then flip to cook the other side, 1 to 2 minutes.

3. Serve: Once both sides of the omelet are golden, transfer it to a plate and season with either light soy sauce to taste or a pinch of sugar or salt. Garnish with the scallion and chile (if using) and serve warm with porridge or rice.

Thai Basil Mushrooms with Yellow Bean Paste

Serves 2 or 3

This quick dish was born out of a night when my husband and I needed to use up leftover king oyster mushrooms and Thai basil in our fridge. It was unexpectedly delicious, one of those instances of lucky improvisation. The basil's peppery, anise-like fragrance melded perfectly with the sauce made of taucu—a chunky fermented yellow bean paste that I always keep around to elevate a quick stir-fry, or to give a braised or steamed dish some subtle depth. It's like umami gold. Feel free to swap out the mushrooms with a pound of tofu for an equally satisfying variation!

1 tablespoon Shaoxing cooking wine

1 teaspoon soy sauce

1 teaspoon sugar

2 teaspoons cornstarch

1 pound (450 g) king oyster mushrooms, roll-cut into bite-sized pieces

2 tablespoons cooking oil

2-inch (5 cm) piece ginger, peeled and thinly sliced

2 garlic cloves, sliced

1 small fresh red chile, sliced

1 cup (20 g) packed fresh Thai basil leaves

2 tablespoons yellow bean paste (taucu)

Kosher salt

Cooked rice, for serving

1. Prepare the sauce: In a bowl, whisk together the cooking wine, soy sauce, sugar, and ¼ cup (60 ml) water until combined.

2. Prepare the slurry: In a separate small bowl, mix the cornstarch and 2 tablespoons water to form a thin slurry.

3. Cook the mushrooms and aromatics: In a dry, large nonstick pan or skillet over medium-low heat, stir-fry the king oyster mushrooms. Cook until the mushrooms release their moisture and continue until they are relatively dry, the edges begin to brown, and they reduce in size by about half, approximately 10 minutes. Transfer the mushrooms to a bowl.

4. In the same pan, heat 1 tablespoon of the oil over medium heat. Add the ginger and stir-fry until the edges start to curl and brown, about 1 minute. Add the garlic, chile, and half of the Thai basil leaves. Stir-fry briskly for about 30 seconds to release their flavors.

5. Push the aromatics to one side of the pan and add the remaining 1 tablespoon oil. Add the yellow bean paste and stir-fry until fragrant, about 20 seconds,

recipe continues

ensuring it doesn't darken too much, as it can turn bitter.

6. Add the prepared sauce mixture to the pan along with the cooked mushrooms. Bring the mixture to a boil, then reduce the heat and simmer for 2 minutes to allow the mushrooms to absorb the flavors.

7. Stir the starch slurry again and add it to the pan gradually, stirring continuously until the liquid thickens into a glossy sauce that coats the mushrooms and aromatics.

8. Serve: Fold in the remaining Thai basil leaves and give everything a final toss. Taste and adjust the seasoning with salt if needed. Serve warm with a bowl of rice.

Lemongrass Sambal Tempeh
(Air-Fried Method)

Serves 2 or 3

Lemongrass's sharp, citrusy notes pair perfectly with the nutty earthiness of tempeh. A little bit of coconut milk rounds things out, adding just enough creaminess to balance the herbaceous lemongrass and spicy sambal (adjust the sambal's heat depending on whether you want mildly warm or mouthwateringly spicy). This is one of my favorite ways to prepare tempeh—it pulls together interesting, fresh flavors without feeling complicated.

Cooking spray

About 8 ounces (250 g) tempeh, cut into 1-inch (2.5 cm) cubes

2 tablespoons cooking oil

3 stalks lemongrass, white parts only, finely chopped (see sidebar, page 91)

1 tablespoon Basic Sambal (page 31)

3 tablespoons (45 ml) full-fat coconut milk

Pinch of kosher salt, plus more as needed

⅛ teaspoon mushroom seasoning

1 teaspoon sugar

¼ each yellow, red, and green bell peppers, cut into 1-inch (2.5 cm) pieces

Cooked rice, for serving

1. **Prepare the tempeh:** Lightly spray the inner basket of the air fryer with cooking spray. Place the tempeh cubes in the basket and spray the top with additional oil. Air-fry at 325°F (165°C) until golden brown, 10 to 15 minutes, shaking the basket a few times to ensure even cooking.

2. **Stir-fry the aromatics:** Heat the oil in a nonstick pan over medium-low heat. Sauté the lemongrass until fragrant and crisp around the edges, about 2 minutes.

3. Stir in the sambal and cook for about 30 seconds to release its flavor. Then add ½ cup (120 ml) water and the coconut milk. Season with the salt, mushroom seasoning, and sugar. Increase the heat to medium-high and bring the mixture to a boil.

4. Add the bell peppers and air-fried tempeh to the pan. Toss everything together quickly until the peppers are crisp-tender and the tempeh has absorbed the sauce, 3 to 4 minutes.

5. **Serve:** Taste and adjust the seasoning with more salt, if needed. Serve warm with rice.

Preparing Lemongrass

In some cases, lemongrass can be used as an aromatic in whatever you're cooking and then discarded. But other recipes, like this one, may call for you to incorporate it into the dish. To prepare lemongrass stalks to be eaten, cut off the root end and peel off the tough outer layers until you see the smooth, pale green part at the bottom. Use just the softer white core, finely mincing it as well as you can, to add a pop of citrus essence to each bite. (And remember to save the dry outer layers for those broths or teas where you want to extract the flavor of the stalk!)

Nai Yau Gu

(Creamy Butter Mushrooms)

Serves 3 or 4

Ask my husband his dad's best dish, and he'd say nai yau shrimp without hesitation. A dish whose name means "milk oil" in Cantonese, this dai chow classic stars shrimp, flash-fried for succulence, enveloped in a rich sauce made with butter and flavored with curry leaves, garlic, and egg floss. My father-in-law, who I call Papa, is its undisputed master, and I love watching him work, especially his patient touch as he scrambles eggs into that silky, golden floss.

As vegetarian and vegan options have grown in popularity, Malaysia's veggie eateries now make nai yau with vegan shrimp or mushrooms. In my recipe, I turn to lion's mane mushrooms—firm and meaty, they crisp up when fried, soaking in the velvety sauce made from plant milk beautifully. One day, my husband, ever thoughtful and creative in the kitchen, suggested adding French green beans for a pop of color and crunch. It's a tweak so perfect it feels like it's always belonged.

3 large (75 g) dried lion's mane mushrooms

Kosher salt

Dash of ground white pepper

Cooking oil, for frying

3 tablespoons (45 g) plant-based butter

1 garlic clove, sliced

1 sprig fresh curry leaves, stems removed

1 fresh Thai bird's eye chile, thinly sliced

4 ounces (110 g) French green beans, thinly sliced diagonally

1 cup (120 ml) unsweetened plant-based milk

1 teaspoon sugar

¼ teaspoon mushroom seasoning

Cooked rice, for serving

1. **Soak the mushrooms:** Place the dried lion's mane mushrooms in a large bowl and cover them with water. Use a bowl or plate to keep them submerged. Soak for 20 to 30 minutes, then gently squeeze the mushrooms to remove the bitter, amber-colored liquid. Drain the water, add fresh water, and soak again for 5 minutes. Squeeze out the liquid and repeat until the water runs clear, about three times total.

2. **Prepare the mushrooms:** Tear the soaked and drained mushrooms into ½-inch (12 mm) chunks, slightly smaller than bite-sized, as they will expand during frying. Squeeze them dry and blot with a paper towel to remove excess moisture. Place in a bowl and toss with a pinch of salt and the white pepper.

3. **Fry the mushrooms:** Heat enough oil to shallow-fry the mushrooms in a small, deep saucepan over

recipe continues

medium heat, bringing it to 350°F (175°C). Working in batches, fry the mushrooms until they are golden brown and very crispy, 3 to 4 minutes, turning them to cook evenly on all sides. Transfer the fried mushrooms to a paper towel–lined plate to drain.

4. **Sauté the aromatics:** In a large skillet or nonstick pan over medium heat, melt the plant-based butter. Add the garlic and curry leaves, allowing them to sizzle to release their flavors for about 30 seconds.

5. Add the chile and green beans to the pan, stir-frying for 1 to 2 minutes, until the beans darken to a vibrant green but remain crisp. Add the plant-based milk, sugar, ½ teaspoon salt, and mushroom seasoning and bring the mixture to a boil.

6. Fold in the fried mushrooms and let them simmer in the flavorful butter sauce, stirring occasionally, for 3 to 5 minutes. The mushrooms will slowly expand as they absorb the sauce.

7. **Serve:** Taste and adjust the seasoning with more salt if needed. Serve warm with rice.

Lion's Mane Mushroom Rendang

For the mushrooms:

5 large (125 g) dried lion's mane mushrooms

½ teaspoon kosher salt

¼ teaspoon mushroom seasoning

2 teaspoons cooking oil

For the kerisik (toasted coconut):

2 tablespoons desiccated coconut shreds or flakes

For the rendang:

3 tablespoons (45 ml) cooking oil, plus more as needed

2 tablespoons finely chopped lemongrass (see sidebar, page 91)

½ tablespoon minced fresh ginger

3 to 4 tablespoons (45 to 60 ml) Basic Sambal (page 31), or to taste

Generous ¾ cup (200 ml) full-fat coconut milk

1 tablespoon palm sugar, plus more as needed

½ teaspoon kosher salt, plus more as needed

¼ teaspoon mushroom seasoning, plus more as needed

1 recipe Nasi Kunyit (page 283; optional)

Serves 4 to 6

I first had rendang at my teacher's house during Hari Raya in Malaysia (see sidebar, page 97). Amid colorful kuih muih and other dishes, this dark, spice-laden curry stole the show: coconut and aromatics cooked low and slow into a deeply fragrant curry. Hailing from Indonesia's Minangkabau culture, it's now a Malaysian dish that shows up at celebrations, a labor of love often paired with turmeric glutinous rice (Nasi Kunyit, page 283). A friend once gifted me rendang and rice for her baby's full moon, alongside a red boiled egg and ang ku kuih—a red tortoise-shaped cake with mung bean paste—to share the joy of her child's birth and wishes for prosperity.

Traditionally rendang is made with beef, slowly cooked until meltingly tender, but my version uses lion's mane mushrooms. Meaty and firm, they fry up crisp, drinking in the rich sauce. I stir in kerisik—grated coconut that's dry-fried until golden—for a sweet, nutty richness that also thickens the curry.

1. **Prepare the mushrooms:** Place the dried lion's mane mushrooms in a large bowl and cover with water. Use a bowl or plate to keep them submerged. Soak for 20 to 30 minutes, then gently squeeze the mushrooms to draw out their bitter, amber-colored liquid. Drain the water, add fresh water, and soak again for 5 minutes. Squeeze out the liquid and repeat until the water runs clear, about three times total.

2. Tear the drained mushrooms into ¾-inch (2 cm) pieces and place them in a large bowl. Add the salt, mushroom seasoning, and oil, tossing gently to combine. Let the mushrooms marinate for 5 to 10 minutes.

3. **Toast the coconut:** While the mushrooms marinate, heat a dry small pan over low heat. Stir-fry the coconut shreds for 2 to 3 minutes, until lightly golden brown.

recipe continues

Once they start to color, immediately transfer to a plate and allow to cool.

4. Fry the mushrooms: Heat the oil in a large skillet or nonstick pan. Pan-fry the marinated mushrooms until golden brown and crispy on all sides, 6 to 8 minutes. Transfer the fried mushrooms to a bowl.

5. Cook the aromatics: Using the same pan and the residual oil, sauté the lemongrass and ginger until aromatic, about 30 seconds. Add the sambal and stir to loosen, adding more oil if necessary to prevent the sambal from burning. Add the coconut milk—be careful, as it may splatter—along with ¼ cup (60 ml) water. Bring the mixture to a boil, then reduce the heat to low.

6. Add the fried mushrooms, palm sugar, salt, and mushroom seasoning. Cover and simmer for 5 to 7 minutes, allowing the mushrooms to expand and absorb the flavors. Taste and adjust with more sugar, salt, or mushroom seasoning as needed.

7. Finish and serve: When ready to serve, stir in the kerisik (toasted coconut). Ladle the dish into serving bowls and enjoy warm with the nasi kunyit, if desired.

What Is Hari Raya?

Hari Raya, or Hari Raya Aidilfitri, is one of the most important festivals for all Muslims in Malaysia, also celebrated around the world, marking the end of the monthlong fast (Ramadan). It's a joyous celebration with families and friends, with feasts of delicious food and gatherings. People also give out green packets (duit raya in Malay) as a token of blessings and good fortune, especially for children and younger family members.

Chapter 3

Reinventing Tradition

(You Can't Believe It's Plant-Based)

Plant-based cooking has always been a place for me to experiment and get creative, and this cookbook reflects that playful spirit. This chapter is dedicated to creations that my husband and I have developed together in our kitchen. We've had fun experimenting and reinterpreting beloved dishes, many of which traditionally rely on meat or seafood.

We've kept the names familiar to honor the classics—lemon "chicken," roast "chicken," and chili "crab"—though the recipes are reimagined with meaty king oyster mushrooms, tofu skin, nori sheets, and other plant-based ingredients, inspired by the playful imitation cuisine of vegetarian traditions I grew up with in Malaysia. This is my way of encouraging my family (and hopefully you!) to try something new.

Sizzling mushroom skewers, grilled to perfection, captured in Thailand.

What's been interesting about this journey is realizing that while I don't miss the traditional proteins, I did miss the sauces and deep flavors that usually come with them. By reworking these dishes with plant ingredients, we get to indulge in the same sense of satisfaction, but in a way that feels kinder. I hope this chapter encourages you to experiment on your own, to learn a few new techniques, and to have your mind blown just a little.

A colorful medley of fresh mushrooms, from Chengdu's market, brimming with earthy allure.

Lemon Mushroom "Chicken"

Serves 3

Lemon chicken is a beloved dish at Malaysian dai chow spots, known for its irresistible combination of golden-fried chicken and sharp lemon sauce. I make a vegan version using king oyster mushrooms, which mimic boneless, skinless chicken with their tender stems. You start by boiling the mushrooms just long enough to soften them, then slice them open like a book to maximize their surface area for battering and soaking up flavor. The mushrooms get a quick dip in a seasoned batter before they're deep-fried until crispy. Drizzle with the sauce and the result is a hearty, crunchy dish with a tart and glossy finish.

For the mushroom "chicken":

Kosher salt

10½ ounces (300 g) king oyster mushroom, caps with stems attached, wiped clean with a damp towel

1 tablespoon soy sauce

1 tablespoon vegetarian oyster sauce

Dash of ground white pepper

1 cup (120 g) dry tempura batter mix (I used Kikkoman)

Cooking oil, for frying

For the lemon sauce:

Zest of 1 lemon

1 tablespoon fresh lemon juice, plus more as needed

2 tablespoons maple syrup, plus more as needed

1 tablespoon sugar

2 teaspoons rice vinegar or distilled vinegar

2 teaspoons cornstarch

2 slices lemon

For serving:

Cooked rice (optional)

1. Cook the mushrooms: Fill a large pot or wok with lightly salted water and bring it to a boil. While waiting for the water to boil, prepare a bowl of ice water. Carefully slide the mushrooms into the boiling water. Cook for about 10 minutes, turning the mushrooms occasionally and immersing them in the water when they float. When the mushrooms develop a glossy outer layer and shrink to about a third of their original size, remove them with tongs and place them in the ice bath to stop the cooking.

2. Make the marinade: While the mushrooms are cooling, in a large shallow plate or baking dish, mix together the soy sauce, vegetarian oyster sauce, and white pepper.

3. Pat the boiled mushrooms dry with a paper towel, gently squeezing to remove any trapped water. To create a cutlet, place a mushroom on a cutting board with the stem end facing you like the number 1. Using a sharp knife, make a ⅜-inch-deep (1 cm) slit lengthwise all the way from the cap of the mushroom to the end of the stem. Then, similar to peeling an apple, cut in a spiral pattern parallel to the mushroom's surface until you get a ⅜-inch-thick

recipe continues

(1 cm) rectangular cutlet. The cutlet will curl up; turn it over and score the side. This should flatten it. Now turn it over and score the other side. Repeat this process with the remaining mushrooms; depending on their size, I usually get 2 or 3 cutlets total.

4. Transfer the cutlets to the marinade plate and coat both sides well. Let them sit for 15 to 20 minutes.

5. **Make the batter:** While the mushrooms marinate, in a wide, shallow bowl, whisk the tempura batter mix with cold water per the package instructions until smooth. Keep chilled until ready to use.

6. **Fry the cutlets:** Pour ¾ inch (2 cm) of oil into a skillet or nonstick pan. Heat the oil over medium-high to about 350°F (175°C) and place the bowl of batter next to your cooking station. When the oil is hot enough, dredge a mushroom cutlet in the batter, shaking off any excess, and carefully slide it into the oil. Fry both sides of the cutlet until golden brown, 8 to 10 minutes, flipping halfway through.

7. Transfer the fried cutlet to a rack to cool slightly and maintain its crispness while you fry the rest. Repeat until all the cutlets are battered and fried. Keep the batter chilled between batches.

8. **Make the lemon sauce:** In a bowl, whisk the lemon zest and juice, maple syrup, sugar, vinegar, cornstarch, and ⅔ cup (160 ml) water until the sugar dissolves. Pour the mixture into a small saucepan and bring it to a boil over medium heat. Taste and adjust the sweetness and tanginess with more maple syrup or lemon juice if needed. Once the sauce begins to simmer, add the lemon slices and continue cooking until the sauce thickens. As soon as you see large bubbles, turn off the heat.

9. **Serve:** Cut the fried cutlets into slices like you'd slice roast chicken cutlets. Spoon the lemon sauce over each cutlet and serve warm with rice or on its own.

Roast Mushroom "Chicken"

Serves 4

This recipe riffs off the traditional roast chicken you'd find in rice eateries in Malaysia, where it's served alongside char siu, or crispy roast pork. It's one of those no-frills comfort dishes craved for its flavor and crispy skin. Just like in my recipe for Lemon Mushroom "Chicken" (page 101), I turn to king oyster mushrooms for their meaty texture. The trick here is twofold: marinating the mushroom stems with a salt rub and then wrapping them in tofu skin, or fu chuk. As the tofu skin crisps up in the pan, it takes on a texture that mimics that golden-brown, crunchy skin you'd expect from a perfectly roasted chicken. Just be patient while pan-frying and I promise the results will be well worth it! I highly recommend serving the cutlets with my "Chicken" Rice Chili Sauce (page 35) for a kick of zesty heat.

For the "chicken":

Kosher salt

4 large (1 pound / 450 g) king oyster mushroom, caps with stems attached, wiped clean with a damp cloth

1 (24-inch / 60 cm) circular semi-dried tofu skin sheet, cut in half to make 2 semicircles

Cooking oil, for frying

For the salt rub:

½ teaspoon kosher salt

½ teaspoon mushroom seasoning

½ teaspoon sugar

Dash of Chinese five-spice powder

For the marinade:

1 tablespoon soy sauce

1 tablespoon maple syrup

¼ teaspoon mushroom seasoning

For serving:

Chile sauce (such as the "Chicken" Rice Chili Sauce, page 35)

1. Cook the mushrooms: Fill a large pot or wok with lightly salted water and bring it to a boil. While the water is heating, prepare a bowl of ice water. Carefully slide the mushrooms into the boiling water and cook them for about 10 minutes, turning the mushrooms occasionally and ensuring they stay submerged. Once the mushrooms develop a glossy outer layer and shrink to about a third of their original size, remove them with tongs and place them in the ice bath to stop the cooking.

2. Make the salt rub: While the mushrooms are cooling, stir together the salt, mushroom seasoning, sugar, and five-spice powder in a small bowl.

3. Pat the boiled mushrooms dry with a paper towel, gently squeezing out any trapped water. To create a cutlet, place a mushroom on a cutting board with the stem end facing you like the number 1. Using a sharp knife, make a ⅜-inch-deep (1 cm) slit lengthwise all the way from the cap to the end of the stem. Then,

recipe continues

similar to peeling an apple, cut in a spiral pattern parallel to the mushroom's surface until you get a ⅜-inch-thick (1 cm) rectangular cutlet. The cutlet will curl up; turn it over and score the side. This should flatten it. Now turn it over and score the other side. Repeat this process with the remaining mushrooms until you have 4 cutlets.

4. Pat the cutlets as dry as possible with a towel. Sprinkle a generous amount of the salt rub over the cutlets and rub it in evenly to coat both sides. Let the cutlets sit for at least 15 minutes to absorb the flavors.

5. Make the marinade: In a small bowl, stir together the soy sauce, maple syrup, and mushroom seasoning with ¼ cup (60 ml) water.

6. On a clean surface, lay out a semicircle of tofu skin. Brush the top with the marinade to soften it. Stack two mushroom cutlets on one end of the tofu skin. Lift the bottom of the tofu skin and fold it over the stack, tucking the end under the bottom cutlet to secure it, similar to wrapping a sandwich in wax paper. Brush on more marinade. Fold both sides toward the center and flip several times to enclose the "sandwich." Repeat to assemble the second "chicken."

7. Fry the cutlets: In a large nonstick skillet, pour in enough oil to reach ¾ inch (2 cm) up the sides of the pan. Bring the oil to 300°F (150°C). To check the temperature, drop a small piece of tofu skin into the hot oil—if it sizzles, the oil is ready. Carefully slide in one cutlet packet and shallow-fry, turning occasionally with tongs, until the tofu skin is crispy and deep golden brown, 1 to 2 minutes per side. Reduce the heat if the tofu skin is browning too quickly. Remove the cutlet from the oil and transfer it to a rack to cool and keep the cutlet crispy. Repeat with the remaining "chicken."

8. Serve: Cut each roast "chicken" into bite-sized slices and serve with the chile sauce.

Eggplant "Unagi" Rice Bowl

For the eggplant:

1 pound (450 g) Chinese or Japanese eggplant (about 3 small eggplants)

2 tablespoons cooking oil

For the sauce:

3 tablespoons (45 ml) mirin

⅓ cup (80 ml) hot water

1 teaspoon kombu dashi powder or kelp powder

2 tablespoons soy sauce

½ tablespoon maple syrup

½ teaspoon sugar

For serving:

3 or 4 scallions, cut into 4-inch (10 cm) sections (optional)

Cooking oil, for drizzling (if using scallions)

Kosher salt

Cooked rice or your favorite grain

1 sheet roasted nori, cut into squares that fit inside the serving bowl

Toasted sesame seeds

Serves 2

Eggplant might not have been love at first bite for me, but now it's one of the vegetables I can't get enough of. Lately, I've been into pairing it with a simple teriyaki glaze that draws out its natural sweetness with savory depth. It reminds me of unagi, or eel, the way the eggplant drinks in the rich, slightly sweet sauce and caramelizes in the pan, becoming buttery and tender.

You can steam the eggplant and let it soak up the marinade in the fridge for a few hours, or even overnight, until you're ready to cook. I like to serve each eggplant "unagi" over a bed of rice with a crisp sheet of nori tucked underneath. That little touch of the sea rounds the dish out perfectly.

1. Steam the eggplant: Trim the tops off the eggplant and cut each into 4- to 5-inch (10 to 12 cm) sections or halves, depending on size. Place the eggplant "logs" in a bamboo steamer or on a rack set over boiling water. Steam over high heat until tender and easily pierced with a chopstick, 8 to 10 minutes. Allow the eggplant to cool until it's easy to handle.

2. Prepare the sauce: While the eggplant is steaming, whisk together the mirin, hot water, kombu dashi powder, soy sauce, maple syrup, and sugar in a small bowl.

3. Using a sharp knife, cut each eggplant lengthwise down the middle, being careful not to cut through the skin so that the two halves remain connected like a book. Then, make an additional lengthwise cut down the middle of the left half (as if quartering the eggplant), then another down the right half. The eggplant should now be able to lie flat. Finally, score the flesh against the grain with shallow ¼-inch (6 mm) lines across the surface to help it absorb the sauce. At

recipe continues

Note:

Any leftover sauce can be reduced and used as a drizzle or stored in a jar in the refrigerator for later use.

this point, you can keep it refrigerated until you're ready to cook the meal.

4. **Sear the eggplant:** Heat the oil in a large skillet or nonstick pan over medium heat. When the oil is hot, place the eggplant in a single layer, flesh side down, and sear until the bottom is golden brown, 2 to 3 minutes. This will help prevent the flesh from tearing apart.

5. Flip the eggplant so that the flesh side faces up. While cooking, baste the top evenly with the sauce, 1 tablespoon at a time, until the eggplant has absorbed the flavor. You may not need to use all the sauce—about 2½ tablespoons for each piece of eggplant should suffice.

6. Flip the eggplant pieces again so that the skin is facing up and the scored sides are on the bottom, allowing the eggplant to absorb any remaining sauce in the pan. Continue cooking until the flesh is tender and starting to sear, 3 to 4 more minutes. Transfer the braised eggplant to a plate.

7. **Char the scallions (if using):** Place the scallions in a heatproof bowl or on a plate. Drizzle with oil and sprinkle with salt. Use a hand torch to char the scallions until they are fragrant and blistered, or broil or grill them for a similar effect.

8. **Serve:** Place a portion of cooked rice in each bowl and top with a piece of nori followed by the braised eggplant. Drizzle with any extra sauce (optional; see Note) and garnish with sesame seeds and the scallions (if using).

Sweet Chili Mushroom "Crab"

For the mushrooms:

¾ cup (90 g) all-purpose flour

¾ cup (85 g) rice flour

½ teaspoon kosher salt

½ teaspoon mushroom seasoning

A few dashes of ground black pepper

1¼ cups (300 ml) cold water, plus more as needed

11 ounces (300 g) oyster mushrooms or shimeji (beech) mushrooms, ends trimmed and separated into clusters

For the sauce:

¼ cup (60 ml) ketchup

3 to 4 tablespoons (45 to 60 ml) Thai sweet chile sauce, or to taste

1 tablespoon soy sauce

½ teaspoon kosher salt, plus more as needed

2 teaspoons cornstarch

2 tablespoons cooking oil

2 tablespoons finely chopped shallot

1 tablespoon minced fresh ginger

1 tablespoon minced garlic

1 tablespoon Basic Sambal (page 31)

2 tablespoons silken or soft tofu

Serves 2 or 3

When I first made this recipe at home, it was an instant hit with my kids—they were literally licking their fingers clean. Chili crab is a beloved dai chow dish with a glossy sauce, typically served with golden fried mantou (plain steamed buns). It brings back memories of family dinners out. But for me, it was never the crab itself that made the dish special. It was the tart heat of the gravy that I missed the most.

Occasionally, a thoughtful chef would serve me just the sauce on the side, no seafood involved, and I started to wonder what else I could pair with one of my favorite flavors. I experimented with a cauliflower and sauce pairing at first, but then I discovered battered mushrooms, which were better at soaking in the sauce without becoming mushy or losing their texture. Oyster mushrooms in particular offer a tender bite and seafood-like umami of their own. This plant-based variation on chili crab has become a regular at our family table, delivering the same joy as the chili crab of my childhood—proof you can recreate the dishes you cherish with a bit of creativity and love!

1. Prepare the batter: In a large bowl, mix the all-purpose flour, rice flour, salt, mushroom seasoning, and black pepper. Add the cold water and whisk until smooth, with a consistency similar to tempura batter. If the batter is too thick, thin it with 1 tablespoon of water at a time.

2. Fry the mushrooms: Preheat an air fryer to 390°F (200°C). Submerge the mushrooms in the batter, shake off any excess, and place them in a single layer in the air-fryer basket. Air-fry for 15 to 20 minutes, or until crispy. (Alternatively, deep-fry the mushrooms in hot oil for 3 to 5 minutes, until golden brown and crispy; it may take a bit longer for larger ones.)

recipe and ingredients continue

For serving:

Thinly sliced scallions, white and green parts

Cooked rice or fried mantou (Chinese buns)

3. Prepare the sauce: In a large measuring cup, whisk together the ketchup, Thai sweet chile sauce, soy sauce, salt, and 1½ cups (360 ml) water. In a small bowl, mix the cornstarch with 2 tablespoons water to make a slurry.

4. Heat the oil in a large skillet or nonstick pan over medium heat. Sauté the shallot, ginger, and garlic until fragrant and slightly translucent, about 2 minutes. Add the sambal and stir to combine.

5. Pour the sauce mixture into the pan and bring to a boil. Let it simmer for 2 to 3 minutes, until slightly reduced. Add the tofu, breaking it up and stirring it into the sauce. Slowly stir in the cornstarch slurry, letting the sauce thicken.

6. Finish and serve: Add the mushrooms to the sauce, tossing them until they're thoroughly coated. Taste and adjust the seasoning with more salt if necessary. Garnish with scallions and serve warm, alongside rice or fried buns.

Dou Bao "Fish"

Makes 1 "fish" (serves 2 or 3)

By now, it's no secret that I'm a huge fan of tofu skin, or fu chuk, and this recipe features two distinct types: the soft, fresh tofu skin (dou bao), layered in square patties, and the frozen semi-fresh tofu skin, with its slick oilcloth texture. I start by pan-frying the dou bao to crisp it lightly—this also makes it more receptive to seasoning. Then I layer the filling and wrap it in the pliable semi-fresh tofu skin, and steam the rolls. During steaming, the filling expands, pressing into the outer layer to hold everything together. After a short cooldown, a final pan-fry turns the outer tofu skin golden and crispy, contrasting beautifully with the soft, savory dou bao and filling within.

I often make a batch ahead and stash them in the fridge, for a quick pan-fry whenever I need a protein on a busy weeknight. Whether you're as obsessed with tofu skin as I am or just looking to try something new, this recipe really shows off tofu skin's versatility.

For the filling:

1 tablespoon cooking oil

8 ounces (225 g) fresh tofu skin (dou bao), thawed if frozen

7 ounces (200 g) enoki mushrooms, ends trimmed

1 tablespoon all-purpose flour

1 teaspoon minced fresh ginger

½ teaspoon kosher salt

¼ teaspoon mushroom seasoning

For the flour paste:

2 tablespoons all-purpose flour

3 tablespoons (45 ml) cold water

For the "fish":

1 (24-inch / 60 cm) circular semi-dried tofu skin (bean curd sheet), cut in half to make 2 semicircles

1 square nori sheet

1. Prepare the filling: Heat the oil in a wok or nonstick skillet over medium heat. Pan-fry the tofu skin until it starts to stick and turn golden brown, 3 to 5 minutes. Transfer to a cutting board, slice into ¼-inch-thick (6 mm) strips, and place in a large bowl.

2. Cut the enoki mushrooms into roughly 2-inch (5 cm) segments and separate them into finger-thick clusters. Add to the bowl with the tofu skin.

3. Add the flour, ginger, salt, and mushroom seasoning to the bowl. Use your hands to toss and combine, allowing the flour to bind the ingredients.

4. Make the flour paste: In a small bowl, mix the flour with the cold water to create a thick paste.

5. Assemble the "fish": Lay out one semicircle of tofu skin on a clean surface (save the other half for

recipe continues

Note:

If you want to braise some of the leftover "fish" with a sauce, I recommend the Sichuan Douban "Fish" sauce (page 135).

another use). Using a spoon or your fingers, smear a thin layer of flour paste in the center, roughly the size of the nori sheet. Press the nori sheet on top to adhere. Place the filling in the center of the nori in a mounded rectangle, about 6 inches long and 2 inches wide (15 by 5 cm). Apply more flour paste to the edges of the tofu skin. Fold the sides tightly over the filling to enclose it in a rectangular fish shape.

6. **Steam the "fish":** Prepare a steamer and bring the water to a boil. Place the wrapped "fish" on a plate and steam over medium-low heat for about 20 minutes.

7. **Serve and store:** Enjoy the steamed "fish" immediately, use it for Douban "Fish" (page 135), or let it cool before storing in the fridge for up to 3 days or freezing for up to 3 months.

Sweet and Sour "Fish"

For the filling:

10 ounces (280 g) king oyster mushrooms

2 teaspoons cooking oil

Kosher salt

One 14- to 16-ounce (390 to 450 g) package firm tofu, drained and pressed

½ teaspoon sugar, plus more as needed

½ teaspoon mushroom seasoning, plus more as needed

Dash of ground white pepper

1 tablespoon cornstarch

For the "fish":

6 large (8½ to 10 inches / 22 to 25 cm) rice paper rounds

6 square nori sheets

Cooking oil, for frying

Cornstarch, for dusting

For the sauce:

2 tablespoons ketchup

1 tablespoon rice vinegar

2 tablespoons sugar

1 teaspoon fresh lemon juice

1 tablespoon soy sauce

½ teaspoon kosher salt

1 teaspoon cornstarch

1 teaspoon cold water

For serving:

1 small tomato, cut into cubes

¼ cup (30 g) peeled and chopped cucumber

Cooked rice

Serves 4

When I first shared this recipe on my blog, I saw a comment that made my day: Someone said it reminded them of ikan tenggiri (mackerel)! Years of experimenting led me to this clever combo of rice paper and seaweed, which is my go-to method for a vegan fish. The casing—a nori sheet for briny depth and rice paper for chewy, fish-skin texture—wraps together a filling of stir-fried mushrooms and tofu. After steaming and pan-frying the "fish" for a golden, crispy shell, I slice and re-fry each piece to hold the filling and douse it with sweet and sour sauce.

1. Prepare the filling: Trim the mushrooms and cut them into 2-inch (5 cm) sections. Tear each section into large chunks. Heat the oil in a medium skillet over medium-low heat and sauté the mushrooms until they release moisture and start to brown on the edges, 3 to 5 minutes. Season with a pinch of salt and transfer to a food processor.

2. Break the tofu into small pieces and add them to the food processor with the mushrooms. Add the sugar, mushroom seasoning, 1 teaspoon salt, the white pepper, and cornstarch. Pulse until thoroughly combined. Taste and adjust the seasoning if needed, with more salt or mushroom seasoning for savoriness or sugar for a sweet hint. Transfer the mixture to a large plate and divide it into six equal portions.

3. Assemble the "fish": Fill a large shallow plate with water and dip a round of rice paper in it, rotating to moisten all sides. Remove from the water—it's okay if the rice paper is slightly firm, as it will continue to soften—and place it on a clean surface.

4. Center a sheet of nori on each round of rice paper, then place a portion of filling on the lower half of the

recipe continues

nori, shaping it into a rectangular mound, leaving about 2 inches (5 cm) of room on each side. Fold the sides of the rice paper in, like wrapping a burrito. Bring the bottom edge up and fold it loosely over the filling, then roll the burrito toward the top edge to seal. (Because the filling will expand during cooking, don't make the roll too tight, as the skin may burst later while cooking.) Repeat for the remaining five portions.

5. **Fry the "fish":** Fill a large skillet with enough oil to reach ⅜ inch (1 cm) up the sides. Heat the oil to 325°F (165°C) over medium-high heat. If you don't have a thermometer, drop a small piece of dried rice paper into the oil—if it sizzles, the oil is ready.

6. Working in batches, fry the rolls in a single layer, leaving generous space between them to prevent the rolls from sticking together. Fry the rolls without disturbing them until a white crust forms on the bottom, 3 to 4 minutes, then turn them with tongs and fry the other side until the surfaces are blistered and white, 8 to 10 minutes in total. If cracks start to form on one side, stop frying that side immediately and turn the roll over (you'll be able to cook it later, after slicing the rolls). Reduce the heat if the rice paper browns too quickly. Reserving the oil in the pan, transfer the rolls to a paper towel–lined plate to drain.

7. Once the rolls have cooled slightly, use a serrated knife to cut them into 2-inch (5 cm) diagonal slices. Dust the open sides with cornstarch.

8. **Sear the slices:** Heat the same pan with the reserved oil. Pan-fry the slices, cut sides down, until golden brown and crisp, 2 to 3 minutes. Flip and repeat with the other sides. Transfer to the paper towel–lined plate (see Note).

Note:

This recipe can be made in advance! After you pan-fry the rolls, you can pop them in the fridge and finish the saucing later.

9. Make the sauce: Clean the skillet and set it over medium heat. Add the ketchup, vinegar, sugar, lemon juice, soy sauce, salt, and 1 cup (240 ml) water. Bring to a boil. In a small bowl, mix the cornstarch with the cold water to create a slurry.

10. Finish and serve: Gradually add the slurry to the sauce and stir until thickened. Fold in the tomato and cucumber, cooking just until the tomato softens, about 1 minute. Add the fried "fish" pieces to the sauce and gently coat them. Cook until they've absorbed the sauce, about 2 minutes. Serve warm with rice.

Chapter 4

A Taste of Sichuan

What captivates me about Sichuan food is the rich history woven into every dish and flavor profile. Living in Chengdu has been transformative for my cooking—the flavors and techniques here have inspired the recipes in this section. From the tingling spice of peppercorns and chiles in Spicy Fried Lion's Mane Mushrooms (page 139) to the bright kick of pickled mustard broth in sour mustard "fish" (page 141), each dish is a nod to Sichuan's culinary spirit.

Over the past few years, I've also experienced the incredible warmth and generosity of the locals. It's been a journey of endless discovery, tweaking recipes in my own kitchen to make them plant-based and sharing them with friends who know these dishes inside and out. Their feedback has been invaluable, helping me refine the recipes to capture the essence of Sichuan cuisine. These are some of my favorite Sichuan recipes, adapted to use ingredients that are easier to find in the US, and this chapter is my way of bringing a bit of Chengdu's vibrant food culture into your kitchen.

A classic noodle shop in Chengdu hums with warmth.

Vibrant Sichuan peppercorns gleam in the market, their zesty aroma igniting the air.

A tranquil afternoon in Chengdu, where four uncles focus on their Chinese chess match.

Chengdu's fall unfurls in golden hues, a crisp breeze carrying whispers of the season.

Kung Pao Button Mushrooms

Serves 3 or 4

Before even setting foot in Chengdu, I was already hooked on kung pao, also known as gong bao. It's a "dry" stir-fry that hits all the right notes—fiery, savory, a bit sweet, with just the right amount of crunch. Although it originates from Sichuan province, you can order kung pao at dai chow joints in Malaysia as well. The dish's distinctive flavor profile is made with red chiles and a rich sauce that usually clings to bite-sized morsels of chicken, studded with crunchy peanuts. But instead of the traditional chicken, I've opted for button or cremini mushrooms for a veg-forward version. As the star of the dish, they hold their shape and act as the perfect vessel for the kung pao sauce.

For the kung pao sauce:

3 tablespoons (45 ml) soy sauce

½ teaspoon dark caramel soy sauce

2 tablespoons Shaoxing cooking wine

1 tablespoon sugar

1 tablespoon cornstarch

For the mushrooms:

1 pound (450 g) button or cremini mushrooms

1 tablespoon Shaoxing cooking wine

1 tablespoon soy sauce

3 tablespoons (23 g) cornstarch

Cooking oil, for frying

For the aromatics:

2-inch (5 cm) piece (15 g) fresh ginger, peeled and thinly sliced

4 large garlic cloves, sliced

5 to 10 dried chiles, such as Kashmiri, for milder heat

For serving:

2 tablespoons fried or roasted peanuts (preferably red-skinned)

2 scallions, white parts only, thinly sliced

Cooked rice

1. **Prepare the kung pao sauce:** In a small bowl, whisk together the soy sauces, cooking wine, sugar, cornstarch, and 2 tablespoons water.

2. **Marinate the mushrooms:** Trim the stems of the mushrooms close to the caps and discard the stems. Wipe the caps clean with a damp towel. Place them in a large bowl. Add the cooking wine and soy sauce, tossing to combine. Let the mushrooms rest for 5 to 10 minutes to release some liquid.

3. Sprinkle the cornstarch over the mushrooms, gently tossing and rubbing them to ensure an even coating.

4. **Fry the mushrooms:** In a large skillet or nonstick pan over medium-high heat, heat enough oil to reach ⅜ inch (1 cm) up the sides. Fry the mushrooms until golden brown on both sides, 2 to 3 minutes per side. Transfer to a paper towel–lined plate to drain.

5. **Stir-fry the aromatics:** Pour out most of the oil from the pan, leaving about 1 tablespoon. Over medium heat, sauté the ginger until the edges start to

recipe continues

curl and brown. Add the garlic and stir-fry until fragrant, then toss in the dried chiles. Stir-fry to release their fragrance, about 1 minute.

6. Before the chiles darken, return the fried mushrooms to the pan and pour in the sauce. Increase the heat to medium-high and quickly toss and stir-fry everything together until the mushrooms have absorbed most of the sauce, about 2 minutes.

7. **Serve:** Fold in the peanuts and scallions. Give everything a final toss and serve warm with rice.

Yu Xiang (Fish-Fragrant) Eggplant

Serves 3

This is one of my daughter Tiffany's favorite dishes, featuring tender eggplant braised with spicy pickled chili and TVP (textured vegetable protein) in every bite. It's become a go-to in our home, especially when we're craving something quick but layered with flavor. The first time I encountered this dish at a Chinese restaurant years ago, the waitress explained that yu xiang, which translates to "fish fragrant," is actually vegetarian. Instead of using any seafood, the recipe relies on a classic Sichuan flavor profile built on garlic, ginger, and pickled chiles that's traditionally used in fish dishes. The result is a sauce that's spicy, garlicky, and just a touch sweet. It reminds me of my early days of exploring Sichuan flavors—an experience I share now with my family, especially Tiffany, whose love for this dish has only deepened my own.

For the sauce:

3 tablespoons (45 ml) soy sauce

1 tablespoon Chinkiang black vinegar or rice vinegar

1½ teaspoons sugar

1 teaspoon cornstarch

For the eggplant:

Cooking oil, for frying

1 pound (450 g) Chinese or Japanese eggplant, roll-cut into 1-inch (2.5 cm) chunks (see Notes, page 128)

For the aromatics:

1 tablespoon minced garlic

1 tablespoon minced fresh ginger

1 tablespoon pickled chiles (duo jiao), coarsely chopped (see Notes, page 128)

2 tablespoons textured vegetable protein (TVP), rehydrated and squeezed to drain

For serving:

1 scallion, white and green parts, thinly sliced

Cooked rice

1. Prepare the sauce: In a small bowl, whisk together the soy sauce, black vinegar, sugar, cornstarch, and ¾ cup (180 ml) water.

2. Fry the eggplant: In a wok or deep skillet, add enough oil to reach about ½ inch (12 mm) up the sides (about 1 cup / 240 ml for a smaller, 8- to 10-inch skillet, or 2 cups / 480 ml for a larger, 12- to 14-inch wok). Heat the oil over medium-high heat to 375°F (190°C), or until an inserted wooden chopstick forms a rapid stream of bubbles. Fry the eggplant in batches for 1 to 2 minutes, until its skin becomes slightly wrinkled. Drain the eggplant on a paper towel–lined plate. Pour the oil into a heatproof container and reserve for another use.

3. Stir-fry the aromatics: In the same wok or skillet, heat 1 tablespoon oil over medium heat. Sauté the garlic and ginger for about 30 seconds, until fragrant. Add the pickled chiles and stir-fry for another 30 seconds to release their flavor.

recipe continues

Notes:

- *Choose Chinese or Japanese eggplants that are firm, with a light purple skin and a slightly frosted look. The top may show hints of white, a sign that it's young and tender. These eggplants have a milder flavor and buttery texture when cooked, perfect for absorbing the bold flavors of the sauce in this dish.*
- *Duo jiao (chopped chiles that are pickled or fermented in a salty brine) are key to this dish. They add heat and acidity, so if pickled chiles aren't available, use fresh chiles and an extra splash of vinegar.*

4. Pour in the prepared sauce, being careful of splattering. Add the rehydrated TVP and bring the liquid to a gentle simmer, about 1 minute. Fold in the eggplant and cook for 2 minutes, until it absorbs the sauce and becomes tender.

5. Serve: Stir in the scallion. Serve warm with rice.

On Eggplant

When I was younger, eggplant wasn't exactly at the top of my list of favorite vegetables. I found it a bit odd and didn't really appreciate its spongy texture. But as time passed, I discovered its charm—especially when it meets robust flavors. In Malaysia, eggplant gets the royal treatment, fried, stuffed, or simmered with fiery sambal or coconut curry until it transforms into something buttery and irresistible. The more I experiment with eggplant in my kitchen, the more I appreciate its versatility. My daughter, for instance, absolutely adores the Yu Xiang Eggplant (recipe above), a quintessential Chinese dish with a garlicky sweet and sour sauce. Watching her savor it makes me love eggplant even more—it's become a bridge between my past and her present.

Lao Gan Ma Thousand-Layer Tofu

For the tofu:

2 teaspoons cooking oil

14 ounces (400 g) thousand-layer tofu (bai ye, aka qianye tofu; see Notes, page 131), cut into ¼-inch (6 mm) slices

For the sauce:

2 tablespoons Lao Gan Ma chili crisp with black beans, including oil from the jar (see Notes, page 131)

½ teaspoon sugar

1 teaspoon soy sauce

Kosher salt, as needed

For serving:

3 scallions, white and green parts, cut into 1-inch (2.5 cm) pieces, or ¼ cup (10 g) chopped fresh cilantro

Cooked rice

Serves 2 or 3

I first encountered this dish at a local restaurant hidden deep in a bamboo forest near Chengdu. Their staff couldn't have been more accommodating, and they offered a selection of vegan dishes just for us. When they ran out of tofu for a dish we were interested in, the chef suggested we try "thousand-layer tofu," a bouncy soy protein I'd often enjoyed in hot pot and braises. We were intrigued! When the tofu arrived, my husband, friends, and I were blown away by the dish's flavors and textures. The protein had this QQ quality (a bouncy, chewy texture) and reminded me of fish cakes. We joked that maybe this likeness was our hunger talking, but the truth was, it was just that good! I knew I had to re-create it at home.

After some experimenting, I found that Lao Gan Ma's black bean sauce—a widely available condiment in the US—along with a touch of sugar and soy sauce, brought me right back to that meal. It's a genuinely amazing combination that's since become a fixture in my dinner rotation.

1. Fry the tofu: Heat the oil in a large skillet or nonstick pan over medium heat. Swirl to coat the bottom. Arrange the tofu in a single layer (working in batches if necessary) and fry until one side is golden brown and begins to puff up, about 3 minutes. Flip and repeat on the other side. Transfer to a paper towel–lined plate to drain.

2. Make the sauce: In the same pan, add the Lao Gan Ma chili crisp and its oil. Stir-fry over medium heat until fragrant, about 30 seconds. Add the sugar and stir until dissolved.

recipe continues

Notes:

- *Thousand-layer tofu—also called bai ye, qianye, or Chiba tofu—has a chewy, layered texture ideal for stir-fries and hot pots. Find it in the fresh or frozen tofu section of Asian markets or online (e.g., Dianfa Chiba Tofu Frozen from Weee!). You can also try searching for "thousand-page tofu." Just be mindful that it's not the same thing as stinky or regular tofu. If it's unavailable, use thin slices of extra-firm tofu.*
- *For another use of qianye tofu, I like to cut the long blocks into thin slices and pan-fry them until they puff up in the middle, and then serve them with a dusting of chili powder for a savory snack.*
- *Instead of the Lao Gan Ma chili crisp, you may substitute 1 tablespoon fermented black beans plus 1 tablespoon Chili Oil including the sediment (page 41).*

3. Return the tofu to the pan and toss until fully coated in the sizzling, aromatic mixture. Stir in the soy sauce and taste, adding salt if necessary.

4. Finish and serve: Fold in the scallions or cilantro and give the dish a final toss to combine. Serve warm with rice.

La Jiao Xiang Gu Si

(Sichuan Chili Mushroom Shreds)

For the sauce:

1 teaspoon soy sauce

1 teaspoon Shaoxing cooking wine

1 teaspoon sweet bean paste (tian mian jiang) or hoisin sauce

¼ teaspoon mushroom seasoning

Dash of ground white pepper

½ teaspoon cornstarch

For the mushrooms and aromatics:

18 ounces (500 g) king oyster mushrooms, cleaned with a damp towel

1 teaspoon Shaoxing cooking wine

1 teaspoon soy sauce

¼ teaspoon ground white pepper

½ teaspoon kosher salt, plus more as needed

1½ teaspoons cornstarch

2 tablespoons cooking oil

1-inch (2.5 cm) piece (10 g) fresh ginger, peeled and thinly sliced

2 garlic cloves, sliced

5 ounces (140 g) fresh green chiles of choice (I used er jing tiao), thinly sliced

For serving:

Cooked rice

Serves 2 or 3

As a lover of spicy food, one of my favorite dishes is la jiao rou si (chile pork strips), a popular stir-fry you can spot on many menus in Chengdu. Here, I swap out the pork for king oyster mushrooms. Their thick, meaty white stalks shred into strips easily, and just a quick crush from a pestle or a bit of hand-shredding pulls apart the fibers, giving them the perfect tender bite.

For that essential heat, I reach for er jing tiao peppers, a Sichuan classic. These long, slender peppers bring a fruity heat. If you can't find them, Korean chile peppers are a good alternative, offering similar heat and crunch. A bit of sweet bean paste deepens the flavors with its salty-sweet umami, and the mushroom strips, dusted in a little starch and tumbled with the peppers and sauce, develop a glossy finish that's impossible to resist.

1. Prepare the sauce: In a small bowl, stir together the soy sauce, cooking wine, bean paste, mushroom seasoning, white pepper, and cornstarch with 2 tablespoons water.

2. Prepare the mushrooms: Gently pound the mushrooms with a pestle or the bottom of a small jar to break them open. Tear them into ½-inch (12 mm) strips. For thicker mushrooms, cut them into 2-inch (5 cm) sections before pounding for easier tearing.

3. Heat a dry large skillet or nonstick pan over medium-low heat. Stir-fry the mushroom strips for about 5 minutes, until they release their moisture. Transfer to a large bowl.

4. Add the cooking wine, soy sauce, white pepper, and salt to the mushrooms. Sprinkle on the cornstarch, then toss with your fingers (or chopsticks) to evenly coat the mushrooms in starch.

recipe continues

5. Fry the mushrooms: In the same skillet, heat 1 tablespoon of the oil over medium-high heat. Add the mushrooms and stir-fry until they're golden brown and slightly crispy, 4 to 5 minutes. Remove to a plate.

6. Stir-fry the aromatics: Heat the remaining 1 tablespoon oil in the pan over medium-high heat. Sauté the ginger and garlic until fragrant, about 30 seconds. Add the chiles and cook briefly to remove their raw taste, about 30 seconds.

7. Finish and serve: Return the fried mushrooms to the pan, pour in the prepared sauce, and stir-fry until the mushrooms absorb all the sauce, about 2 minutes. Serve warm with rice.

Sichuan Douban "Fish"

Serves 2 or 3

This recipe is my homage to douban fish, one of the first dishes I fell in love with when I moved to Chengdu. One of the best parts of making this dish is seeing how locals respond. When I serve it to friends here, they're often surprised and delighted by how the "fish" and sauce capture the textures and tastes they know so well.

Douban (豆瓣), or bean paste, is essential in Sichuan cooking and the backbone of many Sichuan dishes. The douban I like to use in this recipe is Pixian doubanjiang, a deep red fermented bean paste from Pixian County, made with broad beans and chile peppers. You can find it in jars or tubs in most Asian supermarkets. We also add black vinegar to the dish for a sharp acidity that cuts through the rich, spicy douban and lifts the whole flavor profile. The malty undertone of black vinegar balances beautifully with garlic and ginger. Honestly, you could spoon this sauce over a bowl of rice and call it a meal.

For the "fish":

1 Dou Bao "Fish" (page 113), steamed and cooled

3 to 4 tablespoons (45 to 60 ml) cooking oil, or enough to cover the bottom of the pan

For the sauce:

2 tablespoons cooking oil

1½ tablespoons doubanjiang (Sichuan chili bean paste), finely chopped

1 tablespoon minced fresh ginger

1 tablespoon minced garlic

1½ tablespoons sugar

¼ teaspoon mushroom seasoning

1 tablespoon Chinkiang black vinegar

Kosher salt, as needed

1 teaspoon cornstarch

For serving:

2 scallions, white and green parts, thinly sliced

Cooked rice

1. Pan-fry the "fish": Make several deep slits on one side of the bean curd "fish," being careful not to cut all the way through (aim for four or five slanted slits). In a wok or nonstick pan over low heat, warm the oil. Once the oil is hot, carefully place the "fish" into the pan with the slit side facing up. Pan-fry until golden brown on the bottom, then flip to cook the other side. Remove and set on a paper towel–lined plate to drain.

2. Make the sauce: Using the same pan, heat the oil over medium heat. Sauté the doubanjiang over medium heat until it releases its fragrant red oil, about 30 seconds. Be cautious, as the paste may sputter upon contact with the pan. Add the ginger and garlic, stir-frying until fragrant, about 30 seconds more. Add 1 cup (240 ml) water and bring everything to a boil. Add the sugar, mushroom seasoning, and black vinegar. Taste and adjust the seasoning with salt, if needed.

recipe continues

3. Reduce the heat to low to maintain a gentle simmer. Gently place the pan-fried "fish" into the sauce, slit side up. Baste it with a spoon to ensure it absorbs the flavors.

4. Prepare the slurry: In a small bowl, mix the cornstarch with 1 tablespoon water.

5. Drizzle the slurry around the "fish" in the simmering liquid, stirring gently to thicken. Continue basting the "fish" with the sauce until most of the liquid is absorbed and the "fish" is coated in a glossy sauce.

6. Finish and serve: Remove the pan from the heat, fold in the scallions, and serve warm with rice.

La Zi Ji

(Spicy Fried Lion's Mane Mushrooms)

Serves 2 or 3

La zi ji commands attention when it hits the table. It's an overwhelming pile of fiery red chiles and golden, crispy bites of fried chicken, though in my recipe I use lion's mane mushrooms. Originally from Chongqing, a city famous for its intensely spicy food, la zi ji doesn't just embrace heat but flaunts it. In Sichuan locals love to snack on la zi ji, often accompanied by a cold beer. I still remember watching my sister carefully pick out pieces of chicken from the pile of chiles. That's the real fun of this dish—sifting through it like a culinary treasure hunt. And if you're more adventurous, you might dare to nibble on the chiles themselves. Serve this with some steamed rice to balance the heat, or enjoy it straight as an addictive snack.

For the mushrooms:

3 medium heads (60 g) dried lion's mane mushrooms

Cooking oil, for frying

For the batter:

6 tablespoons (50 g) all-purpose flour

6 tablespoons (50 g) rice flour

½ teaspoon kosher salt

¼ teaspoon ground white pepper

For the aromatics:

Cooking oil, as needed

1-inch (2.5 cm) piece (10 g) fresh ginger, peeled and thinly sliced

1 tablespoon red Sichuan peppercorns

2 cups (40 g) dried chiles, cut into 2-inch (5 cm) sections with seeds shaken out

For serving:

1 tablespoon soy sauce

¼ teaspoon mushroom seasoning

Kosher salt, as needed

Cooked rice (optional)

1. Soak the mushrooms: Place the dried mushrooms in a large bowl, covering them with water. Weigh them down with a plate to keep them submerged. Soak for 20 to 30 minutes, then gently squeeze to remove the bitter amber-colored liquid. Drain and soak again with fresh water for another 5 minutes. Repeat this process about two more times, until the water runs clear. Tear the mushrooms into ½-inch (12 mm) chunks.

2. Prepare the batter: In a large bowl, whisk together the all-purpose flour, rice flour, salt, white pepper, and ½ cup (120 ml) water to form a smooth, thick batter. Gently fold the mushrooms into the batter, ensuring each piece is thoroughly coated.

3. Fry the mushrooms: In a wok or deep skillet, add enough oil to reach about ½ inch (12 mm) up the sides (about 1 cup / 240 ml for a smaller, 8- to 10-inch skillet, or 2 cups / 480 ml for a larger, 12- to 14-inch wok). Heat the oil to 350°F (175°C). Fry the battered mushrooms in batches, turning them once a crust forms. Cook until golden brown and very crispy,

recipe continues

3 to 4 minutes. Reserving the oil in the pan, transfer the mushrooms to a paper towel–lined plate to drain.

4. Stir-fry the aromatics: Heat the same pan and remaining oil (or if needed, clean out the wok and start with a fresh ¼ cup / 60 ml oil) over medium heat. Add the ginger and sizzle, about 30 seconds. Add the Sichuan peppercorns and chiles, stir-frying for 1 minute, until fragrant, keeping a close eye so that they don't darken too quickly in the oil.

5. Combine and serve: Return the fried mushrooms to the wok. Add the soy sauce and mushroom seasoning, then stir-fry briskly over high heat for about 1 minute, allowing the flavors to meld. Taste and adjust the seasoning with salt, if needed. Serve immediately, either as a snack or alongside a meal with rice.

Suan Cai Yu

(Sichuan Sour Mustard "Fish")

Serves 4

When I first tried suan cai yu at a vegetarian restaurant in Chengdu, I was hooked. Unlike Sichuan's fiery, red-oil dishes, this was a mellow, cloudy broth—sour, savory, and laced with numbing heat. Growing up with pickled mustard greens in Teochew cuisine, I felt an instant connection. Its delicate appearance contrasted with bold, layered flavors, finishing with tongue-tingling heat and a pleasantly sour note.

Newer than Sichuan's staples, suan cai yu originated in Chongqing (part of Sichuan until 1997) and quickly became a sensation in Chengdu. Its flavor lies in the broth, simmered to extract the essence of pickled mustard greens and fresh aromatics. I swap in king oyster mushrooms for the fish fillets, which, once boiled and lightly pounded, develop a porous texture that soaks up flavors like fish does. This recipe is my tribute to Chengdu's inventive vegetarian scene, where chefs create dishes as beautiful as they are delicious. Whether you're diving into this with rice or solo, suan cai yu's spicy and sour intensity makes you come back for more.

For the broth ***(or substitute 4 cups / 1 L Basic Vegetable Stock, page 37, or store-bought)*****:**

1 tablespoon cooking oil

1½ pounds (675 g) daikon radish, peeled and roll-cut into 2-inch (5 cm) chunks

For the mushroom "fish":

18 ounces (500 g) king oyster mushrooms, sliced diagonally into ¼-inch-thick (6 mm) slices

1 tablespoon Shaoxing cooking wine

¼ teaspoon mushroom seasoning

½ teaspoon kosher salt

Dash of ground white pepper

1 to 2 tablespoons cornstarch, as needed

For the sour mustard soup:

5 tablespoons (75 ml) cooking oil

8 ounces (225 g) pickled mustard greens, coarsely chopped, rinsed, and squeezed dry (about 2 cups)

1-inch (2.5 cm) piece (10 g) fresh ginger, peeled and thinly sliced

1. Make the broth: Heat the oil in a large, heavy-bottomed pot over medium heat. Add the daikon radish and sauté until softened on the edges, about 2 minutes. Pour in 8 cups (2 L) water and bring to a boil. Cover the pot and gently boil until the liquid reduces by half, 25 to 30 minutes. Strain the broth, discarding the daikon or reserving it for another use. Measure out 4 cups (1 L) of the broth.

2. Prepare the mushrooms: Bring a large pot of water to a boil. Blanch the mushroom slices for about 2 minutes, until they shrink slightly. Transfer them to a bowl of ice water, then drain and squeeze out as much liquid as possible. Gently pound the mushroom slices with a rolling pin or meat tenderizer to break

recipe and ingredients continue

3 scallions, finely chopped, white and green parts separated

10 to 12 dried chile peppers (1 cup / 20 g), cut into 2-inch (5 cm) sections with seeds removed

2 tablespoons Pickled Green Chiles (page 39), or store-bought (optional)

½ teaspoon mushroom seasoning

½ teaspoon sugar

1½ tablespoons white vinegar

Kosher salt

1½ teaspoons minced garlic

1 tablespoon green Sichuan peppercorns (preferably fresh), or substitute a drizzle of Sichuan peppercorn (teng jiao) oil

2 tablespoons cooking oil

For serving:

Cooked rice

down the fibers, then toss with the cooking wine, mushroom seasoning, salt, and white pepper. Sprinkle 1 tablespoon of the cornstarch on top of the mushroom slices. Using a claw-like method, toss the mushrooms in the starch until they are well coated, adding another 1 tablespoon of the cornstarch if needed. Set the "fish" aside to marinate.

3. Prepare the soup: Heat 3 tablespoons (45 ml) of the oil in a large wok or saucepan over medium heat. Stir-fry the mustard greens for 2 to 3 minutes to release their flavor and dry them out a little. Push them to one side, then add the ginger, white parts of the scallions, dried chiles, and pickled chiles. Stir-fry for 1 minute, until fragrant. Pour in the reserved broth and bring to a boil. Cover and let it boil for 5 minutes. Season with the mushroom seasoning, sugar, vinegar, and salt to taste. Adjust the seasoning as needed—the broth should be very flavorful.

4. Strain out the solids from the broth and transfer them to a large serving bowl. Bring the strained broth back to a boil over medium-high heat. Carefully drop the "fish" slices into the broth one at a time, spacing them evenly to prevent sticking. Reduce the heat to a simmer and cook for 2 minutes, until tender, gently nudging apart any slices that stick.

5. Prepare the fragrant oil: Heat the remaining 2 tablespoons oil in a small saucepan over medium heat. Add the garlic and Sichuan peppercorns and cook, stirring quickly, for about 15 seconds.

6. Finish and serve: Remove the mushroom "fish" from the broth and place them atop the reserved mustard greens and other solids in the serving bowl. Ladle the hot broth over the top. Place the chopped green parts of the scallions over the mushroom "fish" in a pile. Pour the hot oil mixture over the scallions. They will release a sizzling sound. Serve warm with rice.

Chapter 5

Dim Sum and Dumplings

Loh Mai Gai *(Steamed Glutinous Rice with Mushrooms)*

Chai Kuih *(Crystal Dumplings)*

Si Yao Wong Chao Min *(King Soy Sauce Fried Noodles)*

Sin Jyuk Guen *(Steamed Tofu Skin Rolls)*

Crispy Pan-Fried Tofu Skin Rolls

Lobak Gou *(Pan-Fried Daikon Radish Cake)*

Golden Bottom Potstickers

Sheng Jian Bao *(Pan-Fried Cabbage Buns)*

No-Yeast Crispy Bottom Vegetable Buns

Chao Shou *(Wontons in Chili Oil)*

"Har gao, siu mai, char siu bao!" (Shrimp dumpling, pork dumpling, char siu bun!) call the dim sum cart-pushers as they weave through the restaurant's tables, stacking bamboo steamers and offering up treasures hidden under their lids. Steam rises in swirls as servers pause just long enough to set down the next dish. There's a comforting rhythm in the hum of conversation, the gentle clink of chopsticks, the sound of tea streaming into porcelain cups, and the aroma of charred lobak gou and wok-seared noodles drifting from the kitchen. This is yum cha, or "drink tea" in Cantonese, a ritual my family enjoys on a weekend—a time to gather around shared plates and endless pots of tea.

A server revealing fluffy buns and gleaming loh mai gai at a busy dim sum restaurant.

Dim sum, or "dot heart," is heart in every bite—dumplings, buns bursting with fillings, charred noodles, and sticky sweets. Here, I've reimagined some of my favorites, including two kinds of tofu skin rolls: one steamed (Sin Jyuk Guen, page 157) and one pan-fried (page 161), each with its own charm; there's also pan-fried Lobak Gou, a savory daikon cake (page 163), and vegan Malaysian-style Loh Mai Gai, sticky rice steamed in a bowl (page 149).

In this chapter, you'll find my most popular dumpling recipes and my own favorites, recipes that are crowd-pleasers and great fun to make with friends. A standout is the no-yeast crispy bottom bun, born of the yeast shortage during the pandemic and an instant hit. And of course, there's my Sichuan wontons in chili oil (Chao Shou, page 177), which my whole family can't resist—it's a wonton so good I could easily eat ten in one sitting.

A Note on Dumplings

With my Teochew and Cantonese roots, I've always had a soft spot for dumplings—anything wrapped, pleated, or folded into a little parcel of joy. My first experience was with pleating wontons. I'd often frequent a wonton noodle stall near my home, and when the owner was struggling without help one busy day, I offered to wrap wontons for her. It led to a friendship, and I was even invited to her wedding.

Loh Mai Gai

(Steamed Glutinous Rice with Mushrooms)

Makes 6 rice bowls

Loh mai gai, Cantonese for "glutinous rice chicken," is a must-order for us every time we go out for dim sum. In its classic form, it's steamed in lotus leaves for that subtle, earthy fragrance—a treat at fancier spots. But in Malaysian dim sum restaurants, it often takes a more straightforward, no-fuss approach: the rice steamed in a stainless-steel bowl, soaking up every bit of that rich sauce. In my take, I've swapped the chicken for shiitake mushrooms and textured vegetable protein (TVP), both lacquered in a dark, savory sauce until they're deeply aromatic. Then they're steamed with seasoned sticky rice, allowing all the flavor to meld.

My favorite part of this dish is the reveal. To serve, flip the bowl upside down on a plate and gently lift it off, letting that rich sauce cascade down, coating every bite. Everyone oohs at that final touch of flavor and moisture.

For the rice:

2 cups (420 g) glutinous rice, soaked for at least 4 hours, rinsed three times until the water runs clear, drained

For the sauce:

1 tablespoon cooking oil

3 slices peeled fresh ginger (about ¾ inch / 2 cm piece), finely chopped

2 garlic cloves, finely chopped

6 large or 12 small dried shiitake mushrooms, rehydrated and destemmed (reserve the soaking liquid)

¾ cup (55 g) textured vegetable protein (TVP) slices, rehydrated and squeezed to drain

1 tablespoon soy sauce

1 tablespoon Shaoxing cooking wine

1 tablespoon vegetarian oyster sauce

½ teaspoon dark caramel soy sauce

½ teaspoon sugar

½ teaspoon toasted sesame oil

⅛ teaspoon ground white pepper

1 teaspoon cornstarch

2 tablespoons cold water

1. **Steam the rice:** Spread the soaked, drained rice in an even layer inside a heatproof bowl or container that fits in your steamer. Steam over high heat for 40 minutes, adding ¼ cup (60 ml) water halfway through to help the rice cook evenly. The rice should be fully cooked but still slightly chewy.

2. **Make the sauce:** Heat the oil in a large skillet or nonstick pan. Sauté the ginger and garlic until fragrant, about 30 seconds. Add the drained mushrooms and sauté until they start to color on the edges, about 1 minute. Add the drained TVP, soy sauce, cooking wine, and vegetarian oyster sauce, tossing everything to coat. Stir in the dark caramel soy sauce, sugar, sesame oil, white pepper, and ½ cup (120 ml) water. Simmer for about 3 minutes, letting the TVP and mushrooms absorb the flavors.

3. **Make the slurry:** In a small bowl, whisk the cornstarch with the cold water to form a slurry.

recipe and ingredients continue

For the loh mai gai:

1 tablespoon soy sauce

2 tablespoons vegetarian oyster sauce

1 teaspoon dark caramel soy sauce

2 tablespoons Shallot Oil (page 43)

½ teaspoon toasted sesame oil

⅛ teaspoon ground white pepper

1 teaspoon sugar

¼ teaspoon kosher salt

For serving:

Hoisin sauce and chile sauce

4. Gradually drizzle the slurry into the pan, stirring continuously, until the sauce thickens and coats the TVP and mushrooms. Remove from the heat.

5. **Season the rice:** Transfer the steamed rice to a large bowl. In a small bowl or measuring cup, combine the soy sauce, vegetarian oyster sauce, dark caramel soy sauce, shallot oil, sesame oil, white pepper, sugar, salt, and ½ cup (120 ml) water to make a flavorful broth. Gradually add the broth to the cooked rice, stirring with chopsticks until the rice absorbs all the liquid.

6. **Assemble:** Prepare six heatproof rice bowls. In the bottom of each, arrange 1 or 2 mushrooms along with a spoonful of TVP and sauce. Gently press the seasoned rice into each bowl, leaving about a ⅜-inch (1 cm) gap from the top. Drizzle 2 tablespoons of the reserved mushroom soaking liquid into each bowl.

7. **Steam and serve:** Place the bowls in a steamer basket, cover, and steam over high heat for 40 minutes, until the loh mai gai is sticky and tender. To serve, run a small spatula or knife around the edge of each bowl to loosen the rice, then invert the bowl onto a serving plate. Serve warm with hoisin and chile sauce on the side.

Chai Kuih

(Crystal Dumplings)

Makes 24 dumplings

Every Friday, the Taman Desa pasar malam—a bustling night market in Kuala Lumpur—sprang to life in a swirl of sights, sounds, and the unmistakable aroma of street food. "Bi, it's Friday, let's hit Taman Desa!" I'd say to my boyfriend (now husband), who was just as eager as I was for chai kuih, as is said in Teochew (kaw ji in Cantonese). These savory dumplings, filled with shredded jicama, weren't always found in dim sum establishments, so we'd make a beeline to the stall at the Taman Desa before they sold out. On lucky days, the seller was still there, donning gloves and filling boxes with the delicate dumplings, adding a drizzle of chile sauce or a sprinkle of crispy fried garlic if we asked. Each bite was all about that first tug of steaming translucent skin, followed by the tender jicama.

Chai kuih, it turns out, brought us together—it was on those Friday night pasar malam dates that my husband and I bonded over our shared love for these dumplings. As my kitchen confidence grew, I began making them at home, refining the recipe for a satisfying bite. A starch blend helps provide the perfect chew, while the filling—a stir-fry of jicama, carrot, and a touch of white pepper—keeps the flavors simple. We hope you'll love these traditional Teochew dumplings that wove us together.

For the filling:

- 2 tablespoons cooking oil
- 1 small (80 g) carrot, shredded (about ¾ cup)
- 1 pound (450 g) jicama, peeled and shredded (about 3½ cups)
- ½ teaspoon kosher salt
- ½ teaspoon mushroom seasoning
- Dash of ground white pepper
- 2 teaspoons toasted sesame oil
- 1 stalk fresh cilantro, finely chopped (both stems and leaves)

For the wrappers:

- 1 cup (130 g) wheat starch
- ¾ cup (130 g) tapioca starch, plus more for dusting
- ¼ teaspoon kosher salt
- Scant 1 cup (230 g) boiling water
- 1 tablespoon cooking oil

For assembly and serving:

- Banana leaves or parchment paper, for lining
- Shallot Oil (page 43) or scallion oil, for coating (optional)
- Chile sauce (such as the "Chicken" Rice Chili Sauce, page 35)

1. Cook the filling: In a large pan or wok, heat the oil over medium heat. Add the carrot and stir-fry for about 2 minutes, until it begins to soften. Stir in the jicama and cook until the edges are translucent and any liquid has evaporated (see Notes, page 153). Season with the salt, mushroom seasoning, white pepper, and sesame oil. Fold in the cilantro. Taste and adjust the seasoning if necessary—the filling should be tender and very flavorful. Let cool.

2. Make the wrappers: In a large heatproof bowl, combine the wheat starch, tapioca starch, and salt. Gradually pour in the boiling water, stirring with a

recipe continues

Notes:

- *Cooking time for the filling may vary depending on the moisture content of the jicama. You want the filling to be mostly dry to prevent the wrappers from breaking.*
- *Leftover dumplings can be refrigerated or frozen in a single layer. Reheat by steaming directly from the fridge or freezer until the inside is hot.*

Heaps of fresh jicama at Malaysia's lively pasar.

spatula or thin rolling pin. The starches will begin to clump. Form the mixture into a shaggy, sticky dough. Cover the bowl with a lid and let it rest for 5 minutes to "steam" the dough.

3. After resting, knead the dough in the bowl until it's smooth and pliable. If it's too dry, add room-temperature water, 1 tablespoon at a time. Transfer the dough to a clean surface, add the oil, and continue kneading for 5 to 10 minutes, until it's soft, smooth, and glossy. Roll the dough into a rope and divide it into 24 equal pieces (about ⅔ ounce / 18 to 19 g each) with a sharp knife. Keep the dough covered with a damp towel to prevent drying out.

4. Assemble: Cut 24 squares of banana leaves or parchment paper (about 3 inches / 7.5 cm each). Lightly dust your working surface with tapioca starch.

5. Take one portion of dough and flatten it with your palm. Roll it into a thin disc about 3½ inches (9 cm) in diameter. Place the wrapper in your nondominant hand and spoon about 2 tablespoons of filling onto the center, spreading it out evenly with the spoon. Fold the wrapper in half so that the edges meet, and pinch all along the half-moon rim to seal. You can crimp the edge into pleats if desired. Place each dumpling on a banana leaf or parchment square, with its pleated edge facing upward.

6. Steam: Set up a steamer with water in the bottom half and bring to a rolling boil. Arrange the dumplings on their squares in a single layer, about 1 inch (2.5 cm) apart, in the steamer basket. Steam for 12 to 15 minutes, until the skins become tender and glossy—they will turn translucent as they cool.

7. Finish and serve: Uncover the dumplings and brush the tops with a thin layer of shallot or scallion oil (optional, to prevent the dumplings from drying out). Serve at room temperature with a side of chile sauce.

Si Yao Wong Chao Min

(King Soy Sauce Fried Noodles)

Serves 2

This Cantonese favorite, dubbed "soy sauce king" or "soy sauce supreme" stir-fried noodles, is my dim sum obsession in the US. I'd always beg for extra bean sprouts—I love how their crisp snap cuts through the dish's richness. What hooked me was that intoxicating aroma: soy sauce caramelizing in a screaming-hot wok, mingling with the chewy, slightly charred noodles for a deep hit of umami. Irresistible every time.

I traded egg noodles for vegan ramen, which has a similar bouncy chew and faint alkaline tang. It's a perfect stand-in. A quick tip: I'd dry the noodles post-cooking, letting them air out without clumping, to prep them for the final wok sear. Bean sprouts and chives get a fast toss in hot oil to keep them crisp and vibrant, while a pinch of sugar in the sauce coaxes out smoky wok hei—the elusive aroma. It's Cantonese soul food: humble stuff turned sublime with a little technique.

For the sauce:

1 tablespoon soy sauce, plus more as needed

1 tablespoon dark soy sauce, plus more as needed

1½ teaspoons vegetarian oyster sauce

1 teaspoon sugar

For the noodles:

8 ounces (225 g) fresh yellow noodles, such as ramen

2 tablespoons cooking oil, plus more to keep the noodles from sticking

1½ cups (160 g) mung bean sprouts, ends pinched off

2 stalks Chinese chives or 2 scallions, cut into 2-inch (5 cm) segments (about ½ cup)

1 large shallot, thinly sliced

Sesame seeds, for serving (optional)

1. Prepare the sauce: In a small bowl, combine the soy sauces, vegetarian oyster sauce, and sugar.

2. Prepare the noodles: Bring a large pot of water to a rolling boil. Add the noodles, spreading them out in the water with chopsticks or tongs. Turn off the heat immediately and let the noodles sit for 1 minute to cook. Remove the noodles with tongs and transfer to a large plate, shaking off as much water as possible. Rub a couple teaspoons of oil into the noodles to prevent them from sticking. Let them cool.

3. Stir-fry the vegetables: Heat 1 teaspoon of the oil in a large skillet or wok over high heat. Stir-fry the mung bean sprouts for about 30 seconds, until hot but still crisp. Transfer to a bowl. Add another 2 teaspoons of the oil to the same skillet and sauté the chives and shallot until fragrant, about 30 seconds. Add to the bowl.

recipe continues

4. **Pan-fry the noodles:** Heat the remaining 1 tablespoon oil in the skillet over medium-high heat. Add the oiled noodles, spreading them evenly across the bottom of the pan. Let the noodles sear for 1 to 2 minutes, then flip and cook the other side.

5. Increase the heat to high and pour half the sauce over the noodles. Toss the noodles with tongs or chopsticks to coat evenly. Add the mung bean sprouts, chives, shallot, and the remaining sauce. Continue tossing until the noodles absorb the sauce and start to develop a slight crisp on the edges. Taste and season with more soy sauce if needed, allowing any added liquid to fully evaporate. The noodles should be dry and slightly seared on the edges, fragrant and chewy with a bite to them.

6. **Serve:** Garnish with sesame seeds if desired and serve immediately.

Sin Jyuk Guen

(Steamed Tofu Skin Rolls)

Serves 4 to 6 (makes 16 rolls)

Everyone in my family knows I'm a hardcore fu chuk lover. Tofu skin, formed on the surface of boiling soymilk, can be dried or enjoyed fresh, each version soaking up broth, stew, or sauce with its delicate texture.

The magic of this dish lies in the filling: a simple mix of vegetables and tofu, seasoned well and rolled in large, moistened tofu skin sheets from the frozen section, which resemble oilcloth. Once pan-fried until golden, they are steamed, allowing the skin to absorb the flavors and become chewy and juicy. Making them at home is a bit involved, but once you get the hang of it, they're a crowd-pleaser! Something about the flavors makes people fall in love with tofu skin, even if they've never had it before.

For the filling:

One 14- to 16-ounce (390 to 450 g) package firm tofu, drained and pressed

2 teaspoons cooking oil

2 large dried shiitake mushrooms, rehydrated and finely chopped (3 tablespoons)

¼ ounce (7 g) dried wood ear mushrooms, rehydrated and finely chopped

3 tablespoons sweet corn kernels or edamame

3 tablespoons finely chopped carrot

3 tablespoons peeled and finely chopped water chestnut

3 tablespoons finely chopped fresh cilantro (reserve some for garnish)

½ teaspoon kosher salt, plus more if needed

½ teaspoon mushroom seasoning

¼ teaspoon ground white pepper

Drizzle of toasted sesame oil

2 tablespoons cornstarch

1. Make the filling: Place the tofu on a clean surface and press and mash it into a thick paste using a knife or flat pastry scraper. (Alternatively, squeeze the tofu dry in a nut milk bag or press in a mesh strainer.) Once there are no large lumps, transfer the mashed tofu to a large bowl.

2. Heat the oil in a large skillet or nonstick pan over medium-low heat. Sauté the shiitake mushrooms and wood ear mushrooms until fragrant, about 2 minutes. Transfer to the bowl of tofu. Add the corn, carrot, water chestnut, and cilantro to the mixture. Season with the salt, mushroom seasoning, white pepper, and sesame oil. Taste and add more salt if needed. Stir in the cornstarch and mix using a spatula or your hand until the filling is well-combined and holds together.

3. Prepare the bean curd sheets: Cut the bean curd sheets into 6 by 6-inch (15 by 15 cm) squares (you'll need 16 total). If using frozen bean curd sheets, they should be pliable straight from the packet. If using dried sheets, soak them in cold water until flexible,

recipe and ingredients continue

For assembly and frying:

8 ounces (225 g) semi-dried bean curd sheets, preferably from frozen

1 tablespoon cornstarch

Cooking oil

For the sauce:

1 tablespoon cooking oil

3 slices peeled fresh ginger (about ¾ inch / 2 cm piece)

2 scallions, white and green parts, cut into 2-inch (5 cm) segments

1 tablespoon vegetarian oyster sauce

2 teaspoons soy sauce

½ teaspoon sugar

¼ teaspoon mushroom seasoning

⅛ teaspoon ground white pepper

1 tablespoon cornstarch mixed with 2 tablespoons water

For serving:

Chopped fresh cilantro

Chile sauce (such as the "Chicken" Rice Chili Sauce, page 35)

then gently press out the excess water. Handle carefully, as the sheets are fragile and can tear easily. Keep them covered with a damp towel.

4. **Assemble:** In a small bowl, whisk together the cornstarch and 1½ tablespoons water to make a slurry. Lay out one square of bean curd on a clean surface and brush lightly with slurry to moisten. Place about 2 tablespoons of filling near the bottom edge. Fold the sides in toward the center, then roll the sheet up toward the top like a spring roll. When about 1 inch (2.5 cm) remains, brush with a bit more slurry to seal (save some for the sauce). Roll tightly and set aside. Repeat with the remaining sheets and filling, keeping the finished rolls covered with a damp towel.

5. **Fry the rolls:** Heat a large skillet with about ½ inch (12 mm) oil over medium-high heat to 350°F (175°C). To test the oil temperature, insert a wooden chopstick—it should release a merry stream of small bubbles. Fry the rolls in batches, carefully sliding them into the oil and cooking until golden and crispy. Transfer to a paper towel–lined plate to drain.

6. **Make the sauce:** Wipe out the skillet, then heat the oil for the sauce over medium heat (add a drizzle of oil if the pan is dry). Sauté the ginger and scallions until the ginger is fragrant and the scallions start to brown, about 2 minutes. Add ¾ cup (180 ml) water, bring to a boil, and stir in the vegetarian oyster sauce, soy sauce, sugar, mushroom seasoning, and white pepper. Once the sugar dissolves, discard the ginger and scallions. Slowly whisk in the remaining slurry, stirring until the sauce thickens and turns glossy and pourable like gravy.

7. **Steam and serve:** Divide the fried rolls between two heatproof plates (8 rolls per plate), arranging them in a single layer. Spoon half of the sauce over each plate of rolls. Place the plates in a steamer and steam over high heat for 8 to 10 minutes, until the rolls are tender and glistening, surrounded by a flavorful broth. Garnish with cilantro and serve warm with chile sauce.

Crispy Pan-Fried Tofu Skin Rolls

For the filling:

1 tablespoon cooking oil

1 small carrot (80 g), julienned (about ¾ cup)

4 ounces (115 g) oyster mushrooms, julienned

8 ounces (225 g) cabbage, shredded (about 3 cups)

¼ ounce (7 g) dried wood ear mushrooms, rehydrated and julienned

⅓ cup (50 g) bamboo shoot slices, julienned

¼ teaspoon mushroom seasoning

¼ teaspoon kosher salt, plus more as needed

1 teaspoon soy sauce

1 teaspoon vegetarian oyster sauce

¼ teaspoon ground white pepper

1 stalk fresh cilantro, finely chopped (leaves and stem)

½ teaspoon toasted sesame oil

For assembly, frying, and serving:

8 ounces (225 g) semi-dried bean curd sheets, preferably from frozen

Cooking oil

Thai sweet chile sauce, "Chicken" Rice Chili Sauce (page 35), Chili Oil (page 41), or hoisin sauce, for serving

Makes 6 rolls

Unlike Sin Jyuk Guen (page 157), these tofu skin rolls skip the sauce and steaming, going straight into the pan for a crispy finish. They're one of the meatless options I can reliably find at dim sum spots in the States, and they usually come with a side of chili oil. They're simple to make at home and I love them as breakfast, a side dish, or a quick snack!

For the filling in these rolls, I like a variety of mushrooms. Wood ear mushrooms add a bit of crunch, while oyster mushrooms bring juicy savoriness. Sautéed cabbage and carrot add sweetness and depth, plus they're a great way to sneak in more veggies. When wrapping, I always double up on the tofu skin sheets; this locks in the filling and gives you extra crispy layers.

1. Cook the filling: Heat the oil in a large skillet or nonstick pan over medium-high heat. Sauté the carrot until crisp-tender, about 30 seconds. Add the oyster mushrooms and sauté for another minute. Stir in the cabbage, wood ear mushrooms, and bamboo shoots and cook for 1 minute, until the cabbage wilts. Season with the mushroom seasoning, salt, soy sauce, vegetarian oyster sauce, and white pepper. Taste and adjust the seasoning as needed. Turn off the heat and transfer the filling to a bowl to cool. Stir in the chopped cilantro and sesame oil.

2. Prepare the bean curd sheets: Stack the bean curd sheets and cut them into twelve rectangles, about 10 by 12 inches (25 by 30.5 cm) each. If using frozen bean curd sheets, they will be pliable directly from the freezer. If using dried sheets, soak them in cold water until soft, then gently press out the excess water. Handle with care, as the sheets are delicate and may tear easily.

recipe continues

3. Assemble: Divide the filling into six portions. Lay two bean curd sheets side by side on a clean surface. Place one portion of the filling in the center of the first sheet and roll it like a burrito, folding the sides as you roll to enclose the filling. Place this roll onto the second bean curd sheet and repeat the process; the double layer offers extra structure. Set the finished roll seam side down on a plate. Repeat with the remaining sheets and filling to make six double-layered rolls.

4. Fry the rolls: Heat a large skillet or nonstick pan over medium-low heat with enough oil to cover the bottom. Arrange the rolls seam side down in the pan, making sure there is enough space between them to avoid overcrowding. Fry the rolls, turning occasionally, for 4 to 6 minutes total, until all sides are crispy and golden brown.

5. Serve: Enjoy the rolls warm or at room temperature with your choice of dipping sauce.

Lobak Gou

(Pan-Fried Daikon Radish Cake)

Serves 3 or 4

This is one of my favorite dim sum recipes, right up there with taro cake (Orh Tau Kuih, page 321). I love anything soft and steamed that's made with rice flour. This carrot-laced daikon cake has a melt-in-your-mouth tenderness and a sweet savoriness you only get from cooked radish. Although it can be served straight out of the steamer, I always pan-fry it for extra-crispy edges!

Symbolically, the dish represents hopes for a better year ahead. In Cantonese, *gou* (糕) is a homonym for "tall" or "high" (高), making lobak gou a popular dish to share with loved ones during Chinese New Year for the way it brings rising prosperity to diners. If you want to get extra auspicious, you can say to your coworkers or friends, "Bou bou gou sing," which translates to "Each step going higher."

For the batter:

1½ cups (210 g) rice flour

¼ teaspoon mushroom seasoning

¼ teaspoon kosher salt

2 cups (480 ml) warm water

For the vegetables:

1 tablespoon cooking oil, plus more for frying

8 large dried shiitake mushrooms, rehydrated and finely chopped

1 small (80 g) carrot, shredded (about ¾ cup)

1 pound (450 g) daikon radish, peeled and shredded

½ teaspoon kosher salt

⅛ teaspoon ground white pepper

1 tablespoon Fried Shallots (page 43), or store-bought

For frying and serving:

Cooking oil, for frying

Hoisin sauce

Chili Oil (page 41), or store-bought chile sauce

1. Make the batter: In a large bowl, whisk together the rice flour, mushroom seasoning, salt, and warm water until smooth. Let the mixture rest while you prepare the vegetables.

2. Cook the vegetables: Heat the oil in a large skillet or nonstick pan over medium-high heat. Sauté the shiitake mushrooms for about 30 seconds, until fragrant. Add the carrot and stir-fry for another 30 seconds, until softened. Add the daikon radish and cook for about 2 minutes, until it releases its liquid and takes on a golden hue from the carrots. Continue stir-frying until all the moisture evaporates. Season with the salt and white pepper and fold in the fried shallots. Turn the heat to low.

3. Combine the batter and vegetables: Stir the batter in the bowl to recombine, then pour it into the pan with the carrot-daikon mixture. Swiftly incorporate the batter into the shredded vegetables, stirring and folding continuously until the batter cooks into a very thick paste.

recipe continues

Note:

This a great make-ahead recipe: Steam the cake the night before, let it set in the fridge, and then slice it up to pan-fry for breakfast or whenever you're ready to serve.

4. Lightly grease a 9 by 4-inch (23 by 10 cm) loaf pan. Transfer the mixture to the pan, using a spatula to smooth the top and press the mixture into the corners. I like to use a toothpick or fork to poke all along the surface to ensure there are no large air pockets.

5. **Steam:** Bring a large pot of water to a rolling boil. Place the loaf pan in a steamer basket over the boiling water. Cover the pot with a lid wrapped in a towel to prevent condensation from dripping into the batter. Steam the cake for 45 minutes, until a cake tester inserted into the center comes out clean.

6. **Set overnight:** Let the lobak gou cool completely in the pan, then refrigerate overnight to fully set.

7. **Pan-fry and serve:** The next day, loosen the set lobak gou from the pan. Using a greased knife, cut the cake into 1-inch-thick (2.5 cm) slices. Heat a nonstick pan over medium-high heat with enough oil to coat the bottom. Pan-fry the slices until golden brown and crispy on both sides. Serve with hoisin sauce and chili oil or chile sauce as a breakfast dish or snack.

Golden Bottom Potstickers

Makes 40 to 50 potstickers

After moving to the States in 1999, I started a tradition of making dumplings with our kids during Chinese New Year once they were toddlers and old enough to join in, as a way for my husband and me to share our culture. I'd always tell them that dumplings are more than just food—they're symbols of wealth and prosperity in Chinese tradition. The process became a hands-on ritual that tied us not only to our heritage but to each other. Mixing the filling, pleating the dough, cooking, and of course eating together—it all keeps us connected to a tradition we want to preserve while letting us create something uniquely ours.

The kids adore the messy, tactile fun of it, and it's the perfect time to swap stories about our heritage. Our potstickers may not perfectly mimic the ingot shape of ancient Chinese currency, but their golden-bottomed bellies carry the same wishes for good fortune. We hope these potstickers bring you as much joy in making and sharing them as they do for us!

For the filling:

1 tablespoon cooking oil

1 tablespoon minced fresh ginger

7 ounces (200 g) firm tofu, drained and pressed

1 medium round (8 ounces / 225 g) eggplant, diced into ¼-inch (6 mm) pieces

3½ ounces (100 g) green beans, trimmed and diced into ¼-inch (6 mm) pieces

8 ounces (225 g) cremini mushrooms, diced into ¼-inch (6 mm) pieces

¼ teaspoon kosher salt (see Notes, page 168)

½ teaspoon sugar

2 tablespoons soy sauce, or to taste (see Notes, page 168)

¼ teaspoon ground white pepper

1 teaspoon yellow or white miso paste (see Notes, page 168)

1 tablespoon toasted sesame oil

2 tablespoons (15 g) all-purpose flour or cornstarch, plus more for dusting

1. Cook the filling: Heat the oil in a large skillet or nonstick pan over medium-high heat. Add the ginger and sauté until fragrant and lightly golden. Crumble the tofu into the pan with your hands. Press the tofu with a spatula and let it cook undisturbed until a thin crust forms. Stir occasionally, breaking down the tofu further, and cook for 6 to 8 minutes, until browned around the edges.

2. Stir in the eggplant, green beans, and mushrooms. Stir-fry for about 5 minutes, until the vegetables are tender. Season with the salt, sugar, soy sauce, white pepper, and miso paste, using the back of your spatula to mash any miso clumps. Continue stir-frying over medium-high heat until most of the moisture evaporates. Taste the filling and adjust the saltiness if

recipe and ingredients continue

For assembly and frying:

40 to 50 dumpling wrappers, thawed to room temperature if frozen

2 teaspoons cooking oil

For serving:

Chili Oil (page 41) or Chinkiang black vinegar with slivered fresh ginger

Notes:

- *There are three salty components in this recipe: salt, soy sauce, and miso. Adjust the quantities according to your miso or soy sauce, as their saltiness may vary.*
- *The amount of water needed to cook the dumplings depends on the size of your pan and the number of dumplings. As a rule of thumb, add enough water to just submerge the bottom of the dumplings. For a 10-inch (25 cm) pan, ½ cup (120 ml) water works well.*

needed. Stir in the sesame oil and remove from the heat. If there's any remaining liquid, transfer the filling to a bowl with a slotted spoon to drain it. Once the filling has cooled, stir in the flour or cornstarch to bind the mixture.

3. Assemble: Set up a small bowl of water for sealing the dumplings and generously dust a plate or baking sheet with flour or cornstarch.

4. Take one dumpling wrapper and spoon about 2 teaspoons filling in the center. Wet the edges of the wrapper with a dab of water and fold it in half to form a half-moon shape. Pleat the edges tightly to seal, pressing firmly to ensure the filling stays enclosed. Place the dumpling on the floured surface. Repeat with the remaining filling, keeping the formed dumplings covered with a damp cloth to prevent drying out. You should end up with 40 to 50 dumplings, depending on the amount of filling you use for each.

5. Pan-fry the dumplings: Heat a large skillet or nonstick pan over medium heat. Add the oil and swirl to coat the bottom. Arrange as many dumplings as the pan will comfortably fit in a single layer, with a fingernail-width gap between each so they don't touch. Cook undisturbed for about 3 minutes, until the bottoms are lightly golden.

6. Add ½ cup (120 ml) water into the hot pan, enough to barely cover the bottom of each dumpling (see Notes). Cover the pan tightly with a lid and let the dumplings steam until the water has evaporated and you hear minimal sizzling. Uncover and check if the dumpling skins are semi-translucent and the bottoms are crispy and golden brown. Remove the potstickers to a plate, and repeat steps 5 and 6 with the remaining dumplings.

7. Serve: Serve with a side of chili oil or slivered ginger in Chinkiang black vinegar.

Sheng Jian Bao
(Pan-Fried Cabbage Buns)

Makes 20 small buns

Somewhere between potstickers and steamed buns, sheng jian bao get their name from the method of cooking them directly on a griddle after proofing. The buns are nestled in sizzling oil, crisping on the bottom, then doused with water and covered. As the steam fades, they're showered with sesame seeds and scallions and gently scraped from the pan, their browned bottoms sticking together like pull-apart rolls.

At home, my favorite moment is seeing them puff up under my skillet's glass lid. This recipe, one of the first I shared on social media, has evolved with whatever veggies I have—now a savory mix of cabbage, kale, mushrooms, and carrots. My twist? Dip the buns in sesame seeds before pan-frying for an extra nutty, crunchy crust—perfect with that tender, steamy top!

For the dough:

1¾ cups (210 g) all-purpose flour, plus more for dusting

1 packet (2¼ teaspoons / 7 g) active dry yeast

1 tablespoon sugar

⅔ cup (160 ml) unsweetened plant-based milk, warmed or at room temperature

1 tablespoon cooking oil

For the filling:

1 tablespoon cooking oil

2 teaspoons minced fresh ginger

About 6 medium dried shiitake mushrooms, rehydrated and thinly sliced

3 garlic cloves, minced

1 small (80 g) carrot, shredded or finely chopped

4 cups (14 ounces / 400 g) finely shredded cabbage

1 cup (100 g) shredded kale (or use more cabbage)

2 tablespoons soy sauce

2 teaspoons vegetarian oyster sauce

1. **Prepare the dough:** In a large bowl or the base of a stand mixer, combine the flour, yeast, and sugar. Add the plant-based milk. Knead into a soft dough, about 5 minutes, then add the oil and knead until smooth and elastic, 4 to 5 minutes longer. Cover the bowl and rest the dough for 30 minutes.

2. **Make the filling:** Heat the oil in a large skillet or nonstick pan over medium-high heat. Sauté the ginger, mushrooms, and garlic until fragrant, about 3 minutes. Add the carrot, cabbage, and kale and cook until the vegetables are as crisp-tender as you like, 2 to 4 minutes, stirring continuously to allow the moisture to evaporate. (If there is still liquid in the pan, transfer the mixture to a sieve to drain, squeezing out as much liquid as possible.) Stir in the soy sauce, vegetarian oyster sauce, and sugar, then fold in the scallions and white pepper and add the sesame oil. Taste and add salt if needed. Transfer the filling to a large bowl.

recipe and ingredients continue

1 teaspoon sugar

2 scallions, white and green parts, thinly sliced (reserve some of the greens for garnish)

⅛ teaspoon ground white pepper

1 teaspoon toasted sesame oil

Kosher salt, as needed

For assembling, frying, and serving:

½ cup (70 g) toasted sesame seeds (can be a mix of black and white)

3 tablespoons (45 ml) cooking oil

Chili Oil (page 41), or store-bought, for serving

Soy sauce, for serving

3. **Assemble:** Knead the dough lightly on a floured surface and shape it into a rope. Divide the log into twenty (20 g) portions and roll each one into a ball. Take one portion of dough and flatten it slightly with your palm into a circular disc. Position a rolling pin on the edge of the disc with your dominant hand. Roll the dough by pushing from the outside toward the middle of the circle, turning the dough with your nondominant hand, until the wrapper is 3 inches (7.5 cm) in diameter. There should be a quarter-sized "belly" in the center to hold the filling.

4. Prepare a small plate with water and another with toasted sesame seeds. Holding one wrapper in your nondominant palm, place a heaping tablespoon of filling in the center, leaving a ¾-inch (2 cm) margin of dough around the filling. Pinch the edge of the wrapper around the filling like closing the opening of a pouch, tightly sealing the dough with a final pinch. Dab the bottom of each bun in the plate of water and then press it into the sesame seeds to coat. Repeat with the remaining dough.

5. **Pan-fry the buns:** Heat the oil in a large skillet or nonstick pan over medium heat. When the oil is hot, arrange the buns sesame side down in a single layer, leaving a fingernail-width gap between each bun. Cook, undisturbed, until the bottoms are golden brown, about 2 minutes.

6. Carefully pour hot water into the pan, enough to rise up to a third of the buns' height. Immediately cover with a tight-fitting lid and steam the buns over medium-low heat for 5 to 6 minutes, or until the water has completely evaporated (listen for the sizzling to slow down). Uncover and continue frying until the buns are crispy and deeply browned on the bottom.

7. **Serve:** Serve warm with chili oil and soy sauce.

No-Yeast Crispy Bottom Vegetable Buns

Makes 10 buns

In the initial weeks of the COVID-19 pandemic, when there was a yeast shortage, this recipe was a big hit. Not only is the dough forgiving, needing no time to rise, but it bakes into the softest buns with a slightly crispy exterior and an aromatic sesame crust. The trick to the dough is using boiling hot water to mix it. This denatures the flour's protein and creates less elasticity, making it easy to roll out thin.

The filling is just as easy. I use green beans, carrot, and cilantro for a mix of flavor and crunch, all bound together with tender tofu. Be sure to season the mixture so it's slightly saltier than how you'd eat it on its own, as it mellows out in the bun, creating the perfect crunchy, flavor-packed bite!

For the dough:

2½ cups (300 g) all-purpose flour, plus more for dusting

¼ teaspoon kosher salt

¾ cup (80 ml) boiling water

½ cup (70 g) toasted sesame seeds (can be a mix of black and white)

For the filling:

One 14- to 16-ounce (390 to 450 g) package firm tofu, pressed and mashed

2 teaspoons cooking oil

8 ounces (250 g) green beans, cut into ⅛-inch (3 mm) dice (about 2 cups)

1 small carrot (80 g), finely chopped

Handful of fresh cilantro, finely chopped

1 teaspoon kosher salt, plus more as needed

½ teaspoon ground white pepper, plus more as needed

1 tablespoon toasted sesame oil

1. Make the dough: In a large bowl, combine the flour and salt. Make a well in the center and carefully pour in the boiling water. Stir the mixture with a spatula or chopsticks until it forms shaggy flakes. Once cool enough to handle, knead the dough in the bowl for 3 to 5 minutes to incorporate all the flour. If the dough feels too dry, add 1 tablespoon of cool water at a time. Turn the dough out onto a clean surface and knead until it's smooth and taut, 10 to 12 minutes. Cover with a bowl or a damp towel and let it rest for 30 minutes.

2. Prepare the filling: While the dough is resting, place the tofu in a nut milk bag or over a mesh strainer and squeeze out as much liquid as possible. Transfer the drained, mashed tofu to a large bowl.

3. Heat the oil in a large skillet or nonstick pan over medium-high heat. Sauté the green beans for about 2 minutes, until they become crisp-tender and darkened in color. Transfer to the bowl with the tofu.

recipe and ingredients continue

For pan-frying:

Cooking oil

For serving (choose one):

Chopped scallions and soy sauce

Slivered fresh ginger and Chinkiang vinegar

Chile sauce (such as the "Chicken" Rice Chili Sauce, page 35) or Chili Oil (page 41), or store-bought

Add the carrot and cilantro to the bowl, then season with the salt, white pepper, and sesame oil. Fold and mash the filling into a paste, adjusting seasoning as needed. The mixture should be slightly saltier than you'd eat on its own.

4. **Assemble:** Divide the filling into ten equal portions. Roll each portion into a ball with your palms, then flatten into a patty. Keep the patties covered until you're ready to form the buns.

5. Turn the rested dough onto a lightly floured surface and knead for about 2 minutes, until smooth. Roll the dough into a thick log and divide it into ten equal portions (45 to 50 g each). Keep the dough portions covered with a damp towel while you work.

6. Take one portion of dough and flatten it into a round disc with your palm. Using a rolling pin, roll the edges of the dough toward the center, pressing back and forth, turning the dough with your nondominant hand, until the wrapper is 4½ inches (11 cm) in diameter. There should be a quarter-sized "belly" in the center to hold the filling. Holding one wrapper in your nondominant palm, place a heaping tablespoon of filling in the center, leaving a ¾-inch (2 cm) margin of dough around the filling. Pinch the edge of the wrapper around the filling like closing the opening of a pouch, tightly sealing the dough with a final pinch.

7. Prepare one plate with water and another with toasted sesame seeds. Dab the smooth side of the bun lightly in water, then press it into the sesame seeds. Set the bun on a floured surface. Repeat with the remaining dough and filling.

8. **Pan-fry the buns:** Heat a large skillet (I use a 12-inch / 30.5 cm nonstick pan) over medium heat. Add 1 tablespoon oil or enough to coat the bottom of the pan. Arrange the buns sesame side down in a

single layer, about 1 inch (2.5 cm) apart. Gently flatten each bun with your palm until it's 1 inch (2.5 cm) thick, similar to a hockey puck.

9. Once the bottoms are golden brown, 5 to 8 minutes, flip the buns over. Add 1 to 1½ cups (250 to 375 ml) water to the pan, enough to come up about one-third of the bun's height. Cover with a tight-fitting lid (preferably glass, to monitor the water level) and reduce the heat to medium-low. Steam until all the water has evaporated and the bottoms are crisp and golden again, 5 to 10 minutes.

10. Serve: Serve the buns warm with your choice of scallions and soy sauce, slivered ginger with Chinkiang vinegar, or chile sauce or chili oil.

Chao Shou

(Wontons in Chili Oil)

For the filling and wrappers:

1 tablespoon cooking oil

4 dried shiitake mushrooms, rehydrated, destemmed, and thinly sliced

½ teaspoon minced fresh ginger

½ tablespoon soy sauce

1 large (3½ ounces / 100 g) carrot, chopped into ½-inch (12 mm) slices

7 ounces (200 g) roughly chopped cabbage (about 2 cups)

3 ounces (85 g) firm tofu, drained and pressed

¼ teaspoon mushroom seasoning, plus more as needed

½ teaspoon kosher salt, plus more as needed

⅛ teaspoon ground white pepper, plus more as needed

1 teaspoon toasted sesame oil

30 to 40 square wonton wrappers, thawed to room temperature if frozen

For the garlic water:

2 garlic cloves, minced

Serves 3 or 4

Wonton, or wantan, as we say in Malaysia, translates to "cloud swallow." Wontons are smaller than jiaozi (traditional dumplings) and easy to eat in one bite, and in Malaysia they're served in broth or as a noodle bowl topping (page 229). Wontons were my gateway to making dumplings at home. They don't need much, if any, pleating. Just grab the wrapper, add the filling, and pinch it closed! In Chengdu, my love for dumplings led me to chao shou, wontons in chili oil. These boiled wontons, shaped like little crossed arms or folded wings, are drenched in a spicy, mouth-tingling sauce of ground Sichuan peppercorns and fragrant chili oil. My son, Justin, especially can't get enough!

At street stalls, locals order them by weight, with "one liang" (about 50 grams or 8 to 10 small wontons) being the standard serving. This recipe is designed around that serving size. I like to prep the wontons in big batches and freeze them, so we can quickly boil and toss them in the sauce for an easy meal on busy days. They're small, spicy, and addictively good.

1. Make the filling: Heat the oil in a large skillet or nonstick pan over medium-high heat. Sauté the mushrooms and ginger until fragrant, about 2 minutes. Add the soy sauce—it will sizzle and caramelize as it hits the pan. Immediately add the carrot and stir-fry until it's piping hot, about 1 minute. Add the cabbage and cook to soften, about 1 minute.

2. Transfer the vegetables to a food processor. Add the tofu, breaking it into a few pieces with your hands. Pulse everything in short pulses to combine, until the texture resembles a coarse mixture.

3. Scrape the filling into a large bowl. (If there is still liquid, transfer the mixture to a sieve to drain, squeezing out as much liquid as possible. You don't

recipe and ingredients continue

For the sauce for each serving:

⅛ teaspoon kosher salt

⅛ teaspoon mushroom seasoning

⅛ teaspoon sugar

⅛ teaspoon ground Sichuan peppercorns

1½ teaspoons soy sauce

1 teaspoon Chili Oil (page 41)

1 teaspoon Chili Oil sediment (page 41)

1 teaspoon garlic water with minced garlic (see step 5)

1 to 2 tablespoons thinly sliced scallions, white and green parts

want the filling to be too wet, as it'll break the wonton wrappers.) Season with the mushroom seasoning, salt, white pepper, and sesame oil. Taste and adjust until it is very flavorful.

4. Assemble: Prepare a small bowl of water. Take one wonton wrapper and place it flat on your palm (or a clean surface). Add 1 to 1½ teaspoons filling to the center of the wrapper. Moisten the edges with water. Fold the wrapper in half to form a triangle. Pinch the edges around the filling to seal, pressing out any air bubbles. Bring the two bottom corners toward each other and seal them with a little water. The dumpling will resemble a hat with a top point. (For an alternate way of wrapping a wonton, see the photos on page 230.) Pinch tightly and set on a clean plate or baking

Guiding my daughter, Tiffany, in the tender art of wrapping chao shou, a moment of love.

Note:

When cooking, use a deep pot or wok filled with enough water to allow the wontons to float. A larger pot will prevent the dumplings from clumping together.

sheet. Continue with the remaining filling to make 30 to 40 wontons total. Keep the rest of the wrappers covered under a damp paper towel so they won't dry out.

5. **Make the garlic water:** Place the garlic in a bowl and add 3 tablespoons (45 ml) water. Whisk and set aside.

6. **Prepare the sauce (one per person):** In each serving bowl, combine the salt, mushroom seasoning, sugar, ground Sichuan peppercorns, soy sauce, chili oil, chili oil sediment, garlic water with minced garlic, and a pinch of scallions.

7. Bring a large pot of water to a rolling boil (see Note). Add the wontons (cook them in batches, so they have space to move around in the water). When the water in the pot comes back to a boil, add ½ cup (120 ml) cold water to immediately lower the temperature. When the water returns to a second boil, the wontons will float to the top, meaning they're done!

8. **Serve:** Using a slotted spoon, place a few wontons into each prepared bowl. Toss the wontons in the sauce to coat and serve warm.

Chapter 6

Everything Tofu

Tauhu *(Tofu)* Sambal

Pad Kra Pao Tofu *(Spicy Thai Basil Tofu)*

San Bei Tofu *(Three Cup Tofu)*

Home-Style Tofu

Salt-and-Pepper Tofu *(Air-Fried Method)*

Mama's Thai-Style Tofu

Fried Tofu Balls

Sweet and Sour Tofu "Pork"

Napa Cabbage Tofu Ball Stew

Mapo Tofu

Chilled Tofu Noodle and Celery Salad

Savory Chilled Soft Tofu

Tofu and Carrot Scramble

I've loved tofu since I was a kid. In Teochew or Hokkien we call it tauhu, while in Cantonese it's tau foo. Anything made from this versatile little bean delighted me, especially tofu byproducts like fu chuk (bean curd skin) and tau foo pok (fried tofu puffs). I remember enjoying tau foo pok at the pasar (market) with my grandma. Back then, a handful of eight to ten pieces cost only a few cents. Vendors would deep-fry the tofu until it inflated with a spongelike texture. I'd break a few pieces in half and drizzle soy sauce over them. The open holes in the golden sponge immediately soaked up the sauce, and I'd pop the succulent snack into my mouth as I walked around, a happy camper.

When I first started my vegetarian journey in Malaysia, tofu and beans were my go-to proteins. To this day, I'm amazed at how chefs at food stalls turn a simple block of tofu into a range of incredible dishes, like an artist transforming a blank canvas. Tofu comes in many varieties, but in this chapter, I focus on the easily accessible ones: soft, medium-firm, and firm. You can coat and pan-fry it for a braised dish (page 193), freeze and thaw it for an irresistible sweet and sour "pork" (page 203), use it as a filling for dumplings (pages 167 and 177), or simply enjoy it as is.

There are hundreds of ways to serve, eat, and cook tofu, and I've chosen the ones in this chapter because they can be easily achieved at home. Whether you're a tofu veteran or just starting out, I hope these recipes bring fresh inspiration to your kitchen.

Blocks of handmade firm tofu, glowing with freshness.

A skilled tofu seller deftly slices sheets into threadlike noodles.

How to Cut Tofu into Equal Shapes

I love transforming tofu into playful shapes to make every dish a delight! These steps will guide you in cutting a firm or extra-firm tofu block (4 by 3 by 2 inches / 10 by 7.5 by 5 cm) for the recipes in this book. If you're unsure, you can always just mash the block with both palms for a crumbled texture.

1. **Prepare the tofu:** Drain the tofu, press it to remove excess moisture, and pat it dry. Place it flat on its largest face (4 by 3 inches /10 by 7.5 cm) on a cutting board.
2. **For rectangles or slabs (e.g., tofu steaks):** Use a sharp knife for clean cuts. Slice the block lengthwise into even pieces—½ inch (12 mm) wide for thin slices or 1 inch (2.5 cm) wide for thicker ones. For smaller rectangles, cut each slab into strips or pieces of equal width, like 1 by 2 inches (2.5 by 5 cm).
3. **For small cubes** (e.g., for Salt-and-Pepper Tofu, page 197): Slice the block horizontally into two 1-inch-thick (2.5 cm) slabs. Cut each slab lengthwise into four 1-inch-wide (2.5 cm) strips, then cut each strip crosswise into three 1-inch (2.5 cm) cubes. This yields about 24 cubes (or 12 from half the block).
4. **For large cubes** (e.g., for Home-Style Tofu, page 193): Halve the block crosswise into two 1½-inch-thick (4 cm) slabs. Cut each slab lengthwise into three 1⅓-inch-wide (3.5 cm) cubes. This yields 6 cubes.
5. **For triangles** (e.g., for Tauhu [Tofu] Sambal, page 185): Slice the block horizontally into two 1-inch-thick (2.5 cm) slabs. Cut each slab diagonally from top left to bottom right corner, then from top right to bottom left corner, yielding 4 triangles per slab, 8 triangles total.

Tauhu (Tofu) Sambal

Serves 2 to 4

At Malaysia's banana leaf restaurants—Indian-style spots where you heap rice on a large leaf and pick from stainless-steel trays in a setup called "mixed rice"—tofu sambal was my vegetarian lifeline. You'll spot it everywhere: pasar malam (night markets), Malay nasi lemak stalls, and Indian eateries, where it's nestled among meats, fish, and pickles as a vibrant side. The tofu is deep-fried to a chewy, golden crust, then simmered until it drinks in a fragrant, fiery red sambal. (When dining out, ask if it contains belacan, or shrimp paste, as some cooks may add it.)

In my take, I pan-fry the tofu instead of deep-frying it for a simpler process, marinating it with a touch of curry powder for extra flavor. For the stew, I rely on my homemade sambal (page 31), with onions for sweetness and tomatoes for brightness. It's a twist on this beloved dish that brings all the warmth of the original.

For the tofu:

Two 14- to 16-ounce (390 to 450 g) packages firm tofu, drained and pressed

½ teaspoon kosher salt

2 teaspoons curry powder

Cooking oil, for frying

For the sauce:

½ small red onion, diced

2½ tablespoons Basic Sambal (page 31)

1 teaspoon garlic paste or 2 garlic cloves, minced

1 teaspoon ginger paste or ½-inch (12 mm) piece (3 g) fresh ginger, peeled and minced

1 medium tomato, cut into wedges

¼ teaspoon mushroom seasoning, plus more as needed

½ teaspoon sugar

¼ teaspoon kosher salt, plus more as needed

For serving:

Cooked rice

1. Marinate the tofu: Cut the tofu into 2 by 1-inch (5 by 2.5 cm) rectangles or triangles, slightly larger than bite-sized, as they will shrink with cooking. Place in a large bowl and sprinkle with the salt and curry powder. Gently toss to coat, using your fingers to evenly distribute the spices. Let the tofu marinate at room temperature for 30 minutes.

2. Fry the tofu: Heat a large skillet or nonstick pan over medium-high heat, adding about 2 tablespoons oil, or enough to fully cover the bottom. Arrange the tofu in a single layer (cook in batches if necessary) and let the tofu pieces fry undisturbed until a golden crust forms on the bottom, 4 to 7 minutes. Flip each piece using tongs or chopsticks and cook until the other side is golden and crispy. Transfer to a paper towel–lined plate to drain.

recipe continues

3. Cook the sauce aromatics: In the same pan, reserve (or add) 2 tablespoons oil. Sauté the red onion over medium-high heat until soft and fragrant, 3 to 5 minutes. Stir in the sambal, garlic, and ginger and sauté for about 30 seconds, until fragrant.

4. Add 1½ cups (360 ml) water and the tomato to the pan. Cook, stirring occasionally, until the tomato is tender and starts to break down, about 3 minutes.

5. Return the tofu to the pan, then season with the mushroom seasoning, sugar, and salt. Cook for about 5 minutes, or until the liquid is reduced by half, flipping the pieces occasionally so the tofu absorbs the flavors of the broth evenly.

6. Serve: Taste and adjust the mushroom seasoning and salt as needed. Serve warm with rice.

Pad Kra Pao Tofu

(Spicy Thai Basil Tofu)

Serves 2 to 4

Pad kra pao means "stir-fried holy basil" in Thai—a spicy trio of bird's eye chiles, garlic, and peppery holy basil that lures you in with its aroma and layered heat. Growing up in Malaysia, just south of Thailand, I was no stranger to Thai food—the bold flavors of these two cuisines have much in common, and Thai dishes have a special place in my family's food memories. I first discovered pad kra pao in college, but the traditional minced meat version wasn't an option for me. So I set out to create my own version using tofu.

This recipe transforms the tofu's texture. Firm tofu (essential for the way it holds up during cooking) is mashed and cooked in a dry pan to remove moisture, then stir-fried again in oil until golden and springy. This method gives it a chewiness reminiscent of minced meat. This version delivers the dish's spicy, fragrant, and enticing flavors with a twist that's my own.

For the pad kra pao sauce:

½ teaspoon dark caramel soy sauce, plus more as needed

3 tablespoons (45 ml) Golden Mountain brand Thai seasoning sauce, plus more as needed

¼ cup (60 ml) Vegan Fish Sauce (page 49), plus more as needed

2 teaspoons sugar

¼ cup (60 ml) warm water

For the tofu and aromatics:

Two 14- to 16-ounce (390 to 450 g) packages firm tofu, drained and pressed

2 tablespoons cooking oil

1 medium shallot, minced (about 3 tablespoons)

6 garlic cloves, minced (about 2 tablespoons)

For serving:

2 fresh Thai chiles, thinly sliced

1 cup (20 g) packed fresh Thai basil leaves

Cooked rice

1. **Make the pad kra pao sauce:** In a small bowl, whisk together the dark caramel soy sauce, Golden Mountain seasoning sauce, vegan fish sauce, sugar, and warm water until combined.

2. **Cook the tofu:** Heat a dry large skillet or nonstick pan over medium-high heat. Crumble the tofu into the pan using your hands or a fork. Cook for 8 to 10 minutes, stirring occasionally, until the moisture evaporates and the tofu takes on a light golden color and a slightly springy texture.

3. Drizzle 1 tablespoon of the oil into the pan and continue stir-frying the tofu for 4 to 5 minutes, until it turns golden brown and some bits start to jump from the pan. Reduce the heat if the tofu starts to brown too quickly. Transfer to a bowl and set aside.

recipe continues

4. Cook the aromatics: In the same pan, heat the remaining 1 tablespoon oil over medium heat. When the oil shimmers, add the shallot and garlic, sautéing until fragrant and softened, 2 to 3 minutes.

5. Return the tofu crumbles to the pan and stir into the aromatics until evenly coated. Slowly pour in the prepared sauce, being careful to avoid splattering. Stir-fry for another 2 minutes, until the tofu absorbs most of the sauce.

6. Finish and serve: Fold in the chiles and basil, tossing everything together until the basil begins to wilt. Taste and adjust the seasoning, adding more dark caramel soy sauce, Golden Mountain seasoning sauce, or vegan fish sauce as needed. Serve warm with rice.

San Bei Tofu

(Three Cup Tofu)

Serves 2 or 3

I was introduced to Taiwanese cuisine in college thanks to my godmother, whose son—a talented home cook—became a good friend to both my husband and me. It was during this time that I first tasted san bei or "three cup," a dish named for its equal parts soy sauce, rice wine, and sesame oil. These days, my family and I especially love the tofu version, which many restaurants offer for non-meat eaters. When you order this dish, you can hear it before you see it, with tofu sizzling and popping in the sauce. As you take a spoon and stir everything together, you'll find charred ginger, garlic, and crispy batter bits seared at the bottom of the clay pot, releasing the unmistakable aroma of toasted sesame oil and Thai basil.

At home, I've learned to make a lighter version with less oil than the restaurant style, but it still captures the deep, savory flavors that make san bei so satisfying. I've lost count of how many bowls of rice I've eaten with this dish!

For the sauce:

2 tablespoons mijiu (Chinese rice cooking wine)

1½ tablespoons toasted sesame oil

2 tablespoons soy sauce

2 teaspoons sugar

¼ cup (60 ml) warm water

For the tofu and aromatics:

¼ cup (30 g) cornstarch, plus more if needed

One 14- to 16-ounce (390 to 450 g) package tofu, drained and cut into 2-inch (5 cm) cubes

Cooking oil, for frying

2-inch (5 cm) piece ginger, peeled and thinly sliced (about 10 slices)

3 garlic cloves, thinly sliced

For serving:

1 fresh red chile, thinly sliced (optional)

1 scallion, white and green parts, cut into 2-inch (5 cm) segments and julienned

1 cup (20 g) packed fresh Thai basil leaves (see Note, page 192)

Cooked rice

1. Make the sauce: In a small bowl, whisk the mijiu, sesame oil, soy sauce, sugar, and warm water until the sugar is completely dissolved. Set aside.

2. Prepare the tofu: Place the cornstarch on a deep plate and generously coat each tofu cube, shaking off any excess.

3. Fry the tofu: Heat a large skillet or nonstick pan over medium-high heat and add enough oil to cover the bottom. Arrange the tofu in a single layer (cook in batches if necessary) and let the tofu pieces fry undisturbed until a golden crust forms on the bottom, 4 to 7 minutes. Flip each piece using tongs or chopsticks and cook until the other side is golden and crispy. Transfer to a paper towel–lined plate to drain.

recipe continues

Note:

To enhance the aroma of the Thai basil while preserving its bright color, in step 4 you may briefly sauté the leaves with the ginger for about 15 seconds, then remove them from the pan. Fold them into the tofu toward the end of the cooking time for a vibrant finish.

4. **Cook the aromatics:** Clean the pan and return it to medium-high heat with 1 tablespoon oil. Sauté the ginger until it becomes golden and crispy, about 30 seconds. Add the garlic and stir-fry for another 30 seconds, until fragrant.

5. Pour the prepared sauce into the pan and let it simmer until it slightly thickens. Add the tofu and gently fold it into the sauce, ensuring each piece is thoroughly coated.

6. **Finish and serve:** Fold in the chile (if using), scallion, and Thai basil. Stir everything together for about 30 seconds, until the basil wilts slightly. Serve warm with rice.

Home-Style Tofu

Serves 4 to 6

At pretty much any Chinese restaurant that serves tofu, you'll find a dish called jiachang doufu, which translates to "home-style tofu"—a name that conveys its comforting, home-cooked vibe. Each restaurant puts its own spin on it, and the sauces vary, but the tofu is typically paired with wood ear mushrooms and a colorful mix of vegetables. My version incorporates doubanjiang, or Sichuan fermented bean paste, for a subtle kick. Like so many Chinese dishes, it's a perfect harmony of colors and textures: fragrant ginger and garlic, a savory sauce that clings to the tender braised tofu, and fresh vegetables and scallions for pops of flavor. We love it served over steamed rice.

½ cup (60 g) plus 2 teaspoons cornstarch

Two 14- to 16-ounce (390 to 450 g) packages firm tofu, drained and cut into 2-inch (5 cm) cubes

Cooking oil, for frying

1 teaspoon minced fresh ginger

1 garlic clove, thinly sliced

1½ teaspoons doubanjiang (chili bean paste), coarsely chopped

1 cup (240 ml) hot water

1½ tablespoons soy sauce, plus more as needed

½ teaspoon sugar

½ teaspoon mushroom seasoning

⅓ cup (55 g) bell pepper (any color) cut into 1-inch (2.5 cm) pieces

¼ ounce (7 g) dried wood ear mushrooms soaked in warm water to rehydrate

2 scallions, white and green parts, cut into 2-inch (5 cm) segments and julienned

Cooked rice, for serving

1. Prepare the tofu: Place ½ cup (60 g) of the cornstarch in a deep plate. Generously coat the tofu cubes with cornstarch, shaking off any excess.

2. Fry the tofu: Heat a large skillet or nonstick pan over medium-high heat and add enough oil to cover the bottom. Arrange the tofu in a single layer (cook in batches if necessary) and let the tofu pieces fry undisturbed until a golden crust forms on the bottom, 4 to 7 minutes. Flip each piece using tongs or chopsticks and cook until the other side is golden and crispy. Transfer to a paper towel–lined plate to drain.

3. Cook the aromatics: In the same pan, add 1 tablespoon oil and heat over medium-high. Sauté the ginger and garlic until fragrant, about 30 seconds. Add the doubanjiang and quickly stir-fry for a few seconds, until the paste releases its aroma and the oil turns red. You may want to briefly remove the pan from the heat if the mixture sputters.

4. Add the fried tofu back into the pan along with the hot water. Season with the soy sauce, sugar, and

recipe continues

mushroom seasoning. Cover the pan with a lid and let it simmer for 2 to 3 minutes, allowing the tofu to absorb the flavors and the sauce to reduce by a third.

5. Prepare the slurry: In a small bowl, stir together the remaining 2 teaspoons cornstarch and 1 tablespoon water to create a slurry.

6. Uncover the pan and taste the sauce, adjusting the saltiness with more soy sauce if needed. Add the bell pepper and wood ear mushrooms, cooking for another 2 to 3 minutes, until the peppers become vibrant and the mushrooms are glossy. Fold in the scallions.

7. Serve: Stir the slurry, then drizzle it into the pan a little bit at a time, stirring until the sauce thickens to your desired consistency. Serve warm with rice.

Salt-and-Pepper Tofu
(Air-Fried Method)

Serves 2 or 3 as an appetizer

At dai chow spots, my family loves ordering jiu yim tau foo—Cantonese for "salt-and-pepper tofu." It's a perfect example of the flavors and techniques we love in dai chow cooking. At home, I air-fry the tofu until crisp to skip the oil mess, then toss it with minced garlic, scallion, and red chiles. For a twist, I throw in ground Sichuan peppercorns—not your usual Malaysian dai chow move—adding their wild, numbing buzz.

For the tofu:

One 14- to 16-ounce (390 to 450 g) package medium-firm tofu, drained and cut into 1-inch (2.5 cm) cubes

½ cup (50 g) cornstarch, plus more if needed

Cooking oil spray

For the spice mix:

½ teaspoon ground white pepper

¼ teaspoon ground black pepper

¾ teaspoon kosher salt

¼ teaspoon ground Sichuan peppercorns (optional)

For the aromatics:

1 tablespoon cooking oil

3 garlic cloves, minced

1 fresh red chile pepper, minced

1 scallion, thinly sliced, white and green parts separated

1. **Prepare the tofu:** Place the tofu in a large bowl and gently toss with the cornstarch, ensuring each piece is generously coated. Add more cornstarch if needed.

2. **Air-fry the tofu:** Spray the inner basket of the air fryer with oil. Arrange the tofu cubes in the basket in a single layer and spray their tops with more oil. Air-fry at 390°F (200°C) for about 15 minutes, shaking the basket halfway through, until the tofu is golden brown and crispy.

3. **Make the spice mix:** In a small bowl, combine the white pepper, black pepper, salt, and Sichuan peppercorns (if using). Set aside.

4. **Cook the aromatics:** While the tofu is air-frying, heat the oil in a large nonstick pan or skillet over medium-low heat. Sauté the garlic, chile, and white parts of the scallion for about 45 seconds, until fragrant and the garlic starts to turn golden.

5. Once the tofu is done, add it to the pan with the aromatics. Stir to coat the tofu evenly. Sprinkle half of the spice mix over the tofu and quickly toss to combine, ensuring an even coating. Taste and add more of the spice mix if needed.

6. **Finish and serve:** Garnish the tofu with the green parts of the scallion and serve immediately.

Note:

This recipe is perfect for potlucks. You can prep everything ahead—just keep the toppings separate and toss them with the tofu right before serving.

Mama's Thai-Style Tofu

Serves 4 to 6 as an appetizer

I'm so grateful for my mama, who whips up meatless meals for us whenever we visit Malaysia. In the hot climate, food is designed to be light, refreshing, and bold with flavor to cut through the humidity, and her Thai-style tofu is our favorite. She fries tofu into crisp, golden nuggets, slathers them with a fiery-sweet Thai chile sauce, and adds her neatly sliced cucumbers.

I've tweaked it, taking inspiration from Thai salads like green papaya, and pan-frying the tofu before tossing in fresh herbs and fruits. Each bite is a cool, spicy jolt of flavor: juicy pomelo, crisp cucumber, tart green mango, and peppery mint, all intermixed with lime juice and sweet chile sauce.

For the tofu:

Cooking oil, for frying

Kosher salt

Two 14- to 16-ounce (390 to 450 g) packages medium-firm tofu, drained and cut into 2-inch (5 cm) cubes

For the chili dressing:

3 tablespoons (45 ml) Thai sweet chile sauce, plus more as needed

2 tablespoons fresh lime juice, plus more as needed

For serving:

¼ cup (30 g) peeled, pitted, and shredded green mango

¼ cup (30 g) thinly sliced cucumber

¼ cup (55 g) pomelo (or other citrus) segments, broken into bite-sized pieces

½ cup (35 g) shredded lettuce

1 small shallot, thinly sliced

1 fresh red chile pepper, thinly sliced

Handful of fresh mint leaves, julienned

2 makrut lime leaves, julienned (optional)

1. Pan-fry the tofu: Heat a large skillet or nonstick pan over medium-high heat and add enough oil to cover the bottom. Sprinkle the oil generously with salt. Carefully add the tofu cubes in a single layer, spaced slightly apart. Let the tofu fry undisturbed for 4 to 7 minutes, until a golden crust forms on the bottom. Flip each cube and continue frying, adding more oil if needed, until all sides are crispy and golden brown, about 15 minutes in total. Transfer the tofu to a paper towel–lined plate to drain.

2. Make the chili dressing: In a small bowl, whisk together the Thai chile sauce and lime juice. Taste and adjust the balance of flavors, boosting the acidity with more lime juice or the sweetness with more sweet chile sauce, according to your preference.

3. Combine the toppings: In a large bowl, gently toss the mango, cucumber, pomelo, lettuce, shallot, chile, mint, and lime leaves (if using) with your fingers until well combined. Set aside until ready to serve.

4. Serve: Arrange the tofu on a serving plate. Top with the salad ingredients and spoon on the dressing (see Note). Serve immediately while the tofu is still crispy.

Fried Tofu Balls

Makes twelve 1-inch (2.5 cm) balls or nine 2-inch (5 cm) balls

These deep-fried tofu balls are golden and crispy, outrageously good dipped in a straightforward Thai chile sauce. Add just a squeeze of calamansi for a bright, citrusy kick.

The trick here is to thoroughly drain the firm tofu and press it until it reaches a paste-like consistency. I like to mix in finely chopped veggie stems (an excellent way to cut down on food waste), carrots, mushrooms, and cashews for a savory bite and hint of nuttiness. The smaller you chop the ingredients, the better they will bind with the tofu when forming the balls. You can fry the balls ahead of time, then reheat them in the oven or air fryer when you're ready for a quick snack or appetizer. I also use them as the main protein in dishes like napa cabbage stew (page 207), where they soak up the rich flavors just like tender meatballs.

For the tofu:

One 14- to 16-ounce (390 to 450 g) package firm tofu, drained and pressed

2 large fresh shiitake mushrooms, destemmed and finely chopped

Cooking oil, for frying

3 tablespoons finely chopped vegetable stems, such as kale, broccoli, or cauliflower (use whatever you have on hand)

3 tablespoons finely chopped carrot

Kosher salt

2 tablespoons cornstarch

1 tablespoon finely chopped toasted cashews

¼ teaspoon mushroom seasoning

For serving:

Thai sweet chile sauce

Calamansi or lime wedges

1. Prepare the tofu: Place the tofu in a nut milk bag and squeeze out as much moisture as possible. If you don't have a nut milk bag, crumble the tofu into a fine-mesh strainer set over a bowl and press to drain and crush the tofu. The tofu should resemble a damp paste.

2. Cook the vegetables: Heat a dry skillet or nonstick pan over medium-high heat. Sauté the shiitake mushrooms until most of their moisture evaporates and they start to turn golden brown, about 2 minutes. Add 2 teaspoons oil and continue stir-frying until fragrant. Stir in the chopped vegetable stems and carrot. Cook for about 3 minutes, until the vegetables soften. Season with a pinch of salt and transfer the mixture to a large bowl.

3. To the same bowl, add the squeezed tofu, cornstarch, cashews, and mushroom seasoning.

recipe continues

Using your hands or a spatula, mix everything together until well combined.

4. Divide the mixture into twelve even portions. Roll each portion into a compact ball, about 1½ inches (4 cm) in diameter, using your palms. (If making nine balls, they should be 2 inches / 5 cm in diameter.).

5. Fry the tofu balls: Fill a small deep saucepan or pot with 2 inches (5 cm) oil. Heat the oil to 350 to 375°F (175 to 190°C). Carefully drop the tofu balls into the hot oil using a slotted spoon. Fry until deep golden brown, turning occasionally so that they color evenly, 3 to 5 minutes. Transfer to a paper towel–lined plate to drain.

6. Serve: Serve the tofu balls while hot and crispy, with a dip of sweet chile sauce and a squeeze of calamansi or lime juice.

Sweet and Sour Tofu "Pork"

For the tofu:

Two 14- to 16-ounce (390 to 450 g) packages firm tofu, frozen overnight

½ cup (50 g) cornstarch, for coating

Cooking oil, for frying

For the sauce:

3 tablespoons (45 ml) ketchup

2½ tablespoons sugar

1 tablespoon distilled white or apple cider vinegar

1 tablespoon soy sauce

½ teaspoon kosher salt

Juice of half a lemon (about 1½ tablespoons)

1½ teaspoons cornstarch

For the aromatics:

1 tablespoon cooking oil

¾ cup (125 g) large-diced (¾-inch / 2 cm) red, yellow, and green bell pepper

½ small white or yellow onion, cut into ¾-inch (2 cm) dice

½ small apple (preferably Granny Smith or another tart green variety), cut into ¾-inch (2 cm) dice (see Note, page 205)

For serving:

Cooked rice

Serves 4

If there's one dish that upended my eating habits, it's sweet and sour "pork," or kou lou yuk in Cantonese. At dai chow stalls, my family always ordered the meat version—the crispy battered pork draped in a vibrant bright-sweet sauce, heaped over warm rice, was beloved by every kid in our household. One day when I was a teenager, my best friend took me to a temple for lunch. I picked an orange-hued dish, gravitating toward the zesty flavors—it looked like sweet and sour pork, but it was made with gluten-based "meat". The first bite was a jolt of familiarity: the chewy texture, the flood of flavor, but with no pork in sight. I devoured every last bit. That day, my curiosity about vegan cooking took root, shaping a path that led where I am today—a turning point from a single, mind-blowing dish.

My recipe calls for frozen and thawed tofu, tossed in starch for a crisp, chewy shell and soft core. In the wok, a tangy glaze hugs each piece, with apple chunks lending a juicy snap. It wins everyone over—recipe testers, vegan or not, couldn't get enough. I keep blocks of tofu in the freezer and simply thaw one in the fridge overnight for the perfect texture.

1. Thaw the tofu: Thaw the tofu blocks in a large bowl of warm water until the ice crystals have melted, about 20 to 25 minutes, or wrap the frozen tofu with paper towels and microwave on the defrost setting for 5 to 8 minutes, pausing every 2 minutes to check and avoid cooking the edges. Squeeze each block of tofu between your palms to remove as much water as possible.

2. Tear the thawed tofu into large chunks, 1 to 2 inches (2.5 to 5 cm) in size, and place in a large bowl. Dust the tofu with a thin layer of the cornstarch and toss gently to coat.

recipe continues

Note:

Most sweet and sour "pork" recipes use fresh pineapple cubes, which can be subbed with canned pineapples if preferred. Using apple, especially green apple, instead gives the dish a different, slightly tangier sourness.

3. **Fry the tofu:** Heat a deep saucepan with 2 inches (5 cm) oil to 350 to 375°F (175 to 190°C). Coat the tofu chunks with another generous layer of cornstarch. Fry the tofu in batches, flipping occasionally to prevent sticking, until golden brown and crispy, 3 to 5 minutes. Transfer to a paper towel–lined plate to drain and set aside.

4. **Make the sauce:** In a bowl, whisk together the ketchup, sugar, vinegar, soy sauce, salt, lemon juice, cornstarch, and ¾ cup (180 ml) water until smooth and well combined.

5. **Cook the aromatics:** Heat the oil in a large skillet or wok over medium-high heat. Once the oil shimmers, add the bell peppers and onion. Stir-fry for about 3 minutes, until the pepper is softened and the onion is fragrant and beginning to color. Transfer the vegetables to a separate dish.

6. Pour the prepared sauce into the same skillet and cook over medium-high heat until the sauce begins to thicken and large bubbles form, 2 to 3 minutes. When the sauce can coat the back of a spatula, add the apple and return the tofu and vegetables to the pan.

7. **Finish and serve:** Quickly toss everything in the sauce until the tofu is well coated and the sauce is absorbed. Serve warm with rice.

Napa Cabbage Tofu Ball Stew

For the broth:

5 dried shiitake mushrooms, rehydrated, destemmed, and halved, soaking liquid reserved

For the soup:

2 tablespoons cooking oil

1 tablespoon minced fresh ginger

1 small carrot (80 g), roll-cut into 1-inch (2.5 cm) chunks

1 tablespoon minced garlic

1 tablespoon soy sauce

1½ tablespoons Shaoxing cooking wine

1½ teaspoons vegetarian oyster sauce

1 pound (450 g) napa cabbage (about 7 large leaves), cut into 2-inch (5 cm) pieces, stems and leaves kept separate

¼ teaspoon mushroom seasoning

Kosher salt

2 ounces (55 g) dried tofu skin sticks (fu chu), rehydrated and cut into 2-inch (5 cm) pieces

Fried Tofu Balls (prepared according to the recipe on page 201, formed into 9 balls)

For serving:

Ground white pepper

Cooked rice

Serves 3 or 4

When cold weather hits, this tofu ball stew is my go-to for dinner. Inspired by "lion's head meatballs" (shizi tou), a Chinese New Year dish symbolizing unity and abundance, this vegan version brings the same warmth. Golden tofu balls, simmered with tender napa cabbage and fu zhu (dried bean curd sticks), soak up a savory broth. Silky and veggie-packed, it's pure comfort, perfect over rice.

1. Prepare the broth: Combine the reserved mushroom soaking liquid with enough water to make 3 cups (720 ml) of broth.

2. Cook the soup: Heat the oil in a deep saucepan or clay pot over medium-high heat. Sauté the ginger for about 30 seconds, until fragrant.

3. Add the drained shiitake mushrooms and carrot. Press the mushrooms to release their water and stir-fry until they begin to color and the carrot is crisp-tender, about 5 minutes. Stir in the garlic and cook for another 30 seconds.

4. Add the soy sauce and cooking wine, allowing them to sizzle and release their aromas. Pour in the broth and vegetarian oyster sauce, stirring to blend. Bring the liquid to a gentle boil over medium-low heat. Cover and simmer for 5 minutes.

5. Add the napa cabbage stems and cook until softened, 5 to 8 minutes. Add the napa leaves and cook for another 5 minutes. Season with the mushroom seasoning and salt to taste.

6. Stir in the drained tofu skin sticks and fried tofu balls. Simmer for 2 to 3 minutes so they absorb the broth's flavors.

7. Serve: Remove the soup from the heat and season with white pepper. Serve warm over a bowl of rice.

Mapo Tofu

Serves 2 or 3

When I was growing up in Malaysia, spicy food was a daily staple. But the sensation of "ma" in mala—that numbing, tingling effect from Sichuan peppercorns—was something entirely new. I didn't experience it until I moved to the US and tried dishes like mapo tofu. While I loved the heat, the numbing was unexpected. When I moved to Chengdu, the capital city of China's Sichuan province, locals assured me I'd grow to love and even crave it. They were right. Now I joke that a dish feels incomplete without tingly peppercorns (though I consider myself an amateur in acquiring this taste!).

Mapo tofu in Chengdu is a delightful combination: soft, velvety tofu in a fiery, umami-rich sauce, a worthy match for any bowl of rice. The key is to boil the tofu briefly in salted water to remove any beany flavor and open its pores for better sauce absorption. Cooks here add cornstarch slurry in three stages: to thicken the sauce, lock in moisture, and prevent thinning, creating a thick, glossy gravy that holds its texture from the first bite to the last. Don't forget to use Sichuan Pixian doubanjiang, a fermented bean paste, for its essential salty depth and red color.

For the tofu:

Kosher salt

Two 12-ounce (340 g) packages soft or silken tofu, drained and cut into 1-inch (2.5 cm) cubes (see Notes, page 210)

For the sauce:

1 tablespoon soy sauce

1 tablespoon Shaoxing cooking wine

½ teaspoon sugar

¼ teaspoon mushroom seasoning

½ cup (120 ml) warm or hot water

For the slurry and aromatics:

1 tablespoon cornstarch

3 tablespoons (45 ml) cooking oil

1 tablespoon Pixian doubanjiang, coarsely chopped if chunky

1 scallion or garlic scape, thinly sliced, white and green parts separated

5 garlic cloves, minced

1½ teaspoons Sichuan chili flakes (la jiao mian) or regular chili powder

2 tablespoons textured vegetable protein (TVP)

For serving:

1 teaspoon ground Sichuan peppercorns

Cooked rice

1. Prepare the tofu: In a large saucepan, bring enough water to submerge the tofu to a near-boil over medium-high heat. Add a pinch of salt. Once small bubbles start forming on the surface, gently slide in the tofu cubes. Cook for about 3 minutes. Carefully remove the tofu with a strainer and let it drain.

2. Prepare the sauce: In a small bowl or glass measuring cup, combine the soy sauce, cooking wine, sugar, mushroom seasoning, and warm or hot water. Set aside.

3. Make the slurry: In a separate small bowl, combine the cornstarch and ¼ cup (60 ml) water for the slurry.

recipe continues

Notes:

- *Soft silken tofu works the best for this recipe. Remove the tofu from the box and drain well before cooking to prevent excess water from thinning the sauce.*
- *When simmering the tofu, ensure that the liquid only covers about half of the tofu.*

4. **Cook the aromatics:** Heat the oil in a large, deep saucepan or wok over medium-high heat. Add the doubanjiang and sauté until it releases red oil and becomes aromatic. Stir in the white parts of the scallion, the garlic, and Sichuan chili flakes and stir-fry for about 30 seconds, until fragrant.

5. Pour the prepared broth into the pan and bring to a boil. Add the TVP and gently slide the tofu cubes into the broth (see Notes). Cook for about 5 minutes, occasionally pushing the tofu toward the center of the pan with a spatula. Let the sauce reduce by about one-third.

6. Stir the slurry and drizzle one-third of it over the tofu, swirling the pan to mix it in. The sauce will begin to thicken. Repeat this process two more times, adding the rest of the slurry in stages in a circular motion, until the sauce clings to the tofu. Remove from the heat.

7. **Serve:** Transfer the tofu to a serving dish. Sprinkle the ground Sichuan peppercorns over the top and garnish with the green parts of the scallion. Serve hot with rice.

Chilled Tofu Noodle and Celery Salad

Serves 3 or 4 as a side

I love tofu sheet noodles in this vibrant, chewy salad. A quick boil tenderizes them, and they're tossed with homemade scallion oil, crunchy blanched vegetables, and herbs until every strand is tangled in aroma. This is ideal for meal prep—the flavors are even better the next day!

You can find pressed tofu sheets (sometimes labeled as "soy sheets") at Asian markets near the fresh tofu. They're sold in packs of uncut square sheets or precut into thin noodles—both are already cooked and ready to drop into soups and stir-fries. Tofu sheets are great to keep on hand: Unlike block tofu, they last for a long time in the fridge, and you can also freeze and thaw them quickly.

For the scallion oil:

2 tablespoons cooking oil

1 scallion, white and green parts, thinly sliced

For the salad:

¼ teaspoon kosher salt, plus more as needed

1 celery stalk, thinly sliced on the bias

1 small carrot, shredded (about ¾ cup / 80 g)

7 ounces (200 g) fresh tofu sheets (or thawed from frozen), cut into ⅛-inch (3 mm) noodle-like shreds

1½ teaspoons toasted sesame oil

¼ teaspoon mushroom seasoning

1 teaspoon soy sauce

Dash of ground white pepper

1 fresh red chile, thinly sliced

3 stalks cilantro, finely chopped, both stems and leaves

Toasted sesame seeds

1. Make the scallion oil: Heat a small pan with the oil over medium-low heat. Add the scallion and cook, stirring frequently, until fragrant and beginning to caramelize, 4 to 5 minutes. Reduce the heat if necessary to avoid burning. Strain the oil into a clean bowl and set aside.

2. Blanch the vegetables for the salad: Bring a large pot of lightly salted water to a boil. Add the celery and carrot and blanch for about 30 seconds. Lift the vegetables out with a mesh strainer and rinse under cold water. Squeeze out as much water as possible and transfer to a large bowl.

3. Blanch the tofu sheets: Bring the water back to a boil and add the tofu "noodles." Cook for about 3 minutes, stirring frequently to prevent the noodles from sticking to each other and clumping. Remove the noodles with a mesh strainer and rinse under cold water. Gently squeeze the noodles between your palms to remove excess moisture (no need to wring them completely dry) and add them to the bowl with the celery and carrot.

recipe continues

4. Add the scallion oil, sesame oil, mushroom seasoning, soy sauce, white pepper, and salt to the bowl. Add the chile and cilantro. Toss with both hands in a claw-like manner until everything is well combined.

5. Serve: Taste the salad and add more salt if needed. Garnish with toasted sesame seeds and keep chilled until ready to serve.

Savory Chilled Soft Tofu

Serves 1 or 2

In Malaysia's heat, nothing beats my mom's simple chilled tofu on a sweltering day. What makes hers stand out from any restaurant version is the crispy TVP (textured vegetable protein) she toasts to serve as the "fried lard" and heaps on top. It's a genius move. Another of her tricks is briefly heating the vegetarian oyster sauce and soy sauce in oil before pouring it over the tofu. I used to watch her pour the sauce carefully into the wok without any of it splattering, a technique I only learned to appreciate and master as I got older (the key: Keep the heat low!).

When we were younger, my brother and I would compete for the biggest pieces of tofu, making sure we each got plenty of sauce and crispy TVP. It's fantastic chilled, and I serve it as a refreshing snack, but if you're craving something cozier, you can steam or microwave the tofu for a few minutes before adding the sauce.

2 tablespoons dried textured vegetable protein (TVP; see Note)

One 12- to 14-ounce (340 to 390 g) package soft or silken tofu

1 tablespoon cooking oil

1½ teaspoons vegetarian oyster sauce

1 tablespoon soy sauce

1 tablespoon finely chopped fresh cilantro (both stems and leaves)

Note:

TVP comes in a dry form and often needs to be rehydrated before using. However, in this recipe, we use it in its original form, simply toasted to enhance its aroma and crunchiness. My mom calls this "fried lard"—as with fried lard, the crispiness adds a delightful contrast to the soft, silky tofu.

1. **Prepare the TVP:** In a dry small saucepan over medium heat, toast the TVP for about 2 minutes, until it smells good and starts to darken in color. Transfer the toasted TVP to a small bowl and set aside.

2. **Prepare the tofu:** Carefully remove the tofu from its packaging and gently drain any excess liquid. If desired, gently rinse the tofu with clean drinking water. Place it on a serving dish.

3. Heat the cooking oil in the same saucepan over medium-high heat until the oil is shimmering but not smoking. Remove the pan from the heat and quickly stir in the vegetarian oyster sauce and soy sauce. Be cautious, as the mixture may sputter. Once combined, pour the sauce evenly over the tofu.

4. **Finish and serve:** Sprinkle the toasted TVP on top of the tofu and garnish with the cilantro.

Tofu and Carrot Scramble

Serves 2 or 3

This dish is one of the first I learned from my beloved venerable monk while helping in my temple's kitchen in Dallas. It started as a lunch favorite at daycare and quickly became a hit with my kids, finding its way into their lunch boxes. It's a simple, tasty way to enjoy carrots with tofu, proving how these ingredients can shine together. Sautéing shredded carrots in oil brings out their tender sweetness, and the carrot melds with the soft tofu, giving it a warm, golden tint. I keep the seasoning straightforward, using just salt, mushroom seasoning, and white pepper. My son always asks for extra cilantro, swearing it's the secret that enhances the whole dish.

This is our family's forever staple—eat it with rice, use it as a dumpling filling, tuck it between bread (like an egg sandwich!), or serve as a tofu scramble (try a pinch of turmeric for color) for breakfast.

1 tablespoon cooking oil

1 large (13 ounce / 360 g) carrot, shredded

One 14- to 16-ounce (390 to 450 g) package firm tofu, drained and pressed

½ teaspoon mushroom seasoning

½ teaspoon kosher salt, plus more if needed

Dash of ground white pepper

Drizzle of toasted sesame oil

Handful of chopped fresh cilantro

Cooked rice or toast, for serving

1. **Cook the carrot:** Heat the oil in a large skillet or nonstick pan over medium-high heat until shimmering. Sauté the carrot for about 3 minutes, until the carrot is tender and releasing red oil.

2. **Add the tofu:** Crumble the tofu into the pan using your hands or a fork. Cook for 5 to 6 minutes, stirring occasionally to let the moisture evaporate. The tofu should become slightly springy and start browning around the edges. If you prefer a softer texture, add ½ cup (120 ml) water to the pan and cook for another 2 to 3 minutes.

3. **Finish and serve:** Season the tofu mixture with the mushroom seasoning, salt, and white pepper. Remove from the heat and finish with the sesame oil and the cilantro, plus more salt as needed. Serve warm with rice or toasted bread.

Chapter 7

Noodles

Economy Bihun *(Stir-Fried Vermicelli)*

Pan Mee *(Hand-Torn Noodle Soup)*

Malaysian-Style Wonton Mee
(Dry Tossed Noodles with Wontons)

KL-Style Hokkien Mee
(Dark Caramel Soy Sauce–Braised Noodles)

Wat Dan Hor *(Wide Rice Noodles with Gravy)*

Pad Kee Mao *(Thai Drunken Noodles)*

Pad Woon Sen *(Stir-Fried Glass Noodles)*

Pad Thai

Kon Chau "Ngau" Hor *(Beefless Chow Fun)*

Char Kuey Teow *(Malaysian Stir-Fried Flat Rice Noodles)*

Mee Goreng *(Mamak-Style Fried Noodles)*

Mee Jawa *(Malaysian Javanese Noodles in Tangy Gravy)*

Curry Chee Cheong Fun
(Rice Noodle Rolls with Curry Sauce)

Curry Laksa *(Spicy Coconut Noodle Soup)*

Sichuan-Style Dan Dan Noodles

When I was growing up, the options for noodles were endless. At morning noodle stalls, you'd typically have at least three kinds to pick from: flat rice noodles, rice vermicelli, yellow oiled noodles, and sometimes chewy translucent noodles called lou shu fan ("rat tail" or "silver needle" noodles). A breakfast staple was chee cheong fun—soft, steamed rice sheets rolled up or folded, served with sweet brown sauce or a light curry (page 259). At dai chow restaurants, the dishes were even more abundant. Stir-fried, saucy KL-Style Hokkien Mee (page 231), with its thick, udon-like yellow noodles, and Wat Dan Hor (page 235)—flat rice noodles smothered in a silky gravy—were always on my radar. Just thinking about these dishes gets my mouth watering.

With fresh noodles just a walk down the street, it never occurred to me to make them at home. But moving to the US changed that. I missed the variety of noodle options I had growing up, and this absence sparked a newfound appreciation and desire to re-create them for myself, family, and friends, preserving both the traditions as well as my personal memories. In this section, I gathered all my favorite noodle recipes that I've learned and developed over the years, from the comforting noodle soup my aunties made (Pan Mee, page 225) to dishes inspired by eating out, like Pad Thai (page 243) and Sichuan-Style Dan Dan Noodles (page 265). These are staples in our family's rotation, and I hope they become part of yours as well!

An auntie's wok sizzles, churning out smoky char kuey teow with Malaysian flair.

An uncle slices chee cheong fun at the pasar, nailing my favorite breakfast.

Chengdu's dan dan mian shop blends fiery chili and sesame into noodle bliss.

Economy Bihun

(Stir-Fried Vermicelli)

Serves 2 or 3

Economy bihun is exactly what it sounds like—a cheap, filling breakfast staple. At Malaysia's morning markets, people line up for rice vermicelli (bihun) stir-fried with a handful of vegetables like yu choy, mung bean sprouts, chives, or scallions. The vendors prepare it in large quantities and keep it warm in a giant stainless-steel pan. When it's your turn, they grab a portion from the steaming pile with chopsticks, drop it onto a piece of wax paper or banana leaf, and add a spoonful of sauce—usually something soy-based or a sweet chile sauce. If you're into heat, they'll tuck in a side of chile sauce or a few fresh chili slices too. Then they wrap the pile up tight, charging just 50 cents, and you're good to go.

The appeal of economy bihun is the balance of flavors and textures. It's a reminder that the best food doesn't need to be complicated or expensive.

For the noodles:

8 ounces (225 g) thin dried rice vermicelli

For the sauce:

3 tablespoons (45 ml) kecap manis, or 2 tablespoons dark caramel soy sauce

2 tablespoons soy sauce

½ tablespoon sugar

½ teaspoon kosher salt

For the stir-fry:

2 tablespoons cooking oil

4 garlic cloves, finely chopped

8 ounces (225 g / 2½ cups) mung bean sprouts

4 ounces (110 g / 2 cups) yu choy or other tender greens, leaves separated

For serving (optional):

Pickled Green Chiles (page 39), or store-bought

Kari Jap Choy (page 71)

Basic Sambal (page 31)

1. Soften the noodles: Soak the dried vermicelli in cool water for 20 minutes, until tender, then drain. Snip the noodles in half with scissors for easier handling.

2. Prepare the sauce: In a small bowl, whisk together the kecap manis or dark caramel soy sauce, soy sauce, sugar, salt, and 1½ cups (360 ml) water.

3. Start the stir-fry: Heat a large wok or nonstick pan over medium heat until it starts to lightly smoke. Add the oil, swirling to coat the surface. Stir-fry the garlic until fragrant, about 10 seconds, then add the drained vermicelli, using a pair of tongs to spread them into a single layer.

4. Pour the sauce over the vermicelli in a circular motion. Turn the heat to high and continue cooking, stirring the noodles to fold them into the sauce. For a

recipe continues

breezy way of mixing, I like to use a pair of tongs to pull the strands while using another utensil to gently toss the noodles, similar to tossing a salad. As the vermicelli cook, they will gradually absorb the sauce, expand, and soften.

5. When the sauce has been completely absorbed and the noodles are fully cooked, 5 to 7 minutes, add the mung bean sprouts and yu choy. Stir-fry until the vegetables are wilted but still crisp, about 1 minute.

6. Serve: Transfer to a plate and serve with the optional sides.

"The Longer the Noodle, the Longer Your Life Will Be"

You might hear this phrase: "Never cut the long noodle on your birthday!" These were the kinds of things my parents used to say, making sure I knew that noodles weren't just food, but connected to life itself. In my culture, noodles are symbols of longevity and good luck.

Pan Mee

(Hand-Torn Noodle Soup)

Serves 3

Some of my fondest memories are the afternoons I'd help my aunt prepare pan mee for her market stall ahead of busy Saturdays. The kitchen was always a lively scene on a Friday: me and my cousins kneading dough, cracking jokes, and getting everything ready for the next day's rush. Pan mee, a Hakka noodle dish, is all about its chewy, tender handmade noodles, served either in a traditional clear broth or "dry style" with a few toppings. The noodles can be cut with a pasta machine for neat strips, but I personally love the rustic hand-torn version. Each piece has its own character, thick or thin, depending on how you like it.

Although you can order pan mee at a kopitiam (coffee shop), Malaysian families love making this dish at home, especially to feed a crowd. The recipe is easy to scale up, and you can prep the broth and toppings ahead of time. My vegan broth is made from daikon radishes and mushrooms, a delicious base for the noodles. Before eating, make sure to mix everything up in the bowl!

For the soup:

1 tablespoon cooking oil

2 large daikon radishes (about 1¾ lbs / 800 g), peeled and cut into 1-inch (2.5 cm) chunks

2 large dried shiitake mushrooms, rinsed to remove dirt

1½ teaspoons kosher salt, plus more as needed

½ teaspoon mushroom seasoning, plus more as needed

8 ounces (225 g) leafy greens, such as yu choy, bok choy, or yin choy

For the dough:

2 cups (240 g) all-purpose flour

¼ teaspoon kosher salt

1. Prepare the soup: Heat the oil in a large pot or wok over medium-high heat. Stir-fry the radishes until their edges turn translucent, about 2 minutes.

2. Add 14 cups (3.5 L) water and the shiitake mushrooms to the pot. Bring to a boil, then add the salt and mushroom seasoning. Lower the heat and simmer until the soup has reduced to two-thirds of its original volume, 30 to 45 minutes. Skim off any foam or scum that rises to the surface. Taste the soup and adjust the seasoning with more salt or mushroom seasoning if needed.

3. Prepare the dough: While the soup simmers, make the dough. In a large bowl, combine the flour and salt. Create a well in the center and add ¼ cup (60 ml) water to start. Using chopsticks or a spatula, stir the

recipe and ingredients continue

For the topping:

2 tablespoons cooking oil

8 to 10 dried shiitake mushrooms, rehydrated and thinly sliced

½ ounce (14 g) dried wood ear mushrooms, rehydrated and thinly sliced

3 tablespoons textured vegetable protein (TVP), rehydrated and squeezed to drain

1 tablespoon vegetarian oyster sauce

1 tablespoon soy sauce

¼ teaspoon sugar

Dash of ground white pepper

1 teaspoon cornstarch

For serving:

Fried Shallots (page 43), or store-bought

Thinly sliced fresh Thai chile in soy sauce, with a squeeze of lime or calamansi juice

Chile sauce (such as the "Chicken" Rice Chili Sauce, page 35)

flour until it forms shaggy flakes. Knead the mixture into a soft dough, adding more water as needed, 1 tablespoon at a time (you may need to add up to 4 tablespoons / 60 ml in dry weather). Continue kneading until the dough is smooth and elastic and no longer sticks to your hands, 3 to 5 minutes. Cover the dough and let it rest for at least 30 minutes. Alternatively, you can refrigerate it overnight and bring it back to room temperature before proceeding.

4. Cook the topping: Heat the oil in a saucepan over medium heat. Sauté the shiitake mushrooms until fragrant and beginning to brown, 3 to 5 minutes. Add the wood ear mushrooms and TVP, being cautious, as the wood ear mushrooms may pop. Stir in the vegetarian oyster sauce and soy sauce, coating the mixture evenly. Pour in 1 cup (240 ml) water and bring the mixture to a boil. Season with the sugar and white pepper. Reduce the heat and let the mushrooms absorb the sauce, 2 to 3 minutes.

5. While the topping simmers, in a small bowl whisk the cornstarch with 3 teaspoons water to create a thin slurry. Gradually add the slurry to the pan, stirring continuously until the mixture thickens. Remove from the heat and set aside.

6. Strain the soup: Once the soup is ready, strain out the radishes and mushrooms. You can discard them, or you could serve the radishes as a side dish and slice the mushrooms thinly and add them to the topping.

7. When ready to cook the noodles, keep the stock at a low simmer.

8. Make the noodles (see Notes): Remove the dough from its bowl. It should be soft enough to sag when held up. Divide the dough into two portions, keeping one covered while you work on the other.

Notes:

- *There are several methods to form the noodles. My mom prefers tearing the dough inside a bowl of cold water. This method helps wash off the extra starch, resulting in silkier noodles with an optimal texture.*
- *You can also roll out the dough to a rectangle of your desired thickness (or use a pasta machine) and then use a knife to cut it into ribbons or squares. Stretch and drop the noodles into boiling water as directed in the main recipe.*
- *Alternatively, tear and cook the noodles in a separate pot of boiling water before adding them to the soup with the green vegetables for more control.*

9. Hold one portion of the dough with one hand and tear off bite-sized pieces with the other. Pinch and stretch each piece into a shaggy piece roughly the size of an ear. The thickness of the noodle is up to your preference—you can keep it thick or stretch the dough until it's almost see-through.

10. Drop each torn piece of dough directly into the simmering stock. Continue pulling and dropping pieces into the stock, keeping the heat low. Occasionally stir the pot gently to prevent clumping.

11. Add the greens: Once all the noodles are in the pot, increase the heat to a gentle boil. Add the tender greens and cook for 1 minute, until the noodles float to the top. Be careful not to overcook the noodles, as the soup will become starchy. Remove the pot from the heat when the noodles are al dente.

12. Serve: Ladle a portion of noodles, greens, and soup into each bowl. Add a generous spoonful of the mushroom topping and garnish with fried shallots. Enjoy immediately with a side of sliced Thai chile in soy sauce and chile sauce.

Three Shines

In Chinese cooking, there's a saying when you're working with dough: "three shines" (三光), meaning the dough is ready when your hands, the dough, and the bowl are all clean and smooth. This indicates that the dough has been kneaded to perfection, with a smooth, soft surface, and is ready for proofing or use.

Malaysian-Style Wonton Mee

(Dry Tossed Noodles with Wontons)

Serves 2

In Malaysia, wonton mee comes in two styles: clear broth and "dry style." Each vendor puts their own spin on the dish with their sauces, and in Kuala Lumpur, dry style means noodles tossed in a glossy, dark soy coating. I've always preferred dry style, maybe because it's what I grew up on. I can still picture my mom carefully curling the noodles with chopsticks, making sure I could easily manage each bite.

The thin yellow noodles have a distinctive QQ texture—chewy, springy, with just the right amount of bite. Made with alkaline water, they develop a unique flavor. Ramen noodles make a good stand-in: A quick boil, a shock in cold water, and a final dip in hot water before serving achieve the perfect texture. They're paired with wontons, delicate, one-bite dumplings that are served either in a small bowl of broth or right on top of the noodles. Wonton mee is often served with sweet glazed char siu, which you can make ahead (Tofu Char Siu, page 289), and Pickled Green Chiles (page 39)—a bursting bite of that tart, zesty chile plays a perfect counterpoint to the richly coated noodles. This recipe is my version of a dish that's been close to my heart for as long as I can remember.

For the sauce:

2 tablespoons Shallot Oil (page 43)

2 tablespoons soy sauce

2 teaspoons vegetarian oyster sauce

2 teaspoons dark caramel soy sauce or dark soy sauce

1 teaspoon toasted sesame oil

Ground white pepper

For the wontons and noodles:

Drizzle of cooking oil

10 uncooked wontons (page 177), folded according to the photos on page 230, or use frozen store-bought

2 servings (8 ounces / 225 g) fresh alkaline yellow noodles, such as ramen or chow mein

1 cup (60 g) leafy greens, like yu choy or choy sum

For serving:

1 recipe Tofu Char Siu (from Tofu Char Siu Rice, page 289)

Pickled Green Chiles (page 39), or store-bought

1. Prepare the sauce: In a small bowl, combine the shallot oil, soy sauce, vegetarian oyster sauce, dark caramel soy sauce, sesame oil, and white pepper. Whisk until smooth, then divide the sauce between two large serving bowls and set aside.

2. Cook the wontons: Bring a large pot of water to a rolling boil over high heat. Add the oil. Drop in the wontons and cook for 2 to 3 minutes (or 3 to 4 minutes if using frozen), or until they float to the surface. Cook for an additional 30 seconds, then use a strainer to transfer to a plate. Bring the water back to a boil.

recipe continues

3. Cook the noodles: Add the noodles to the boiling water and cook for 1 to 2 minutes, or until al dente. Remove the noodles from the pot (reserve the boiling water) and rinse them under cold water to stop the cooking process and make them springier.

4. Add the leafy greens to the boiling water and blanch until crisp-tender, about 30 seconds. Drain and remove from the heat. Add the noodles back to the pot and stir to combine with the vegetables.

5. Serve: Divide the noodles and vegetables between the two serving bowls. Toss the noodles in the sauce until well coated. Top with the cooked wontons and the tofu char siu. Serve immediately with a side of pickled green chiles.

How to wrap wontons

KL-Style Hokkien Mee

(Dark Caramel Soy Sauce–Braised Noodles)

For the noodles:

2 servings (about 1 pound / 450 g) fresh or frozen udon noodles (usually 225 g per serving)

For the sauce:

1 tablespoon soy sauce

2 tablespoons dark caramel soy sauce

For the tofu topping and cooking the udon:

2 tablespoons cooking oil

2 ounces (55 g) firm tofu, cut into tiny ¼-inch (6 mm) dice (about ½ cup)

Kosher salt

2 garlic cloves, finely chopped

3½ ounces (100 g) fresh oyster or king oyster mushrooms, torn into large strips

½ teaspoon mushroom seasoning

1 cup (90 g) cabbage, cut into 2-inch (5 cm) pieces

1 cup (60 g) yu choy or bok choy, leaves separated

For serving:

Basic Sambal (page 31; optional)

Chopped fresh Thai chile in soy sauce (optional)

Serves 2

When my kids were toddlers, my mama told them, "Hokkien lang ai jiak Hokkien mee"—"Hokkien people need to eat Hokkien noodles." I loved that cute connection between grandma and grandkids as they slurped noodles. At dai chow eateries—open-air spots with Kuala Lumpur's best stir-fries—Hokkien mee is a must-try. These thick, chewy noodles are like udon but yellow from alkaline, coated in a rich, dark gravy with wok hei aroma.

Traditionally, Hokkien mee is packed with meats, seafood, veggies, and crispy lard. I swap out the lard for finely diced firm tofu, pan-fried crisp and seasoned for savoriness, and use udon since traditional yellow noodles are hard to find. But the dark caramel soy sauce in this recipe is essential—it's thicker, sweeter, and more intense than regular soy sauce, giving the noodles a caramelized flavor and signature dark color. Fair warning: The dark sauce can get a bit messy, and these noodles are meant to be slurped, so maybe skip the white shirt!

1. Prepare the noodles: If using refrigerated udon noodles, soak them in a bowl of water until the strands can be separated. If the noodles are frozen, cook them in boiling water for 1 minute to separate, then rinse under cold water. Drain the noodles in a colander.

2. Prepare the sauce: In a small bowl, whisk together the soy sauces.

3. Make the tofu topping: Heat 1 tablespoon of the oil in a large wok or nonstick skillet over medium heat. Pan-fry the diced tofu until golden brown and crispy, 5 to 8 minutes. Season with salt to taste, then transfer to a bowl and set aside as a topping.

4. Cook the udon: Return the wok to medium-high heat and add the remaining 1 tablespoon oil. Sauté the

recipe continues

garlic until fragrant, about 15 seconds. Add the mushrooms and cook for about 2 minutes to give them a sear. Add the drained udon noodles and the sauce mixture, tossing until the noodles are evenly coated. When the noodles start to stick, add 2 cups (480 ml) water and the mushroom seasoning. Cover with a lid and let the noodles boil, absorbing the sauce.

5. When the liquid has reduced by half, after 8 to 10 minutes, uncover the pan and fold in the cabbage and yu choy. Continue to cook, stirring continuously, until most of the liquid has been absorbed and the noodles are thick, glossy, and chewy. Taste and adjust the seasoning if needed.

6. **Serve:** Serve the noodles warm, topped with the crispy tofu, and enjoy with a side of sambal or chopped Thai chile in soy sauce, if desired.

Wat Dan Hor

(Wide Rice Noodles with Gravy)

For the noodles:

1 tablespoon cooking oil

2 servings (1 pound / 450 g) fresh flat rice noodles (usually 225 g per serving)

1 tablespoon soy sauce

For the tofu:

½ tablespoon cooking oil

4 ounces (110 g) firm tofu, drained and cut into ½-inch-thick (12 mm) rectangles

For the aromatics and slurry:

1 tablespoon cooking oil

2 garlic cloves, minced

¼ cup (28 g) carrot slices

½ cup (50 g) fresh oyster or king oyster mushrooms, torn into bite-sized pieces

1 tablespoon soy sauce

½ tablespoon vegetarian oyster sauce

¼ teaspoon mushroom seasoning

½ teaspoon kosher salt, plus more as needed

Dash of ground white pepper

1 tablespoon cornstarch

1 cup (60 g) yu choy or gai lan, cut diagonally into 2-inch (5 cm) pieces

For serving:

Pickled Green Chiles (page 39), or store-bought

Serves 2 or 3

At dai chow spots in Kuala Lumpur, wat dan hor and KL-Style Hokkien Mee (page 231) are my must-orders. This dish stars hor fun, wide rice noodles The flat noodles are tossed in a scorching hot wok until they get a perfect char, then draped with a rich gravy of stir-fried aromatics, protein, and crisp vegetables. Wat dan hor, Cantonese for "silky egg river," gets its name from the egg swirled into the gravy, not the noodles themselves. My vegan version swaps egg for a silky, umami-rich blend with soy sauce and cornstarch to preserve that irresistible richness and silky texture. I serve it with Pickled Green Chiles (page 39) to cut the savory depth—a harmony of textures and flavors.

1. **Sear the noodles:** Heat a large nonstick pan or seasoned wok over high heat until lightly smoking. Add the oil and swirl to coat. Spread the rice noodles in a single layer in the pan. Let them cook undisturbed until the bottom begins to sear and crisp up, about 1 minute.

2. Drizzle the soy sauce over the noodles, then toss them using a pair of tongs or chopsticks. Continue to sear the noodles, flipping and folding them until both sides are slightly charred, about 1 minute more. Transfer the noodles to a serving plate.

3. **Pan-fry the tofu:** In the same pan, heat the oil over medium-high heat. Pan-fry the tofu in a single layer until both sides are golden brown, 5 to 8 minutes. Transfer the tofu to a plate.

4. **Cook the aromatics:** Heat the oil in the pan over medium-high heat. Sauté the garlic until fragrant, about 15 seconds.

recipe continues

5. Add the carrot and oyster mushrooms and stir-fry until softened, about 1 minute. Pour in 1½ cups (360 ml) water and season with the soy sauce, vegetarian oyster sauce, mushroom seasoning, salt, and white pepper. Bring the mixture to a boil.

6. Prepare the slurry: In the meantime, whisk the cornstarch and ¼ cup (60 ml) water in a small bowl to form a slurry.

7. Add the yu choy to the simmering sauce. Gradually stir in the slurry, a little at a time, until the sauce thickens to the consistency of hot-and-sour soup and the yu choy is crisp-tender, about 1 minute. Taste and adjust the seasoning with more salt, if needed.

8. Serve: Remove the pan from the heat. Pour the flavorful thickened sauce and vegetables over the seared flat rice noodles. Serve warm, with a side of pickled green chiles.

Pad Kee Mao

(Thai Drunken Noodles)

Serves 2

Despite my best efforts to explore other dishes on the menu at a Thai restaurant, I always find myself ordering pad kee mao, better known as drunken noodles. There's just something inevitably delicious about the trifecta of garlic, Thai basil, and chiles, and the way the aromatic herbs fuse with those charred noodles keeps you hooked. When I was in Chiang Mai, Thailand—a mecca for vegan food—I made it my mission to eat as many plates of vegan pad kee mao as I could.

What I love about making these at home is the control you get over the process. You can dial the spice level up with bird's eye chiles (or down by using a long red chile pepper) and toss in whatever veggies you've got on hand for added nutrition and color. For the best results, I recommend stir-frying in small batches. This way, each ingredient cooks evenly, and you get that ideal balance of chewy, tender noodles and smoky flavor that makes pad kee mao intensely craveable.

For the sauce:

1½ tablespoons vegetarian oyster sauce

1 tablespoon soy sauce

½ tablespoon Golden Mountain brand Thai seasoning sauce, plus more as needed

½ teaspoon dark caramel soy sauce

2 tablespoons Vegan Fish Sauce (page 49)

1 teaspoon sugar

For the chili garlic paste:

2 fresh Thai bird's eye chiles or 1 long red chili

3 or 4 garlic cloves, finely chopped

For the aromatics and noodles:

2 tablespoons cooking oil

1 cup (60 g) yu choy or gai lan, cut to separate stem and leaves

8 ounces (225 g) firm tofu, pan-fried (see page 65)

1 pound (450 g) fresh flat rice noodles

1 cup (20 g) packed Thai basil leaves

Kosher salt, as needed

1. **Make the sauce:** In a small bowl, whisk together the vegetarian oyster sauce, soy sauce, Golden Mountain seasoning sauce, dark caramel soy sauce, vegan fish sauce, and sugar until well combined.

2. **Make the chili garlic paste:** Using a mortar and pestle, pound the chiles and garlic into a coarse paste. Alternatively, you can chop them finely with a knife or pulse them in a food processor.

3. **Stir-fry the aromatics:** Heat the oil in a wok over medium-high heat. Stir-fry the chili garlic paste until fragrant, about 30 seconds.

4. Add the yu choy stems and tofu and stir-fry briefly, until they are coated in the aromatic paste and piping hot, about 1 minute.

recipe continues

A vegan food stall with stir-fried dishes in Thailand.

Thailand's river market buzzes with tradition and colors.

5. Sear the noodles: Push the vegetables and tofu up one side of the wok. Add the rice noodles, spreading them into a single layer on the bottom. Let them sear undisturbed over high heat for 30 to 45 seconds. Flip the noodles and allow the other side to develop a char.

6. Pour the sauce mixture evenly over the noodles, then toss and stir to coat the noodles thoroughly. Add the yu choy leaves and Thai basil, stir-frying until they are wilted, 1 to 2 minutes.

7. Serve: Taste the dish and season with salt or more Golden Mountain seasoning sauce if needed. Serve hot to enjoy the best flavor and noodle texture.

Pad Woon Sen

(Stir-Fried Glass Noodles)

For the noodles:

3½ ounces (100 g) dried mung bean vermicelli (bean thread)

For the sauce:

2 tablespoons vegetarian oyster sauce

3 tablespoons (45 ml) Golden Mountain brand Thai seasoning sauce

½ teaspoon dark caramel soy sauce

½ teaspoon sugar

¼ teaspoon mushroom seasoning

Dash each of ground white pepper and ground black pepper

For the tofu and vegetables:

2 tablespoons cooking oil

7 ounces (200 g) firm tofu, drained, pressed, and cut into 1-inch (2.5 cm) cubes

3½ ounces (100 g) fresh oyster or king oyster mushrooms, torn into bite-sized pieces

1 small onion, thinly sliced

3 garlic cloves, finely chopped

¼ cup (30 g) carrot slices

Serves 2

Thai-style pad woon sen—a soft tangle of glass noodles aromatic with garlic and onion and mixed with vegetables—was once a dish I was too nervous to try making at home. I used to watch the vendors making a similar glass noodle dish at char kuey teow stalls in Malaysia, stirring like their lives depended on it, making sure every noodle was coated in rich sauce, and I'd think, "How do they pull it off?"

When I finally decided to try making this in my own kitchen, I found a few tricks that made things way easier: Prep the sauce in advance and use a big pan so the noodles have plenty of surface area to absorb the sauce. Use both hands when you're stirring, one with tongs to tease apart stubborn clumps, and one with a spatula to make sure the sauce reaches every corner. At the very end, increase to high heat for a slight sear. With these tips in your back pocket, this dish is fully achievable!

1. **Soften the noodles:** Soak the mung bean vermicelli in warm water for 10 minutes, until tender, then drain. Snip the noodles into shorter lengths with scissors for easier handling and stir-frying.

2. **Prepare the sauce:** In a small bowl, whisk together the vegetarian oyster sauce, Golden Mountain seasoning sauce, dark caramel soy sauce, sugar, mushroom seasoning, white pepper, black pepper, and ½ cup (120 ml) water.

3. **Pan-fry the tofu and mushrooms:** Heat 1 tablespoon of the oil in a large wok or nonstick pan over medium-high heat. Pan-fry the tofu cubes in a single layer until golden brown on both sides, 5 to 8 minutes. Transfer the tofu to a bowl.

4. In the same pan, add the mushrooms and sauté until they are fragrant and starting to sear on the

recipe and ingredients continue

½ cup (60 g) chopped cabbage

½ cup (50 g) chopped yu choy or gai lan

1 small (60 g) tomato, cut into wedges

1 scallion, white and green parts, cut into 2-inch (5 cm) sections and julienned

For serving:

1 or 2 fresh red Thai chiles, thinly sliced, in Vegan Fish Sauce (page 49)

Red pepper flakes

edges, about 2 minutes. Transfer them to the same bowl as the tofu.

5. Sauté the vegetables: Using the same pan or wok, heat the remaining 1 tablespoon oil over medium heat. Sauté the onion, garlic, and carrot for about 2 minutes, until the onion is slightly translucent. Add the cabbage, yu choy, and tomato, then add 2 tablespoons of the sauce mixture. Stir-fry the vegetables until they are softened, about 2 minutes. Return the tofu and mushrooms to the pan, pushing everything to one side.

6. Cook the noodles: Spread the noodles evenly in the pan in a single layer. Pour the remaining sauce over the noodles and increase the heat to medium-high. Using a pair of tongs, toss and stir the vermicelli to combine with the sauce and vegetables. The noodles will gradually expand and soften. If the pan becomes dry before the noodles are fully cooked, add more water, 1 tablespoon at a time.

7. When the sauce is completely absorbed and the noodles are fully cooked, 2 to 3 minutes, fold in the scallion. Increase the heat to high and toss for another minute to combine and lightly sear.

8. Serve: Transfer to a plate and serve with Thai chiles in vegan fish sauce and red pepper flakes.

Pad Thai

Serves 2 (or 1 if you're hungry)

It's no secret that I have a deep love for rice noodles, and pad Thai has been a staple in our house for years, especially back when my kids were just starting to dip their toes into spicy food. This dish hits the perfect notes: sweet, sour, salty, and savory with a balance of soy sauce, tamarind juice, and a touch of palm sugar. The secret addition is tamarind, a flavor I've adored since childhood. Its complex acidity is uniquely fragrant and quite different from the sour notes of citrus.

Everything comes together in a hot wok: a mix of tofu, fresh veggies, and crunchy bean sprouts and chives. Serve with a squeeze of lime and a sprinkle of crushed peanuts, and make sure you stir it up before eating to get everything in each bite. This is a dish where every element is important, but you can prep ahead: Make a batch of the sauce and keep it in a jar in the fridge. This lets you whip up pad Thai whenever the craving strikes—which, in my house, is often.

For the noodles:

3½ ounces (100 g) dried pad Thai rice noodles

For the sauce:

1 golf ball–sized clump (28 g) of tamarind paste

1 cup (240 ml) hot water

3 tablespoons (45 ml) Vegan Fish Sauce (page 49), plus more as needed

1 tablespoon Golden Mountain brand Thai seasoning sauce, plus more as needed

For the tofu and aromatics:

3 tablespoons (45 ml) cooking oil

2 ounces (55 g) firm tofu, cut into cubes (about ½ cup)

2 small shallots, finely chopped

2 large garlic cloves, finely chopped

1 tablespoon palm sugar, coarsely chopped

2 tablespoons preserved radish (sweet variety), coarsely chopped

2 Chinese chives, cut into 2-inch (5 cm) segments, stems and tender tops separated

1½ cups (110 g) mung bean sprouts, plus more for garnish

Kosher salt, as needed

For serving:

Lime wedges

Crushed roasted peanuts

Red pepper flakes

1. **Soften the noodles:** Soak the rice noodles in cool water for 45 minutes, until tender.

2. **While the noodles soak, prepare the sauce:** In a small bowl, combine the tamarind paste with ¾ cup (180 ml) of the hot water. Use your fingers to mash the paste, creating a dark, acidic liquid. In a separate bowl, whisk together 3 tablespoons (45 ml) of the tamarind liquid with the vegan fish sauce, Golden Mountain seasoning sauce, and the remaining ¼ cup (60 ml) hot water.

3. **Pan-fry the tofu:** Heat ½ tablespoon of the oil in a pan or wok over medium-high heat. Pan-fry the tofu in a single layer until both sides are golden brown, 5 to 8 minutes. Transfer the tofu to a plate.

recipe continues

4. **Cook the aromatics and noodles:** In the same pan or wok, heat the remaining 2½ tablespoons oil, swirling to coat the sides. Sauté the shallots and garlic until fragrant, about 30 seconds. Add the palm sugar and stir until it caramelizes.

5. Spread the drained noodles across the bottom of the pan using tongs. Pour in half of the sauce and increase the heat to high. Stir and toss the noodles to incorporate the sauce, cooking until the noodles absorb all the liquid, 3 to 5 minutes.

6. Add the tofu and the preserved radish to the pan. Pour in the remaining sauce and continue stir-frying until the noodles are fully cooked and al dente. If the noodles start to stick, add 1 tablespoon of water at a time and continue to stir-fry.

7. Fold in the stem portion of the chives and the mung bean sprouts. Toss briefly until the chives are wilted, about 30 seconds. Taste and adjust the seasoning with salt or more tamarind juice, vegan fish sauce, or Golden Mountain seasoning sauce as needed.

8. **Serve:** Serve the pad Thai immediately, garnished with more mung bean sprouts, lime wedges, crushed roasted peanuts, red pepper flakes, and the tender tops of the chives.

Kon Chau "Ngau" Hor

(Beefless Chow Fun)

For the soy chop "beef":

8 slices (2 ounces / 55 g) soy chop, rehydrated as directed on the package (can substitute TVP or vegan beef slice, such as Verisoy)

1½ teaspoons soy sauce

1 tablespoon dark caramel soy sauce

2 teaspoons sugar

1 tablespoon hot water

1 tablespoon cornstarch

1 tablespoon cooking oil

For the noodles:

1 tablespoon cooking oil

2 servings (1 pound / 450 g) fresh flat rice noodles (usually 225 g per serving)

1 heaping cup (100 g) fresh mung bean sprouts, shaken dry

2 tablespoons soy sauce

1 tablespoon dark caramel soy sauce

¼ teaspoon mushroom seasoning

For serving:

4 scallions, white and green parts, cut into 2-inch (5 cm) sections

Serves 2

My vegan take on kon chau hor—Cantonese for "dry stir-fried rice noodles"—swaps out the ngau, or beef, for slices of soy protein, which soak up the sauce and bring a chewy bite. I first ate these noodles at a dim sum spot, where I ordered them without the beef, and they quickly became my favorite dish to make vegan. There's a trick to handling the noodles. When you add them to the wok, don't stir right away. Let them sit undisturbed to sear one side deliciously. Then flip them to char the other side. You're aiming for those crispy, golden-brown bits that add texture to every bite, a charred effect that's the hallmark of this dish.

1. Marinate and cook the soy chop: Drain the rehydrated soy slices and squeeze out any excess water. In a small bowl, combine the soy sauces, sugar, and hot water, stirring until the sugar dissolves. Add the soy slices and toss to coat them in the sauce, gently squeezing the slices to help them absorb the marinade. Sprinkle with the cornstarch and toss to evenly coat the soy slices.

2. Heat the oil in a large wok or nonstick pan over medium heat. Pan-fry the marinated soy slices in a single layer, flipping them to sear both sides until golden brown, 5 to 8 minutes. Transfer the soy slices to a bowl and set aside.

3. Char the noodles: In the same wok, heat the oil over medium-high. Add the fresh rice noodles, spreading them in a single layer in the pan. Allow the noodles to sear on one side, undisturbed, for about 1 minute. Flip the noodles and continue cooking until both sides develop char marks, about 2 more minutes.

4. Spread the mung bean sprouts over the noodles. Drizzle with the soy sauces, then season with the

recipe continues

mushroom seasoning. Turn the heat to high and toss the noodles until they are evenly coated with the sauce and the bean sprouts are wilted, about 1 minute more.

5. **Serve:** Add the pan-fried soy slices back to the wok, then fold in the scallions and cook until the scallions are slightly wilted. Remove from the heat and serve the dish warm.

Char Kuey Teow

(Malaysian Stir-Fried Flat Rice Noodles)

For the sauce:

1 teaspoon sweet caramel soy sauce or dark caramel soy sauce

2 tablespoons soy sauce, plus more as needed

¼ teaspoon mushroom seasoning

Pinch of sugar

For the tofu, "egg," and noodles:

2½ tablespoons cooking oil

5 ounces (130 g) firm tofu or vegan fish cake, cut into ½-inch-thick (12 mm) triangles or rectangles

3 garlic cloves, finely chopped

1½ tablespoons sambal oelek or other chile sauce (optional)

½ cup (120 ml) plant-based egg liquid

2 servings (1 pound / 450 g) fresh flat rice noodles (usually 225 g per serving)

1½ cups (110 g) mung bean sprouts

½ cup (20 g) Chinese chives cut into 2-inch (5 cm) segments

Basic Sambal (page 31), for serving

Serves 2

At Malaysia's morning markets, you can always tell when you're near a char kuey teow stall. Metal spatulas clang against woks in a frantic beat, while the air swirls with the unmistakable smell of smoky noodles. Vendors sling it fast over roaring flames—there's a reason people line up for this. Though it's traditionally tossed with shrimp and cockles, I've made this version vegan, keeping all the smoky, savory soul intact. The trick to char kuey teow is using high heat. Garlic sizzles and then the wide, slippery rice noodles hit the heat, soaking up the chef's seasoning sauce with mung bean sprouts snapping in every bite. It lands savory, smoky, and a hint of sweet—a plate that fights back the morning haze.

Every bite yanks me to those mornings and my uncle Ah Cheong, my eldest aunt's husband. On Sundays, he'd sweat over his wok, frying char kuey teow for me, handing it to me with a cup of kopi bing—iced coffee that he'd swirl just right—before I dragged myself to Monday school. He's gone now, and I miss his wok cooking, but this dish keeps him close.

1. Prepare the sauce: In a small bowl, whisk together the soy sauces, mushroom seasoning, and sugar until well combined.

2. Pan-fry the tofu: Heat 1 tablespoon of the oil in a wok or large nonstick pan over medium heat. Add the tofu or vegan fish cake in a single layer and pan-fry, flipping as needed, until golden brown on all sides, 5 to 8 minutes. Transfer to a bowl.

3. In the same pan, heat 1 tablespoon of the oil over medium heat. Stir-fry the garlic until fragrant, about 15 seconds. Add the sambal oelek (if using) and tofu, being careful, as the sambal may splatter. Gently fold the tofu into the mixture until it's heated through and coated in the aromatic sauce.

recipe continues

4. Cook the "egg": Push the tofu to one side of the pan and add the remaining ½ tablespoon oil to the center. Pour in the plant-based egg liquid and cook for about 15 seconds, until the egg is halfway set.

5. Cook the noodles: Spread the flat rice noodles over the egg in the pan. Add the prepared sauce. Increase the heat to high and toss the noodles, stirring rapidly to combine with the egg and the sauce. Cook until the noodles take on color and begin to char, 1 to 2 minutes.

6. Add the mung bean sprouts and chives to the pan, stir-frying for about 30 seconds until wilted but still crisp. Taste the noodles and season with additional soy sauce if needed.

7. Serve: Serve the char kuey teow warm with a side of sambal.

Mee Goreng

(Mamak-Style Fried Noodles)

Serves 2 or 3

Mee goreng, Malay for "stir-fried noodles," comes in many variations, each with its own personality. The one that takes me back is from a mamak stall, an open-air haven where, as a kid, I'd go to escape school or home. No air-conditioning, just good company and the joy of sharing great food under the night sky.

One mamak stall felt like a second home. Alkaline noodles sizzled in a blazing wok, spices mingled with the air, and the vendor's deft tosses were a comforting ritual. We'd start with roti canai (page 333), tearing into the flaky bread, then dig into a plate of mee goreng to cap off the night. My hearty version packs veggies, bean sprouts, tofu, and youtiao—a crisp Chinese cruller that I cut into rounds for a unique crunch, swapping for the fritter-like toppings from those stalls. Those golden, puffed rounds lift the noodles' texture, a twist on the same magic.

For the potato:

1 small potato (120 g)

For the sauce:

2 tablespoons soy sauce

2 tablespoons vegetarian oyster sauce

1 tablespoon dark caramel soy sauce

2 tablespoons sambal oelek

3 tablespoons (45 ml) ketchup

½ tablespoon sugar

½ tablespoon curry powder

1 cup (240 ml) warm water

For the noodles:

1 pound (450 g) fresh yellow oiled noodles

2 tablespoons cooking oil

3 shallots, thinly sliced

3 garlic cloves, finely chopped

1 small tomato (7 ounces / 200 g), cut into thin wedges

4 ounces (110 g) store-bought fried tofu or pan-fried firm tofu (page 65), sliced

Half a fried youtiao (Chinese cruller), baked and sliced into 1-inch (2.5 cm) pieces

1 cup (60 g) yu choy or another tender green, chopped

1 cup (70 g) mung bean sprouts

Kosher salt, as needed

1. Cook the potato: In a large pot, cover the potato with enough water to submerge it. Bring the water to a boil and cook the potato until it's fork-tender, 10 to 15 minutes. Once it's cool enough to handle, peel and cut it into 1-inch (2.5 cm) bite-sized cubes.

2. Prepare the sauce: In a small bowl, whisk together the soy sauce, vegetarian oyster sauce, dark caramel soy sauce, sambal oelek, ketchup, sugar, curry powder, and warm water. Stir until the sugar dissolves, then set the sauce aside.

3. Prepare the noodles: Place the fresh noodles in a strainer and rinse with cold water to remove the oil. Alternatively, you can blanch the noodles in boiling water for 30 seconds. Drain well.

4. Heat the oil in a large wok or nonstick pan over medium heat. Sauté the shallots and garlic until fragrant, about 30 seconds. Add the tomato and fried

recipe and ingredients continue

For serving:

Lime wedges

Chopped chiles

Mee goreng flares in the wok at the mamak stall. The Mamak are Malaysia's Indian-Muslim community, whose street food stalls are a way of life, where I'd savor roti canai and mee goreng with my dad and brother, from dawn breakfasts to late-night feasts, full of warm, familiar vibes.

tofu to the pan. Continue stir-frying until the tomato skins start to blister and the tofu is heated through, about 1 minute.

5. Spread the drained noodles evenly across the pan using tongs. Turn the heat to medium-high. Add the prepared sauce and use the tongs and a spatula to toss the noodles until they are well coated.

6. Add the cubed potato, fried youtiao, and yu choy to the pan. Stir-fry until the greens are heated through, about 1 minute. Add the mung bean sprouts and fold them in until just wilted, about 30 seconds. Taste and adjust the seasoning with salt if needed.

7. Serve: Serve the dish immediately. Add a squeeze of lime juice and accompany with chopped chiles for an extra-spicy kick.

Mee Jawa

(Malaysian Javanese Noodles in Tangy Gravy)

Serves 2

Mee jawa is a favorite breakfast dish at kopitiams in Malaysia: a piping bowl of chewy yellow noodles bathed in thick, comforting gravy. The hearty sauce is made from sweet potatoes, sambal, tomato paste, and palm sugar for caramelly sweetness. Fresh yellow oil noodles at the Asian supermarket are the best option here—I rinse and boil them to al dente texture before ladling on the hot gravy. Topped with crisp shredded lettuce, slices of fried tofu, boiled potato cubes for extra heartiness, and fried fritters, each bite of noodles comes with a crunch. I like using youtiao (Chinese crullers) that I buy frozen and bake until they're perfectly crispy, and I double up on the gravy so I can dip them!

For the potatoes:

1 small (120 g) golden or russet potato

1 large (200 g) sweet potato

For the gravy:

2 tablespoons cooking oil

1 tablespoon Basic Sambal (page 31)

2 tablespoons tomato paste (use 1 tablespoon for a less sour taste)

½ teaspoon mushroom seasoning

½ teaspoon kosher salt

1 tablespoon palm sugar

For the sprouts and noodles:

1 cup (70 g) fresh mung bean sprouts

2 servings (about 8 ounces / 225 g) fresh yellow alkaline noodles, such as ramen (usually about 115 g per serving)

1. Cook the potatoes: Place the golden potato and sweet potato in a large saucepan or pot and cover with enough water to submerge. Bring the water to a boil. Cook the potatoes, covered, until they are fork-tender, 10 to 15 minutes. (The sweet potato may cook faster, so remove it when done to allow the golden potato to continue cooking.)

2. When the golden potato is cool enough to handle, peel it and cut it into 1-inch (2.5 cm) cubes. Set it aside for serving.

3. When the sweet potato is cool enough to handle, peel it and place it in a blender. Add 3 cups (720 ml) water and blend until smooth.

4. Make the gravy: In a deep saucepan or pot over medium heat, heat 1 tablespoon of the oil. Add the sambal and sauté until fragrant, about 30 seconds. Pour in the sweet potato purée and cook until it's bubbling. Stir in the tomato paste, mushroom seasoning, salt, and palm sugar. Keep the gravy at a

recipe and ingredients continue

For serving:

8 ounces (225 g) pan-fried firm tofu (page 65), sliced

Fried Shallots (page 43), or store-bought

Thinly sliced fresh chiles

Half a fried youtiao (Chinese cruller), baked and sliced into 1-inch (2.5 cm) pieces

1 scallion, white and green parts, chopped

½ cup sliced lettuce

Lime or calamansi wedges

gentle simmer, stirring occasionally, while you prepare the noodles and other ingredients.

5. **Blanch the bean sprouts:** Bring a large pot of water to a boil over high heat. Blanch the mung bean sprouts for 30 seconds, then remove and drain in a colander.

6. **Cook the noodles:** Using the same pot of boiling water, cook the yellow alkaline noodles until al dente, 1 to 2 minutes.

7. **Serve:** Divide the noodles and mung bean sprouts between two bowls. Ladle a few spoonfuls of the sweet potato gravy over the top. Add the golden potato cubes, tofu, fried shallots, chiles, youtiao, scallion, and lettuce.

8. Before serving, squeeze some lime or calamansi juice over the dish. Stir everything together and enjoy.

Curry Chee Cheong Fun

(Rice Noodle Rolls with Curry Sauce)

Serves 2

Chee cheong fun is the breakfast item I missed most when moving to the US. In Cantonese, chee cheong means "pig intestine," which sounds odd until you see the long, rolled shape of these delicate rice noodles. At the food stalls back home in Malaysia, they come folded or rolled into neat logs. As a child, I loved the rolled ones for easy dipping, but now I crave the flat, thick ribbons, perfect for slurping with rich sauce or curry.

When you visit a chee cheong fun stall, you're looking at a lineup of sauces: soy sauce, shallot oil, plain curry sauce, sweet bean paste, and chile sauce. The classic move is to go with soy sauce and shallot oil, but my favorite option is mixing curry sauce, sweet bean paste (similar to hoisin sauce), and a good hit of chile. I started making this dish at home using either homemade or store-bought rice noodle sheets and my own homemade sambal (page 31). The result is a dish that transports me right back to those breakfast stalls!

For the curry:

2 teaspoons cooking oil

3 tablespoons Basic Sambal (page 31), plus more as needed

2 cups (480 ml) Basic Vegetable Stock (page 37) or store-bought, or water

Mushroom seasoning, as needed

Kosher salt, as needed

½ cup (120 ml) full-fat coconut milk

For the cheong fun ***(or use 1 pound / 450 g store-bought fresh rice noodles)*****:**

1 cup (120 g) rice flour

⅓ cup (40 g) tapioca starch

¼ teaspoon kosher salt

Cooking oil, for brushing

For serving:

Fried Shallots (page 43), or store-bought

Toasted sesame seeds

1. Cook the curry: Heat the oil in a medium saucepan over medium heat. Add the sambal and stir-fry for about 30 seconds to release its flavor. Add the stock or water and bring to a rolling boil. Taste and adjust the seasoning by adding more sambal, mushroom seasoning, and salt as needed. Slowly stir in the coconut milk and let the mixture simmer until slightly thickened, 5 to 8 minutes. Keep warm while you prepare the cheong fun.

2. Prepare the batter: *(If using store-bought noodles, skip to step 10.)* In a large bowl, combine the rice flour, tapioca starch, and salt. I highly recommend measuring by weight here instead of volume for the most consistent results. Gradually whisk in 1½ cups plus 1 tablespoon (370 ml) water until you have a thin batter with no visible lumps. Let the batter rest at room temperature for 15 minutes.

recipe continues

3. Prepare the steaming setup: You'll need a wok or pot with a lid, large enough to hold a 9 by 13-inch (23 by 33 cm; quarter sheet) baking pan or a similar heatproof dish like an 8 by 8-inch (20 by 20 cm) brownie pan. Fill the pot with enough water that the pan will float on the surface of the water—it's okay if the pan's edges touch or rest on the wok's sides, as this helps stabilize it. Place a large baking sheet filled halfway with cold water on the countertop—this is an optional water bath, but it will help quickly cool down the pan and speed up your process.

4. Steam the noodles: Bring the water in the wok to a rolling boil over medium-high heat.

5. Brush the tray that will float on the water with a thin layer of oil. Stir the rested batter well, as the starch tends to settle. Add ¼ cup or ⅓ cup (60 or 75 ml) batter (depending on the size of your pan) to the tray, just enough to thinly cover the surface. Tilt the tray so that the batter reaches the corners.

6. Using heatproof gloves or tongs, transfer the tray to the boiling water. Quickly tilt the tray again to ensure the batter evenly coats the entire surface. Cover the wok and steam the batter for 2 to 3 minutes over high heat, until you see large bubbles appear under the noodle and the edges start to pull away from the sides of the pan. The glossy white will turn matte white and slightly translucent. It's okay if a few cracks form.

7. Brush the top of the steamed noodle with a thin layer of oil. Using heatproof gloves or tongs, carefully transfer the tray to the baking sheet filled with cold water. Wait until the noodle is cool enough to touch. (Tip: If you have a second pan, you can start steaming the next sheet of noodle while the first one cools.)

8. Using a rubber spatula or plastic pastry scraper, gently loosen and lift the cooled noodle from one end of the pan, rolling it toward the other end or folding it into thirds. Transfer the noodle to a cutting board.

9. Repeat to steam the rest of the batter. You don't have to wash the pan in between batches, as long as you brush the pan with a fresh layer of oil before each batch. Refill the water in the pot as needed.

10. Cut the noodles: Slice the cooled rice sheets or store-bought fresh rice noodles into 1-inch (2.5 cm) ribbons (if not precut). Place them on a plate until ready to serve.

11. Assemble the bowls: If using store-bought noodles, warm them by steaming them for 2 to 3 minutes, or by soaking them in hot water for 1 to 2 minutes, then drain well. Place the store-bought or rolled and cut homemade noodles in serving bowls. Ladle the warm curry over the noodles and garnish with fried shallots and toasted sesame seeds. Serve immediately.

Curry Laksa

(Spicy Coconut Noodle Soup)

Serves 3

Eating a steaming bowl of spicy curry laksa for breakfast might sound intense, but it's an incredible start to the day. Imagine yourself in Malaysia's hot and humid weather, leaned over a deep bowl of steaming aromatic broth, tissues ready for that first fiery slurp. It's pure satisfaction—shiok, as locals say for "deliciously awesome"—waking all your senses at once.

In Kuala Lumpur, curry laksa, or kari mee, usually features curry chicken, fish cakes, and sometimes shrimp for extra richness. This vegan version, which blends creamy coconut milk with sambal and curry paste, keeps the spicy soul intact with plant-based swaps that still hit that shiok spot. I love it especially for the tofu puffs—fried pockets that soak up curry like sponges, bursting with hot, flavorful broth when bitten. I've burned my lips countless times from my excitement. Fried wontons, an extra-charge treat at kopitiams, add a crispy bite—always worth it!

For the mushrooms, eggplant, and wontons:

Cooking oil, for frying

8 ounces (225 g) king oyster mushrooms, trimmed and cut into 3-inch (7.5 cm) sections, then torn into finger-width strips

Kosher salt

1 small (200 g) Chinese or Japanese eggplant, cut into 3-inch (7.5 cm) sections, then torn into finger-width strips

10 uncooked wontons (page 177), folded according to the photos on page 230, or use frozen store-bought

For the curry, vegetables, and noodles:

¼ cup (60 ml) Basic Sambal (page 31) or vegan Malaysian curry laksa paste, plus more for serving

6½ cups (1.5 L) Basic Vegetable Stock (page 37) or store-bought, or water

½ teaspoon mushroom seasoning, plus more as needed

One (14-ounce / 400 ml) can full-fat coconut milk

10 fried tofu puffs (3½ ounces / 100 g), cut in half

Handful of curry leaves

1. Pan-fry the mushrooms: Heat a drizzle of the oil in a large skillet or nonstick pan over medium-high heat. Pan-fry the mushrooms until they release their moisture and start to brown, 3 to 4 minutes. Season with a pinch of salt, then transfer to a bowl.

2. Fry the eggplant: Fill a small saucepan halfway with oil and heat it to 300°F (150°C), or until an inserted wooden chopstick emits a slow stream of bubbles. Fry the eggplant, flipping to cook evenly, until the skin is glossy purple but not yet wrinkled, about 1 minute. Use a slotted spoon to transfer the eggplant to a paper towel–lined plate to drain.

3. Fry the wontons: Increase the oil temperature to 350°F (170°C). Add a few wontons at a time to the hot oil (do not thaw if using frozen) and fry until they turn

recipe and ingredients continue

Kosher salt

Sugar, as needed

1 cup (85 g) vegetables of choice (such as mung bean sprouts, long beans, yu choy)

3 servings (about 12 ounces / 335 g) fresh noodles of choice, such as ramen

For serving:

Lime wedges

golden in the center and the edges are dark golden and crispy, 20 to 30 seconds. Transfer to a paper towel–lined plate to drain.

4. **Make the curry:** In a deep saucepan or pot large enough to hold 10 cups (2.5 L) of liquid, stir-fry the sambal or curry laksa paste over medium heat to release its fragrance. Add the stock or water and bring to a rolling boil. Add the mushroom seasoning, coconut milk, tofu puffs, and curry leaves.

5. Cover and simmer on medium-low for 5 to 8 minutes to meld the flavors. Taste and season with salt. Adjust with more sambal, mushroom seasoning, or sugar if needed.

6. Add the eggplant and cook for 2 to 3 minutes, allowing it to absorb the flavors.

7. **Blanch the vegetables:** Bring a large pot of water to a boil and blanch the vegetables, keeping the cooking time brief to preserve their crispness and color, 30 seconds to 2 minutes (bean sprouts are quick; long beans take a bit longer).

8. **Prepare the noodles:** Boil the noodles according to the package instructions. Drain in a colander.

9. **Serve:** Place a portion of the noodles in each bowl, along with the vegetables. Ladle the hot curry over the noodles and top with the wontons and mushrooms. Serve warm, accompanied by extra sambal and a squeeze of lime juice.

Sichuan-Style Dan Dan Noodles

For the topping and ya cai:

3 tablespoons (45 ml) cooking oil, plus more as needed

1 tablespoon minced fresh ginger

½ tablespoon Pixian doubanjiang (spicy chili bean paste)

½ cup (45 g) textured vegetable protein (TVP), rehydrated and squeezed to drain

1 tablespoon soy sauce

1 tablespoon Shaoxing cooking wine

¼ teaspoon dark caramel soy sauce

¼ teaspoon mushroom seasoning

2 teaspoons ya cai (preserved mustard greens)

For the sauce:

2 teaspoons sesame paste, or more for a creamier version

½ teaspoon sugar

2 teaspoons garlic water (page 177) or 1 teaspoon minced garlic

3 teaspoons Chili Oil (page 41), or store-bought

4 teaspoons roasted peanuts, lightly crushed with a knife or mortar and pestle

2 pinches of ground Sichuan peppercorns

Serves 2

Back in the day, noodle vendors in Sichuan province slung baskets on bamboo poles—one with noodles and the other with toppings and sauce, called zuo liao. They'd yell "Dan dan mian," luring folks with the promise of a bowl of this street food. Fast-forward to today, and dan dan noodles are still a favorite—ordered by the liang (50 g portion), typically two liang unless you're extra hungry.

Vegetarian spots in Chengdu now offer vegan dan dan mian, and I've sampled some stellar ones. My version, when shared with friends, stuns them with the TVP (textured vegetable protein) mimicking minced meat's texture. I lean on Pixian doubanjiang, fermented bean paste, for that deep umami kick. In a perfect bowl, the flavors play off each other beautifully: Chili oil brings just the right amount of heat, ya cai (preserved mustard greens) add funk and saltiness, and sesame paste lends a nutty aroma and creamy richness that slicks every bite.

1. Cook the topping: Heat the oil in a wok or saucepan over medium heat. Sauté the ginger until fragrant, about 1 minute. Add the doubanjiang and stir briefly to release its flavor, being cautious, as the sauce may splatter in the hot oil.

2. Stir in the TVP, followed by the soy sauce and cooking wine, allowing them to sizzle and release their flavors. Add the dark caramel soy sauce, mushroom seasoning, and ½ cup (120 ml) water.

3. Bring the liquid to a boil, then reduce the heat to a simmer. Cook the TVP, stirring occasionally, until it absorbs all the liquid and resembles ground mince, 3 to 4 minutes. Transfer the topping to a bowl.

4. Sauté the ya cai: Clean the wok or pan and set it over medium-low heat. Add another drizzle of oil and

recipe and ingredients continue

For the noodles and greens:

7 ounces (200 g) fresh noodles, such as ramen, or 5 ounces (150 g) dried wheat noodles

½ cup (50 g) tender greens, such as bok choy or yu choy

For serving:

2 teaspoons finely chopped scallion greens

sauté the ya cai, stirring continuously until piping hot, fragrant, and slightly crisped—"frizzled"—30 to 45 seconds. Divide the frizzled ya cai between two serving bowls.

5. Prepare the sauce ingredients: To each bowl with the ya cai, add 1 teaspoon sesame paste, ¼ teaspoon sugar, 1 teaspoon garlic water, 1½ teaspoons chili oil, 2 teaspoons roasted peanuts, and a pinch of ground Sichuan peppercorns.

6. Cook the noodles: Bring a large pot of water to a boil. Cook the fresh noodles until al dente, stirring often to separate the strands, 1 to 2 minutes. If using dried noodles, cook according to the package instructions. In the last 30 seconds of cooking, add the greens to blanch just until they turn bright green. Reserve ¼ cup (60 ml) of the cooking liquid, then drain the noodles and greens in a strainer.

7. Add 2 tablespoons of hot noodle water to each bowl and stir to form the sauce.

8. Assemble and serve: Divide the noodles and greens between the two bowls. Add a few spoonfuls of the mince topping to each bowl, then garnish with scallion greens. Stir the noodles until they're fully coated in the sauce and mince. Serve immediately.

Chapter 8

Rice and Porridge

Spicy Thai Basil Fried Rice

Ginger–Sesame Oil Fried Rice

Dragonfruit Fried Rice

Jade Fried Rice *(Spinach Fried Rice)*

Nasi Kunyit *(Turmeric Glutinous Rice)*

Savory Laba Porridge

Tofu Char Siu Rice

Hainanese Mushroom "Chicken" Rice

Nasi Lemak Bungkus *(Malaysian Coconut Rice)*

XO Sauce Fried Rice

"Jiak beng!" "Sik fan!"—whether it's Hokkien, Teochew, or Cantonese, these phrases mean "Eat rice," the shorthand for calling everyone to the table. Growing up, every time I called home from the US, the first thing my baba would ask was, "Jiak ba buay?" or "Have you eaten?" Which really meant, "Have you had your rice?" It's a question that's less about food and more about how I am, a simple question that carries the weight of love and care.

Rice is more than sustenance—it's a tradition and symbol that honors the growers of our food and the customs passed down across generations. In our culture, rice is life. Whether steamed, served in a warm porridge, or pounded into kuih, it's ever-present on the family table. Our household rice bucket is sacred; when we moved, my mama insisted I fill it to the brim as a sign of 满 (man), or fullness—a promise from leaner times that a full bucket wards off hunger.

Freshly made dishes lined up at a bustling Malaysian economy rice or chap fan stall.

This chapter's recipes carry memories: nasi lemak, my childhood breakfast (page 295); ginger fried rice, my postpartum lifeline (page 275); Jade Fried Rice, my kids' lunch box favorite (page 281); Nasi Kunyit with mushroom rendang, a Hari Raya treat (page 95). They've grown with me from novice to confident cook, blending Malaysian roots with plant-based twists. Rice isn't just a side, but the center of life's moments—births, festivals, quiet nights. These dishes, from fragrant stir-fries to soothing porridges, invite you to fill your own bucket and pass it on.

Spicy Thai Basil Fried Rice

Serves 2

I ate Thai basil fried rice during my college days. Back then, vegetarian and vegan options were hard to come by, but the owner of a small Thai restaurant was more than happy to make something special for me and my boyfriend, now husband. He brought out a steaming plate of Thai basil fried rice with tofu, and I was hooked. That owner's friendliness and the surprise of that dish—the way the chili heat played off the fragrant jasmine rice and the aroma of the Thai basil—stayed with me.

The combination became a staple as I started cooking in college, and after a trip to Thailand to chase down this dish's flavors, I finally developed my own version. It's a perfect fridge-cleaner dish that welcomes improvisation—I make it whenever I find fresh Thai basil at the market or in my husband's herb garden. Sweet basil can work in a pinch for the Thai basil, and you can dial the heat of the chiles up or down depending on your preference.

For the sauce:

2 tablespoons vegetarian oyster sauce

1 tablespoon Vegan Fish Sauce (page 49)

1 tablespoon soy sauce

½ teaspoon dark caramel soy sauce

For the chile-garlic paste:

1 fresh red chile pepper, seeded (or 2 Thai chiles, for more heat)

3 garlic cloves

For the vegetable fried rice:

1 tablespoon cooking oil

¼ medium white or yellow onion, thinly sliced

⅓ cup (30 g) green beans, cut into 1-inch (2.5 cm) pieces

8 ounces (225 g) pan-fried firm tofu (page 65), cut into 1-inch (2.5 cm) cubes

3 cups (450 g) cooked and cooled rice

½ cup (20 g) packed fresh Thai basil leaves

1 teaspoon red pepper flakes (optional)

Kosher salt

1. Make the sauce: In a small bowl, combine the vegetarian oyster sauce, vegan fish sauce, and soy sauces.

2. Make the chile-garlic paste: Place the chile and garlic in a mortar and pound with a pestle until a coarse paste forms. Alternatively, you can pulse the ingredients in a food processor.

3. Cook the vegetable fried rice: Heat the oil in a large skillet or wok over medium-high heat for about 30 seconds. Add the onion and the chile-garlic paste, stirring to break up the paste and coat the onion. Cook until the paste becomes very fragrant and the onion turns slightly translucent, about 2 minutes.

4. Add the green beans and tofu to the pan. Stir-fry until the cubes of tofu are piping hot and the green beans are tender, about 3 minutes.

recipe and ingredients continue

For serving:

Tomato slices

Cucumber slices

Lime or calamansi wedges

1 or 2 Thai chiles, thinly sliced, in Vegan Fish Sauce (page 49)

5. Add the rice and swirl in the sauce. Gently fold and stir everything together, using the back of your spoon or spatula to break up any large clumps of rice. Continue to stir-fry, tossing the rice, until the grains are evenly coated with the sauce and begin to dry out slightly. To know when it's done, just look for the "dancing rice grains" (see below).

6. Gently fold the basil into the rice until wilted and aromatic, about 30 seconds. Add the red pepper flakes for more heat, if desired. Season with salt to taste.

7. Serve: Serve the rice warm with sliced tomato and cucumber and lime or calamansi wedges. Include a side of Thai chiles in vegan fish sauce. Squeeze fresh lime or calamansi juice over the rice just before eating.

Dancing Rice Grains

My kakak, a sister who cared for my grandma when I was thirteen, taught me the "dancing grain" trick—when the rice jumps in the pan, the fried rice is ready. Stir-fry the rice over medium-high heat, tossing till it's coated with sauce and just dry enough—and you'll see those grains pop and dance after 2 to 4 minutes! (Fresher rice might need an extra minute or so.) I still use her tip to this day, every time I fire up the wok.

Ginger–Sesame Oil Fried Rice

Serves 2 to 4

Ever heard of the confinement period? Zuo yue zi, or "sitting the month," is big in Malaysia and across East Asia—the period of care thirty to forty-five days after birth for new moms, when a woman's body is believed to be in a cold, vulnerable state and in need of warmth and nourishment. Spicy, potent ginger becomes essential, finding its way into nearly every dish and drink. After the births of my children, Tiffany and Justin, I was lucky enough to have my mama and mom with me for over a month both times, handling my confinement period, especially the cooking. This ginger-infused fried rice was the only way I ate my rice then—it always made the kitchen smell delicious with the rich aroma of nutty sesame oil. These days, I make it whenever I need something warm and comforting. Here's a tip: You can skip the soy sauce if you prefer and just use salt. Ginger and sesame oil create a fragrant, flavorful base all on their own.

For the fried rice:

2 teaspoons cooking oil

½ cup (120 ml) plant-based egg liquid (optional)

4 to 5 button or cremini mushrooms, stemmed and cut into ¼-inch-thick (6 mm) slices

1 tablespoon toasted sesame oil, plus more if needed

1 tablespoon minced fresh ginger

½ cup (30 g) finely diced kale stems (¼-inch / 6 mm pieces)

⅛ ounce (3.5 g) dried wood ear mushrooms, rehydrated and thinly sliced

2 cups (300 g) cooked and cooled rice

1 tablespoon soy sauce (optional; see headnote)

For serving:

Kosher salt, as needed

Ground white pepper, as needed

Chopped Thai chiles in soy sauce (optional)

1. Scramble the "egg" (if using): Heat a wok or large nonstick skillet over medium heat. Add the oil and pour in the plant-based egg liquid. Scramble until fully cooked, about 3 minutes, then transfer to a bowl.

2. Cook the mushrooms and kale: In the same pan, dry stir-fry the mushrooms over medium heat until they release their moisture, 2 to 3 minutes. Continue cooking until the edges start to brown, about 3 minutes more. Push the mushrooms to the side of the pan.

3. Add the sesame oil and ginger to the center of the pan. Sauté until the ginger is golden and fragrant, 1 to 2 minutes. Add a little more sesame oil if the pan gets too dry.

4. Stir in the kale stems and wood ear mushrooms. Stir-fry until the kale stems are tender and dark green

recipe continues

and the wood ear mushrooms begin to pop, about 2 minutes.

5. Stir-fry the rice: Add the cooked rice to the pan and drizzle with the soy sauce (if using). Gently press the rice with the back of the spatula to break up any large clumps. Continue stir-frying until the rice is hot and has very little visible moisture. The rice is ready when some grains begin to "dance" or jump in the pan (see sidebar, page 273).

6. Combine and serve: If using, fold in the scrambled egg and toss until well combined. Taste and adjust the seasoning with salt and white pepper as needed. Serve warm with chiles in soy sauce, if desired.

Dragonfruit Fried Rice

Serves 2 to 4

The inspiration for this dish came from my favorite vegetarian restaurant in Malaysia, where I once found myself staring down at a plate of fried rice topped with dragonfruit. At first, it seemed like a wild choice (dragonfruit, or pitaya, was still something of a rarity in Malaysia at the time). But then I took a bite and the whole thing clicked. The delicate, juicy sweetness of the dragonfruit cubes tamed the sambal's heat, cooling it down in a way that was surprising and strangely addictive.

The restaurant eventually closed, but that dish stuck with me, and I knew I had to re-create it at home. I've always been a fan of pineapple fried rice, but dragonfruit takes that combination of sweet and salty to another level. Feel free use whatever vegetables you like for variety and color!

For the fried rice:

1 tablespoon cooking oil

1 tablespoon Basic Sambal (page 31), or store-bought Malaysian sambal

½ cup (70 g) diced mixed vegetables, such as carrots, green beans, peas, corn, celery, and/or mushrooms

3 cups (450 g) cooked and cooled rice

1 cup (140 g) fresh (not frozen) peeled, cubed dragonfruit (see Note and sidebar, page 279), either white or red (the latter will color the rice pink)

Kosher salt as needed or about ⅛ teaspoon mushroom seasoning

For serving:

Tomato slices

Cucumber slices

Lime or calamansi wedges

Shredded lettuce

1. **Cook the vegetables:** Heat a large skillet or wok over medium-high heat. Add the oil and sambal, and when the sambal starts sizzling, toss in the vegetables. Stir-fry for about 3 minutes, until the vegetables are brightly colored but still crisp, with minimal moisture visible in the pan.

2. **Incorporate the rice:** Add the cooked rice, using the back of the spatula to gently break up any large clumps. Stir-fry the rice until the grains are piping hot and most of the moisture has evaporated. The rice is ready when some grains start to "dance" or jump from the pan (see sidebar, page 273).

3. **Add the dragonfruit:** Gently fold in the dragonfruit and stir-fry for 1 to 2 minutes, until the cubes are heated through and beginning to soften around the edges. Taste and adjust the seasoning with salt or mushroom seasoning as needed.

recipe continues

Note:

Dragonfruit, a vibrant cactus fruit, also known as pitaya, comes in several varieties, with skin that can be bright pink or golden yellow and flesh ranging from deep red to ivory or white, dotted with tiny edible black seeds. Red-fleshed types may tint dishes, while golden-skinned varieties with yellow-tinged flesh are often sweeter. One medium dragonfruit (about 200 g) yields approximately 1 cup (140 g) flesh.

4. **Serve:** Plate the fried rice with tomato and cucumber slices, lime or calamansi wedges, and shredded lettuce on the side.

How to Prepare Dragonfruit

1. Choose a ripe dragonfruit (slightly soft when pressed) and rinse under cold water to remove any dirt.
2. Slice off both ends, then cut in half lengthwise. Scoop out the flesh with a spoon or peel back the skin like a banana's. Discard the skin.
3. Cube or cut the flesh into your desired shapes. Tip: Use fresh dragonfruit for the best texture. If using frozen, thaw completely in the fridge and pat dry to remove excess moisture before use.

Jade Fried Rice

(Spinach Fried Rice)

Serves 2 to 4

I started cooking as a teenager, but my skills were honed volunteering at my Dallas temple's cafeteria, where I loved chopping veggies, cooking, and serving. A venerable monk taught me to make jade fried rice, a vibrant green dish that's been a staple in my kids' lunch boxes since kindergarten. Originally, we'd blend spinach with water into a paste and stir-fry it to remove moisture. In my streamlined version, you finely chop the spinach to cling to the rice, turning the grains a deep emerald green. Bonus: fewer dishes to wash! Toasted pine nuts add crunch, and fresh corn brings sweetness, my favorite additions.

4 teaspoons cooking oil

2 tablespoons pine nuts

2 cups (40 g) packed spinach leaves

3 tablespoons (30 g) fresh corn kernels

3 cups (450 g) cooked and cooled rice

Kosher salt

⅛ teaspoon mushroom seasoning

½ teaspoon toasted sesame oil

1. Toast the pine nuts: Heat the oil in a large skillet or wok over medium-low heat. Add the pine nuts and toast, stirring occasionally and watching closely to prevent burning, until the nuts turn a light golden brown, about 2 minutes. Remove the nuts with a slotted spoon or fork and set them on a plate to cool. Do not rinse the pan.

2. Prepare the spinach: Roughly chop the spinach leaves or process them in a food processor with up to ½ cup (120 ml) water into a smooth purée.

3. Stir-fry the vegetables and rice: Using the oil remaining in the pan, briefly stir-fry the corn over medium-high heat until fragrant. Add the spinach. If using chopped spinach, stir-fry until the leaves wilt and lose their raw taste, about 1 minute. If using a purée, stir until the liquid evaporates and the paste darkens in color, about 20 seconds.

4. Add the rice to the spinach mixture, breaking up clumps with a spatula. Stir-fry until fully coated, hot, and dry. To know when it's done, just look for the "dancing rice grains" (see sidebar, page 273). Season with salt to taste and the mushroom seasoning.

5. Serve: Remove from the heat and fold in the pine nuts. Drizzle with the sesame oil before serving.

Nasi Kunyit

(Turmeric Glutinous Rice)

1 cup (210 g) sticky (glutinous) rice

½ lime, cut into ¼-inch (6 mm) slices

¼ teaspoon kosher salt

1½ teaspoons ground turmeric

2 fresh or thawed pandan leaves, rinsed and tied into a knot

1 teaspoon whole peppercorns, either white or black

½ cup (120 ml) full-fat coconut milk

Lion's Mane Mushroom Rendang (page 95; optional)

Serves 2 or 3

Turmeric glutinous rice—nasi kunyit—is a cherished Malaysian dish that graces the table during celebrations like Hari Raya, the joyous holiday that marks the end of Ramadan with feasting and gratitude. I learned to make it from a good friend, who prepared nasi kunyit for a vegetarian fair in Texas to showcase Malaysian food. The yellow hue is thanks to the turmeric, and my friend adds a teaspoon of whole white or black peppercorns to the rice before steaming, providing a gentle heat that deepens the aroma. Nasi kunyit is special because of the vibrant gold color, which symbolizes prosperity and good fortune, turning any meal into a celebration. Rendang, a spicy braised meat dish that I make using mushrooms instead (as shown in the photo), is a delicious accompaniment to this fragrant sticky rice, but it's equally comforting on its own.

1. **Soak the rice:** Rinse the rice thoroughly until the water runs clear to remove excess surface starch—about three rinses should do the trick. Drain well. In a large bowl, combine the rice with the lime slices, salt, turmeric, pandan leaves, and enough water to cover the rice by about ½ inch (12 mm). Stir with chopsticks until the turmeric is evenly dispersed. Set aside to soak at room temperature for at least 4 hours or overnight in the fridge.

2. Drain the turmeric water (reserving the liquid if you're using the pressure cooker method in step 4 to cook the rice) and remove the lime slices and pandan leaves.

3. **Steam the rice:** Transfer the rice to a deep, heatproof dish that fits in your steamer. Stir in the peppercorns. Cover and steam over medium-high heat for 25 minutes, or until the grains are tender and sticky and still hold their shape.

recipe continues

4. Or pressure-cook the rice: Place the drained rice, peppercorns, and ⅔ cup (160 ml) of the reserved liquid into the insert pot of an electric pressure cooker. Seal the cooker and manually set it to 12 minutes on high pressure. Let the pressure naturally release for 10 minutes before removing the lid.

5. Finish and serve: Drizzle the coconut milk evenly over the rice. Cover and steam for an additional 5 minutes, until tender, or cover and keep warm in the pressure cooker. You can pick out the peppercorns or eat them along with the rice. Serve with mushroom rendang, if desired.

Savory Laba Porridge

Serves 3 or 4

Each year, the arrival of warm laba porridge from my temple feels like a small gift. This quiet tradition marks the start of the Laba Festival, a Buddhist celebration honoring the day Sakyamuni attained enlightenment on the eighth day of the twelfth lunar month. Every temple has its own take on laba porridge, shaped by the local ingredients, but this recipe was inspired by the venerable monks at Fo Guang Shan International Buddhist Progress Society (IBPS), a Buddhist monastery in Dallas.

The dish starts with white and glutinous rice, simmered until thick, paired with beans and vegetables, giving it nourishing heft. Each spoonful, warmed with soy sauce and a hint of white pepper, fills both belly and soul. It's a symbol of harmony: ingredients coming together to create something beautiful. During winter's coldest days, the Laba Festival and its porridge remind me and my community of the abundance we share.

For the porridge:

2 tablespoons raw peanuts

2 tablespoons dried black-eyed peas

2 tablespoons dried soybeans

3 tablespoons (45 g) dried white beans (cannellini, Great Northern, navy, or lima beans)

½ cup (100 g) short-grain or jasmine rice

⅓ cup (70 g) sticky (glutinous) rice

2 tablespoons cooking oil

5 thin slices peeled fresh ginger

⅓ cup (50 g) diced carrot (½-inch / 12 mm pieces)

⅓ cup (50 g) diced taro (½-inch / 12 mm pieces; see Note, page 323)

2 tablespoons soy sauce

½ teaspoon ground white pepper

4 fried tofu puffs, sliced in half

For serving:

½ cup (50 g) roughly chopped bok choy

¼ teaspoon mushroom seasoning

Kosher salt

Toasted sesame oil

Fried youtiao (Chinese cruller), baked and sliced (optional)

1. Soak the legumes: In a large bowl, cover the peanuts, black-eyed peas, soybeans, and white beans with cool water. Soak at room temperature for at least 4 hours or overnight. If using large white beans, remove any tough skins. Rinse and drain.

2. Cook the legumes: Place the soaked legumes in a small pot and cover with 3 inches (7.5 cm) fresh water. Simmer until tender, about 1 hour. Alternatively, use a pressure cooker: Place the beans in the insert pot of an electric pressure cooker with enough water to cover. Seal the cooker and manually set it to 25 minutes on high pressure. Let the pressure naturally release for 10 minutes before removing the lid. Drain the cooked legumes and transfer them to a bowl.

3. In a large bowl, swish the short-grain or jasmine rice and sticky rice under water until the water turns clear, about three times. Drain well using a sieve.

recipe continues

4. **Prepare the aromatic oil:** In a deep saucepan or wok, heat the oil over medium-low heat until shimmering. Sauté the ginger until fragrant and the edges begin to frizzle. Remove the ginger and discard or save it as a topping for the porridge.

5. **Cook the vegetables and rice:** Add the carrot and taro to the pan, stirring until the carrot softens and the taro starts to brown at the edges, about 2 minutes. Transfer to a bowl.

6. Add the drained rices, soy sauce, and white pepper. Stir-fry until the rice is fragrant and glossy and starting to stick to the pan, 2 to 3 minutes.

7. **Simmer the porridge:** Add 2 quarts (about 1 L) water and all of the cooked legumes. Bring the mixture to a boil, then reduce to a gentle simmer. Cover and cook for 20 minutes, stirring occasionally to prevent the rice from sticking.

8. Uncover and add the tofu puffs along with the taro and carrot. Cover and continue to cook over medium-low heat for 30 minutes, stirring occasionally, until the broth is fully absorbed by the rice and thickened into a velvety porridge, about 1 hour total.

9. **Finish and serve:** Fold in the bok choy and cook for another minute to wilt. Season with the mushroom seasoning and salt to taste. Drizzle with sesame oil and garnish with the reserved fried ginger and youtiao, if you like, before serving. Enjoy hot.

Tofu Char Siu Rice

For the ginger-garlic butter rice:

2 cups (370 g) short-grain or jasmine rice

1½ teaspoons cooking oil

1½-inch (4 cm) piece (12 g) fresh ginger, peeled and thinly sliced

3 garlic cloves, lightly pounded

1 tablespoon plant-based butter

1 teaspoon kosher salt

For the char siu sauce:

1 tablespoon soy sauce

1 tablespoon vegetarian oyster sauce

1 tablespoon hoisin sauce

1½ teaspoons maple syrup

1½ teaspoons toasted sesame oil

¼ teaspoon dark caramel soy sauce

Ground white pepper

For the tofu:

One 14- to 16-ounce (390 to 450 g) package firm tofu

¼ cup (30 g) cornstarch, plus more if needed

Cooking oil, for frying

For serving:

Cucumber slices

Chile sauce (such as the "Chicken" Rice Chili Sauce, page 35)

Serves 4

Char siu, which translates to "fork roasted" in Cantonese, is all about that sweet, sticky glaze and perfectly charred finish. Traditionally, it's made with pork marinated in a mix of honey, soy sauce, hoisin sauce, and spices, then roasted until caramelized and tender. But this glaze isn't just for meat. It works wonders on tofu too. Just coat pressed tofu with cornstarch, pan-fry it until golden and crisp, and baste it with the char siu glaze. The result? Crispy edges with that irresistible sweet-savory flavor.

In Malaysia, char siu fan isn't just served over rice—it's also a popular topping for wonton mee, adding a smoky-sweet element to the springy noodles. To complete the meal, don't forget the Homemade "Chicken" Rice Chili Sauce (page 35). Pair it with sides of vegetables like soy sauce blanched lettuce (page 63) or Soy Sauce Okra (page 61), and you've got a full, restaurant-style experience right at home.

1. **Prepare the rice:** Rinse the rice under clean water until the water runs clear, about three times. Drain well using a sieve.

2. In a large skillet or nonstick pan over medium-high heat, warm the oil. Stir-fry the ginger and garlic until fragrant and the ginger begins to color, about 1 minute. Add the drained rice, plant-based butter, and salt. Stir-fry over medium-low heat, stirring occasionally to coat the rice grains with the butter. Cook until the rice starts to dry and develops a fragrant aroma, 3 to 5 minutes (see Notes, page 290). Remove from the heat.

3. Transfer the mixture to the inner pot of a rice cooker. Add 2½ cups (600 ml) water (see Notes, page 290). Cook using the "white rice" setting and fluff the rice before serving. Alternatively, if cooking on a stovetop, transfer the sautéed rice mixture to a

recipe continues

Notes:

- *When cooking rice, I use about 1¼ cups (300 ml) water per 1 cup (185 g) of dry rice, but this may vary depending on the brand of rice and your rice cooker. It's important to sauté the rice until no moisture remains before adding water for the best texture.*
- *Any leftover glaze can be served as a dipping sauce for the tofu char siu.*

heavy-bottomed saucepan. Add 2½ cups (600 ml) water and bring to a boil over medium-high heat, stirring occasionally to prevent sticking. Reduce the heat to low, cover with a lid slightly ajar or vented, and simmer for 15 to 20 minutes, until all the water is absorbed and the rice is tender. Turn off the heat, let rest for 5 minutes, then fluff gently with a fork or spatula.

4. Make the char siu sauce: In a small bowl, combine the soy sauce, vegetarian oyster sauce, hoisin sauce, maple syrup, sesame oil, dark caramel soy sauce, a few dashes of white pepper, and ⅓ cup (80 ml) water.

5. Pan-fry the tofu: Drain and gently press the tofu to remove excess moisture. Cut the tofu into 3 horizontal slabs, each about 1 inch (2.5 cm) thick. Place the cornstarch on a large plate and coat all sides of the tofu slabs generously, adding more if needed.

6. Heat a large skillet or nonstick pan with ¼ cup (60 ml) oil over medium heat. Arrange the tofu in a single layer (cook in batches if necessary) and let the tofu pieces fry undisturbed until a golden crust forms on the bottom, 4 to 7 minutes. Flip each piece using tongs or chopsticks and cook until the other side is golden and crispy. Add more oil if necessary. Transfer to a paper towel–lined plate to drain.

7. Make the char siu glaze: Clean the pan and set it over medium-high heat. Stir the sauce mixture and pour it into the pan. When it begins to bubble, return the tofu to the pan in a single layer, leaving space between each piece. Use tongs or chopsticks to turn each piece, basting each side until the sauce thickens and clings to the tofu like a glaze (see Notes).

8. Finish and serve: Remove the tofu char siu from the pan and let it cool slightly. Once cool enough to handle, slice the tofu crosswise into ¼-inch-thick (6 mm) slices. Serve with the ginger-garlic butter rice, cucumber slices, and chile sauce for a delicious meal.

Hainanese Mushroom "Chicken" Rice

Serves 3 or 4

"Hello, sap chuht gok" still cracks me up. I'd hear it when my little brother dashed to the chicken rice stall down the road, dimes rattling in his hand. Sap chuht gok—"seventeen dimes" in Cantonese—was what a pack of Hainanese chicken rice cost back then, and he'd grab one for lunch in the mornings before heading to elementary school. He'd count out every coin, all serious like he'd just cracked math, and the seller would yell, "Here comes Seventeen Dimes!" Our neighborhood was like that—everyone knew each other, and my brother was the chicken rice kid.

I'm all about mushrooms, so I've re-created that childhood favorite with king oyster mushrooms in this vegan take on Hainanese chicken rice. The texture of these mushrooms is a perfect stand-in, creating meaty, silky, and tender morsels. I pile them over ginger-garlic butter rice, and it's comfort food that hits me right in the childhood feels, with a little extra nostalgia on the side.

For the mushroom "chicken":

1½ pounds (670 g) fresh king oyster (trumpet) mushrooms, trimmed, cut into 4-inch (10 cm) sections, then torn into finger-width strips

2 tablespoons cooking oil

½ teaspoon kosher salt

For the sauce:

½ teaspoon cornstarch

1 tablespoon yellow bean paste (taucu)

1 tablespoon cooking oil

1 garlic clove, minced

1 teaspoon sugar

⅛ teaspoon mushroom seasoning

For serving:

1 recipe Ginger-Garlic Butter Rice (page 289)

Cucumber slices

Ginger Scallion Sauce (page 47)

Chile sauce (such as the "Chicken" Rice Chili Sauce, page 35)

1. Cook the mushrooms: Heat a dry large skillet or nonstick pan over medium heat. Add the mushroom strips and press them against the pan's interior. Cook until they release moisture and begin to stick to the bottom of the pan, about 2 minutes.

2. Drizzle the oil evenly across the mushrooms and sprinkle with the salt. Continue stir-frying until the mushroom strips soften and turn golden brown, 3 to 4 minutes. Transfer to a bowl.

3. Prepare the sauce: In a small bowl, whisk together the cornstarch and 1 tablespoon water to create a slurry. In another bowl, measure out ½ cup (120 ml) water. Finely chop the yellow bean paste to achieve a smooth texture, ensuring it will release its flavors during cooking.

recipe continues

4. In the same pan used for the mushrooms, heat the oil over medium-low heat. Sauté the garlic until fragrant. Add the yellow soybean paste, stirring quickly for a few seconds to release its flavor. Immediately pour in the measured water and bring to a boil. Season with the sugar and mushroom seasoning. Stir the slurry, then slowly drizzle it into the sauce, allowing it to thicken to your desired consistency.

5. **Assemble and serve:** Place a serving of the ginger-garlic butter rice in a bowl and invert it onto a plate to create a mound. Serve with a portion of the cooked mushrooms and spoon over the prepared sauce. Plate with cucumber slices, ginger scallion sauce, and chile sauce. Repeat for the other servings.

Nasi Lemak Bungkus

(Malaysian Coconut Rice)

Serves 3 or 4

There's a saying that if you visit Malaysia without trying nasi lemak, you haven't truly been there. "Makcik, nasi lemak bungkus satu, tambah sambal" ("Auntie, one wrapped nasi lemak, with extra sambal") is my go-to order. Nasi lemak, or "rich rice," is a savory dish of rice subtly infused with coconut milk and pandan leaves, served alongside sambal, crispy ikan bilis (anchovies), cucumber, and a boiled egg. I'd often take it wrapped (bungkus) for a portable, banana-leaf version to go.

When I was growing up, savory breakfasts like nasi lemak were a staple. At the morning market with my grandma, or mamak stalls with my parents, we'd eat it with roti canai and sips of teh tarik, hot pulled tea. My vegan version of nasi lemak brings all those flavors back with fragrant coconut rice, spicy sambal, crunchy peanuts, crisp cucumber slices, and a plant-based egg. It's all about celebrating those flavors and textures I remember from the streets of Malaysia.

For the coconut rice (nasi):

2 cups (370 g) jasmine rice, thoroughly rinsed

1 small shallot, thinly sliced

1 lemongrass stalk, trimmed to the white part, bruised to release flavor

2 fresh or thawed pandan leaves, rinsed and tied into a knot

2 slices peeled fresh ginger

½ can (7 ounces / 200 ml) full-fat coconut milk

½ teaspoon kosher salt

For the peanuts:

1½ cups (360 ml) cooking oil

1 cup raw peanuts (preferably red-skinned)

For the sambal ***(makes 3 to 4 cups / 720 to 960 ml)*****:**

1½ cups (45 g) dried chiles, destemmed, seeds removed

1 golf ball–sized clump (30 g) of tamarind paste

½ cup (120 ml) hot water

5 fresh red jalapeño peppers

2 medium tomatoes, cut into wedges

5 large shallots

One 4 by 5-inch (10 by 12 cm) piece of dried kombu, soaked in ¾ cup (180 ml) water

1. Cook the rice: Combine the rinsed and drained rice, shallot, lemongrass, pandan leaves, ginger, 2 cups (480 ml) water (or 1¾ cups / 420 ml for fluffier rice), coconut milk, and salt in a rice cooker. Cook using the "white rice" setting (it should be ready in 35 to 40 minutes). For the stovetop method, see the sidebar on page 297.

2. Fry the peanuts: In a large wok or skillet, combine the oil, at room temperature, and the raw peanuts. Set the wok over medium-low heat and fry the peanuts for 10 to 12 minutes, stirring occasionally, until the skins darken. Remove the peanuts with a fine-mesh spider and transfer to a paper towel to drain. The peanuts will continue to cook and become crispy as they cool. Reserve the oil in the wok.

recipe and ingredients continue

1 medium white or yellow onion, cut into thin wedges

2 fresh or thawed pandan leaves, rinsed and tied into a knot

2 rounds palm sugar or 1½ ounces (40 g) granulated sugar

1 teaspoon kosher salt

½ teaspoon mushroom seasoning

For serving:

Banana leaves, cleaned and wiped dry with a paper towel (optional)

Cucumber slices

Plant-based egg liquid, pan-fried like an omelet and cut into slices

3. **Meanwhile, rehydrate the chiles for the sambal:** Combine the chiles and 1½ cups (360 ml) water in a medium saucepan. Bring to a boil and simmer for 5 to 8 minutes, until softened. Strain, reserving the liquid.

4. **Make the tamarind juice:** In a bowl, combine the tamarind paste with the hot water. Use your fingers to mash and dissolve the tamarind into a dark brown liquid.

5. **Make the sambal:** Place the softened chiles, tamarind juice, jalapeños, tomatoes, shallots, and kombu with its soaking liquid in a high-speed blender. Blend on high for 2 minutes, until a fine paste forms.

6. Heat the oil remaining in the wok over medium-low heat. Sauté the onion until fragrant and translucent, 2 to 3 minutes. Carefully add the blended chile paste and knotted pandan leaves, taking care to avoid splashes. Cook the mixture for 40 to 45 minutes, stirring frequently as it thickens. As the moisture evaporates, the sambal will deepen to a dark reddish color. Once the oil begins to separate from the paste (a stage known as pecah minyak), the sambal is ready.

7. Add the palm sugar or granulated sugar, salt, and mushroom seasoning to the sambal. Cook, stirring occasionally, for another minute, until the seasonings are fully dissolved. Remove from the heat and allow the sambal to cool. Transfer to a clean jar and store in the refrigerator for up to 1 month.

8. **Assemble and serve:** Once the rice is ready, remove the pandan leaves, ginger, and lemongrass. Fluff before serving. Place a portion of rice on a cleaned banana leaf (for the bungkus style) or a plate. Add a handful of fried peanuts, a few cucumber slices, the plant-based egg slices, and your desired amount of sambal. Serve warm.

Stovetop Rice Cooking Method and Tips

Combine the rinsed and drained rice, shallot, lemongrass, pandan leaves, ginger, 2¼ cups (540 ml) water (or 2 cups / 480 ml for fluffier rice), coconut milk, and salt in a medium, heavy-bottomed saucepan. Bring to a boil over medium-high heat, stirring occasionally to prevent sticking. Reduce the heat to low, cover with a lid slightly ajar or vented, and simmer for 15 to 20 minutes, until the liquid is absorbed and the rice is tender. Turn off the heat, let rest for 5 minutes, then gently fluff with a fork or spatula. Remove the pandan leaves and lemongrass before serving.

Tips:

- Use a medium, heavy-bottomed saucepan (2 to 3 quarts / 2 to 3 L) for even heating.
- Stir occasionally during boiling to prevent sticking; keep the lid slightly ajar to regulate steam.
- If the rice is still hard at 15 minutes, add 1 to 2 tablespoons water and simmer for an additional 2 to 3 minutes.
- If the rice sticks, lower the heat and add a splash of water.
- If making fluffier rice with 2 cups (480 ml) water, check early to avoid overcooking.

XO Sauce Fried Rice

Serves 2

If you've been enjoying the sauces from chapter 1, "The Basics," and wondering what else to do with that delicious XO Sauce, try making fried rice. It's so simple it almost doesn't need a recipe. But there are two reasons I included it here: first, to show off the flavors of homemade XO sauce, an umami bomb that transforms even the simplest dishes. But more importantly, this fried rice is my go-to when I'm just cooking for myself. It's comforting and takes minimal effort, and I often toss in any leftover veggie bits or tofu from the fridge (see Note)—a great way to reduce food waste. And if you have cooked rice ready, this dish comes together in minutes.

4 teaspoons cooking oil

½ cup (120 ml) plant-based egg liquid

2 scallions, finely chopped, white and green parts separated

3 cups (450 g) cooked and cooled rice

2 tablespoons Vegan XO Sauce (page 45), plus more as needed

¼ teaspoon kosher salt

Note:

Here are some ideas for optional add-ins in step 4: bits of tofu, corn, diced bell peppers, tomatoes, less-than-prime leafy greens or cabbage, wilted herbs, peas, diced onions, chives, Thai chiles for heat.

1. Scramble the "egg": Heat a wok or large nonstick skillet over medium heat. Add 2 teaspoons of the oil to the pan and pour in the plant-based egg liquid. Scramble until fully cooked, 2 to 3 minutes, then transfer to a bowl.

2. Cook the aromatics and rice: In the same wok over medium-high heat, warm the remaining 2 teaspoons oil. Add the white parts of the scallions and sauté briefly until fragrant, about 1 minute.

3. Add the cooked rice to the wok, using the back of the spatula to break up any large clumps. Stir-fry until the rice is hot and mostly dry. Look for the "dancing grain"—the rice is ready when you see some grains start to jump and dance in the pan (see sidebar, page 273).

4. Add the XO sauce, scrambled "egg," and salt. Stir-fry until the rice is evenly coated and heated through. Fold in the green parts of the scallions.

5. Serve: Taste and adjust with more XO sauce, if needed. Serve hot.

Chapter 9

Sweets and Snacks

When my children, Tiffany and Justin, were little, they would often say, "Mama, I still have another tummy for sweets." It was their endearing way of asking for more dessert. I love sharing savory recipes, but I'll let you in on a secret: I've got a sweet tooth too. Instead of cakes or pastries, I'm drawn to the traditional treats of my Malaysian upbringing, including kuih muih; luscious, rich spreads (such as Pumpkin Kaya, page 315); and soothing tong sui, dessert soups to warm the soul (like Red Bean Soup with Glutinous Rice Balls, opposite).

Kuih muih is a catchall Malay term for an assortment of small snacks or desserts, either sweet or savory. These bite-sized treats, with their multiple layers and colors, are crafted from staples like rice flour, glutinous rice, coconut milk, and fragrant pandan. They dazzle the eyes with their striking hues—soft greens from pandan, blues, pinks, and creamy whites—and their intricate forms. Some are molded, some wrapped in banana leaves, and others grilled or fried to a gentle crisp, offering a contrast of textures. They're a must at festive gatherings like Hari Raya but are just as cherished in everyday moments: nibbled over morning tea with the family or grabbed from a bustling wet market stall. My recipe for Kuih Seri Muka is on page 307.

Colorful kuih muih tempt shoppers at the pasar.

But this chapter isn't just about sweets—there are recipes for street snacks too. Think crispy Thai Basil Zhua Bing (page 337) and savory Suan Pan Zi (Hakka Taro "Abacus Seeds," page 325), a Hakka dish traditionally enjoyed during Chinese New Year, or Roti Empat Segi (page 333), the square-shaped roti canai I can't resist dipping into dal for breakfast. This chapter blends handheld street foods and festive treats, and there's plenty to satisfy the sweet and savory tooth alike.

Red Bean Soup with Glutinous Rice Balls

Serves 4 to 6

Red bean soup was one of the first dessert soups I made for my children, a warm and comforting way to start the day before sending them off to school. I would often serve it with chewy glutinous rice balls or alongside youtiao, fried dough sticks that we dipped into the velvety broth and munched on with each sip.

I'm fond of the mashed red bean texture in this dish, known in Cantonese as sa, which basically means "sandy": that satisfying, slightly grainy texture you get when the beans are cooked until they split. I like to use rock sugar for a milder, cleaner sweetness that doesn't overpower the flavors of the soup. An optional but standout ingredient in this recipe is dried orange peel. It introduces a slightly bitter, aromatic hint of orange that complements the sweet and earthy red beans.

1 cup (200 g) dried adzuki (small red) beans, soaked for at least 6 hours or overnight and drained

2 pandan leaves, tied into a knot (optional)

¼ cup (50 g) rock sugar, plus more if needed

2 small pieces dried mandarin orange peel (optional)

Frozen glutinous rice balls (see Note, page 305)

1. Cook the beans and pandan (if using): In a large stockpot, add the beans, pandan leaves (if using), and 3 quarts (3 L) filtered water. Bring to a boil over medium-high heat, then reduce to a gentle boil and continue cooking uncovered. Stir occasionally and skim off any foam or residue that appears on the surface. Cook for about 2 hours, checking toward the end—the beans should be fully cooked but not falling apart. The liquid will reduce to about a third of its original amount. Remove and discard the pandan leaves.

2. Blend half of the beans: Ladle half of the beans and broth into a high-speed blender, being careful with the hot liquid. Blitz until completely smooth, about 1 minute.

3. Return the blended bean mixture to the pot. Add the rock sugar and dried orange peel (if using). Simmer over medium heat for another 20 minutes,

recipe continues

Note:

You can find glutinous rice balls in the frozen section at Asian supermarkets. I like both the small, plain glutinous rice balls, which add a nice texture to the soup, and the larger filled rice balls for a sweeter version (I like black sesame and peanut the best). Cook them directly from the package without thawing.

or until the sugar has completely dissolved and the remaining beans are soft and beginning to split. You can keep the orange peel in the soup for added flavor or remove it once it has infused the soup. Taste and adjust the sweetness with more sugar if desired.

4. Cook the glutinous rice balls: Meanwhile, in another saucepan, cook the rice balls according to the package instructions. Transfer them to a bowl of cold water until ready to use.

5. Serve: Ladle the hot red bean soup into bowls and top each serving with a few glutinous rice balls. Enjoy immediately. For a cold treat, refrigerate the red bean soup until thoroughly chilled, and then top with the glutinous rice balls before serving.

Kuih Seri Muka

(Steamed Layer Cake)

Makes one 8-inch (20 cm) round cake

I love picking up a few sticky pieces of kuih seri muka at the market for breakfast. Dubbed "pretty face cake," it's a stunner: a fragrant glutinous rice base and soft custard top, melded together while steaming. It's the star of celebrations and festive gatherings, but you'll also find it at Nyonya stalls selling kuih muih, Peranakan snacks born from Chinese-Malay roots across Malaysia, Singapore, and Indonesia.

Peranakan flair shines here through brightly colored, creative variations (see sidebar, page 309). Pandan lends a green color, but I personally crave a pumpkin-y twist, with its warm, earthy sweetness. You can even tint the rice with butterfly pea flowers for gorgeous specks of psychedelic blue, as I've done here. At the market, kuih seri muka often comes with a small packet of kaya (page 315). A squeeze of creamy, coconutty kaya over the chewy rice and silky custard takes it to the next level!

For the rice layer:

1½ cups (300 g) glutinous rice, soaked for at least 4 hours or overnight

Scant ½ cup (100 ml) full-fat coconut milk

½ teaspoon kosher salt

2 pandan leaves, one 4-inch (10 cm) segment torn off, the rest tied into a knot

25 dried butterfly pea flowers (about 2 tablespoons; see Notes, page 308)

Cooking oil, for greasing the pan

For the custard layer:

8 ounces (230 g) peeled kabocha squash, cut into 1½-inch (4 cm) cubes (see Notes, page 308)

4¼ ounces (120 g) gula melaka or other palm sugar (about 8 rounds; see Notes, page 308)

¾ cup (100 g) rice flour

¼ cup (30 g) tapioca starch

1 cup (240 ml) full-fat coconut milk

¼ teaspoon kosher salt

Cleaned banana leaf (optional; can sub greased parchment paper)

1. Prepare the rice: Drain the rice well and transfer it to a heatproof dish or rimmed plate that fits in your steamer. In a measuring cup, whisk together the coconut milk, a scant ½ cup (100 ml) water, and the salt. Pour this diluted coconut milk evenly over the rice. Tear the 4-inch (10 cm) piece of pandan in half and add it to the rice. Cover and steam over high heat for 25 to 30 minutes. The rice should be cooked through, but it doesn't have to be completely soft yet, as it will be steamed further later on.

2. Prepare the squash: While the rice is cooking, place the squash, palm sugar, 2 pandan leaves tied in a knot, and 1½ cups (360 ml) water in a large saucepan and bring to a boil over medium heat. Cover and cook until the squash is fork-tender, 15 to 20 minutes.

3. Remove and discard the pandan leaves. Reserve a generous ¾ cup (200 ml) of the hot sweetened cooking

recipe continues

Notes:

- *To reduce the total cooking time to about 1 hour, prepare the butterfly pea flower tea and cook the kabocha squash while the rice is steaming.*
- *Palm sugar or coconut sugar is generally less sweet than regular sugar. Adjust the amount if using granulated cane sugar.*

liquid. Strain the squash and transfer it to a blender or food processor. Add the reserved sweet cooking liquid to the blender. Blend the kabocha into a fine purée.

4. Transfer the kabocha purée to a bowl and sift in the rice flour and tapioca starch. Add the coconut milk and salt, stirring until the batter is well incorporated.

5. **Steep the pea flowers:** In a small pot, bring the pea flowers and ¼ cup (60 ml) water to a boil, submerging the flowers in the water using a fork as they steep. Reduce the heat and simmer for another 5 to 8 minutes to extract the pigment, until the liquid is a dark, concentrated blue. Turn off the heat and let the tea cool in the pot. Strain out the flowers with a fine-mesh sieve, squeezing out as much liquid as possible. (You can reserve the flowers to steep again for more tea.)

6. **Tint the rice:** When the rice is done, fluff it with a fork and let it cool slightly. Remove and discard the pandan leaves. Drizzle the butterfly pea flower liquid over the rice, 1 tablespoon at a time, and fold it in until fully absorbed. Continue drizzling and folding until the rice reaches your desired shade of blue.

7. **Assemble:** Lightly oil an 8-inch (20 cm) cake pan with tall sides and line it with a cleaned banana leaf (or greased parchment paper) cut to fit the base and sides with a slight overhang. Using a fondant smoother or the back of a spatula, firmly press all of the rice into the pan in an even layer. Strain the kabocha purée to remove any lumps and pour it over the rice. Smooth with a spatula to form an even layer. Tap the pan on the countertop a few times to remove any air bubbles.

8. **Steam:** Set the cake pan in a steamer over boiling water. Wrap the pot lid with a clean towel to catch any condensation. Cover and steam for 25 to 30 minutes, or until the kabocha layer is set and a toothpick inserted in the center comes out clean. Remove the cake from the steamer and allow it to cool completely to firm up the layers.

9. **Serve:** Run an oiled knife around the pan's edges to loosen the cake. Lift it out using the banana leaf or parchment overhangs, or use a wide oiled spatula. (You can also just cut it in the pan.) Slice a small edge piece to start, to make more room for the knife to cut, then cut into even strips and then into squares or diamonds, wiping the knife between cuts for neat edges. Lift out pieces with an oiled spatula if you cut it in the pan. Serve at room temperature with tea or coffee. Store leftovers in an airtight container in the fridge for up to 3 days; steam gently before serving.

Peranakans are descendants of early Chinese immigrants who settled in Southeast Asia, mainly in Malaysia, Singapore, and Indonesia. They intermarried with local Malays and adopted parts of their culture. Peranakan means "locally born" in Malay, reflecting their blended Chinese-Malay heritage. Baba and nyonya, the men and women of this community, are known for their distinctive cuisine, which mixes Chinese cooking techniques with Malay spices and ingredients. My favorites are nyonya laksa and assorted kuih muih (bite-sized sweets and snacks). If you visit Malaysia, Melaka and Penang are great places to explore their vibrant food, culture, and Peranakan shophouses.

Kuih Bingka

(Baked Cassava Cake)

8 to 10 pandan leaves, washed and snipped into 2-inch (5 cm) pieces

1 pound (450 g) peeled and finely grated cassava (yuca) root, either fresh or frozen

1½ tablespoons plant-based butter, softened, plus more for greasing

¼ teaspoon kosher salt

¾ cup plus 2 tablespoons (200 ml) full-fat coconut milk

Pumpkin Kaya (page 315), for serving

Makes one 8-inch (20 cm) loaf

In Malaysia, cassava (ubi kayu) gets steamed and tossed with coconut shreds, or transformed into cassava kuih—a tender cake of cassava cooked with coconut milk. Called kuih bingka in Malay, the baked version is my favorite. As the cassava absorbs the buttery coconut milk and browns in the oven, it releases a warm, toasty aroma that will draw everyone into your kitchen. In our family, this cake, often spread with kaya (page 315), is our go-to dessert when we're craving something sweet after dinner. It requires only four ingredients and a pinch of salt. A few tips: Use full-fat coconut milk for the richest flavor, and grate the cassava instead of chopping it. This ensures even cooking and gives the recipe that toothsome, slightly chewy bite. I hope this cake finds a place in your dessert repertoire, especially if you're new to cassava!

1. Preheat the oven to 400°F (205°C).

2. Prepare the pandan: Place the pandan pieces in a blender with ¾ cup (180 ml) water and blend until smooth. Strain through a fine-mesh strainer to extract the juice. Discard the pulp.

3. Make the batter: In a large bowl, stir together the cassava, plant-based butter, salt, coconut milk, and ½ cup (120 ml) of the pandan liquid to form a thick batter.

4. Bake: Grease an 8 by 4 by 2-inch (20 by 10 by 5 cm) loaf pan. Pour in the cassava mixture and smooth the top with a spatula. Bake for 1 hour, or until the cake is fully cooked through, the top is starting to brown, and the edges begin to pull away from the pan.

5. Serve: Let cool before cutting into slices. Enjoy with the kaya.

Chwee Kuih

(Teochew Steamed Rice Bowl Cake)

Serves 6 (makes 6 to 10 rice bowls, depending on size)

As a kid, I'd count down to Tuesdays and Thursdays at the market, because that's when my favorite vendor would be there selling chwee kuih, Malaysia's take on Teochew "water cakes." Steamed in little bowls, this uncle's version of this treat was extra wobbly and soft, piled with stir-fried chai po (preserved radish) and homemade crispy fried garlic, a rare addition.

I never thought about making chwee kuih at home until I moved to the US and wanted to introduce my kids to foods I grew up eating. There are two main steps: preparing the topping and steaming the cakes. To get the best texture and flavor, try to find whole preserved radish at an Asian grocery store, and chop it up finely for an even mouthfeel. The secret to the batter is the water temperature: First mix in cold water, then vigorously stir in boiling water to kick-start the cooking of the rice flour. Once they've been steamed, enjoy the cakes fresh or serve for a potluck—they are best eaten at room temperature!

For the batter:

1 cup plus 1 tablespoon (150 g) rice flour

2 tablespoons tapioca starch

1 tablespoon wheat starch

½ teaspoon kosher salt

1½ cups (360 ml) cold water

2¼ cups (540 ml) boiling water

For the topping:

3½ ounces (100 g) chai po (preserved radish), soaked for at least 30 minutes

Cooking oil, for frying

1 medium shallot, finely chopped

2 garlic cloves, minced

½ teaspoon dark caramel soy sauce

¼ teaspoon mushroom seasoning

1½ teaspoons sugar

For serving:

Hoisin sauce

Crispy fried garlic, store-bought or homemade (optional)

Chile sauce (such as the "Chicken" Rice Chili Sauce, page 35)

1. Prepare the batter: In a large heatproof bowl, combine the rice flour, tapioca starch, wheat starch, and salt. Add the cold water and whisk until the mixture is smooth and free of lumps. Pour in the boiling water (it's important that it's freshly boiling), stirring vigorously until the batter thickens and the ingredients are fully incorporated, about 1 minute.

2. Steam the cakes: Arrange 6 to 8 small ramekins or steam-safe bowls (4 to 8 ounces / 120 to 240 ml each) upside down in a steamer set over a pot of boiling water. Cover and steam for 2 to 3 minutes to heat the bowls. Using heatproof gloves, carefully flip the bowls over.

3. Give the batter a stir and ladle it into the bowls, filling each three-quarters full. Steam over high heat

recipe continues

for 15 minutes, until the batter is fully set. You'll notice the mixture bubbling as it steams, and a dimple may form in the middle.

4. Let the bowls rest in the steamer for about 10 minutes, then remove the bowls with care using a spatula or a butter knife. Let the kuih cool completely.

5. Prepare the topping: Rinse the preserved radish thoroughly, then drain well. Finely mince the radish or pulse it in a food processor (you should have about 1 cup). Heat 2 to 3 tablespoons oil (enough to coat the bottom of the pan) in a medium pan or wok over medium-high. Sauté the shallot and garlic until aromatic, about 30 seconds. Add the preserved radish and stir-fry until fragrant and starting to dry around the edges. Season with the dark caramel soy sauce, mushroom seasoning, and sugar.

6. Add 1½ cups (360 ml) water to the pan and bring the mixture to a boil. Simmer until the liquid is completely absorbed into the radish, but the radish is not fully dry, about 10 minutes. Transfer the topping to a small bowl and set aside. (The preserved radish topping can also be enjoyed as a side dish with porridge, rice, or noodles.)

7. Serve: Run a small silicone spatula along the sides of each bowl to release the cooled kuih, then invert onto a plate. Top with the preserved radish mixture, hoisin sauce, and crispy fried garlic (if using). Serve with a side of the chile sauce.

Pumpkin Kaya

(Coconut-Pumpkin Jam)

Makes about 2 cups (480 ml)

Kaya is a rich, velvety spread made from coconut milk, sugar, and eggs, with deep butterscotch notes from slow caramelization. Some versions are green because they're infused with pandan juice for a vanilla-like aroma. Served with toasted bread as kaya butter toast, it's a beloved breakfast staple at kopitiams and wet markets across Malaysia, often paired with a cup of kopi-o (black coffee with sugar). For my vegan version sans egg, I turn to pumpkin for its natural thick creaminess and gold color, and coconut palm sugar (gula melaka) to lend a rich, smoky depth.

Making kaya isn't a quick affair: My aunt used to temper it over low heat for more than an hour, stirring constantly until it reached a perfect silky texture. I've experimented with shortcuts, but slow stovetop cooking with pandan leaves yields the best results, infusing the kaya with their fragrance. This method takes less time than my aunt's traditional approach but still delivers that luxurious texture.

1 pound (450 g) pumpkin or kabocha squash, peeled, cored, and cut into ¼-inch (6 mm) slices (about 14 ounces / 400 g flesh)

1⅔ cups (400 ml) full-fat coconut milk

4¼ ounces (120 g) gula melaka or other palm sugar (about 8 rounds; see sidebar, page 317)

2 pandan leaves, tied into a knot

1. Prepare the pumpkin: Steam the pumpkin or squash slices in a steamer basket over medium-high heat until tender and almost falling apart, 8 to 10 minutes.

2. Transfer the cooked pumpkin or squash to a blender, add the coconut milk, and blend on high speed until smooth, about 1 minute.

3. Cook the mixture: In a large nonstick pan, combine the blended pumpkin or squash mixture, the palm sugar, and pandan leaves. Cook over medium-low heat, stirring occasionally, for about 15 minutes. For maximum flavor, use the pandan leaves like a clock hand to stir the mixture around in the pot. You can also use the spatula to push the leaves. This movement helps release the pandan's flavors.

recipe continues

Fun fact:
Kaya means "wealthy" in Malay. While the connection is symbolic, I like to think a spoonful of kaya brings a little extra fortune your way!

4. After 15 minutes, the mixture should be thick enough to coat the back of a spatula. Continue cooking and stirring until the mixture darkens into a paste, another 10 minutes. To test if the kaya is ready, draw a line through the kaya with a spatula—if the line holds for longer than 3 seconds, it's done.

5. Finish and store: Remove the pan from the heat and discard the pandan leaves. Allow the kaya to cool before serving. Transfer to an airtight jar and keep in the fridge for up to 1 week.

Gula Melaka

Gula melaka, a traditional Malaysian sweetener, is a sugar derived from the sap of coconut palms. It has a deep, caramel-like sweetness with hints of toffee and smoke. It's usually molded into distinctive cylindrical blocks, often with a dent on top. I'll normally shave or chop these blocks into smaller chunks for use in desserts or sauces. It's my favorite sweetener for Bubur Cha Cha (page 319) and other Malaysian desserts for its distinct sweetness that's not too overpowering.

Bubur Cha Cha

(Coconut Milk Mixed "Porridge")

Serves 4 to 6

This vibrant and colorful dessert's name translates simply as "porridge" in Malay, but bubur cha cha is so much more for me. It's a nostalgic throwback to my school days: A vendor uncle would park his motorbike near the gates of our neighborhood, selling tong shui (Cantonese sweet soups) from large containers hooked up to a propane gas cylinder. Every day, he had three types of sweet soup, but my favorite was his bubur cha cha. It was fragrant with aromatic pandan leaves, and the rich, freshly blended coconut milk wrapped everything in a sweet hug.

What set his bubur cha cha apart was the homemade tapioca jellies he would add on request. I adored their chewy, QQ texture and how they turned translucent but wouldn't melt in the hot broth. I'd always ask for a scoop, just to savor the jellies alongside the soft chunks of sweet potato and taro. It's a simple combination that hits all the right spots for me: creamy, chewy, sweet, with a hint of savory depth from the coconut milk.

For the root vegetables:

2 or 3 pandan leaves, plus more for cooking

7 ounces (200 g) peeled red sweet potato, cut into 1½-inch (4 cm) cubes (about 1½ cups)

7 ounces (200 g) peeled purple sweet potato, cut into 1½-inch (4 cm) cubes (about 1½ cups)

10½ ounces (300 g) peeled taro, cut into 1½-inch (4 cm) cubes (about 2¼ cups; see Note, page 323)

For the tapioca jellies (optional; see Notes, page 320):

5 tablespoons (50 g) tapioca starch, plus more as needed

2 tablespoons boiling water (I used about 33 ml), plus cold water if needed

For the bubur cha cha:

4½ ounces (125 g) gula melaka or other palm sugar (about ½ cup or 8 rounds), plus more as needed (see Notes, page 320, and sidebar, page 317)

Pinch of kosher salt

1⅔ cups (400 ml) full-fat coconut milk, at room temperature, plus more as needed (see Notes, page 320)

1. Steam the root vegetables: Set up a steamer and bring the water to a boil over medium-high heat. Tear up the pandan leaves and use them to line the steamer basket. Place the red and purple sweet potatoes and taro on the pandan leaves. Cover and steam until fork-tender, about 15 minutes. This step infuses the vegetables with pandan flavor. Reserve the pot of water to cook the jellies.

2. Make the tapioca jellies (if using): Place the tapioca starch in a heatproof bowl. While stirring with chopsticks, slowly pour in the boiling water, gathering the dry flour from the sides of the bowl to form a shaggy dough. Clean the chopsticks with the residual starch and knead the dough into a smooth ball with your hands in the bowl (be careful, as the dough may still be hot). If the dough is too wet or soft, add more

recipe continues

Notes:

- *If you don't have time to make the tapioca jellies, you can use ¼ cup (40 g) of store-bought sago and cook according to the package instructions. (Sago, small, dried pearls from the sago palm, turn from white to clear and chewy once cooked, giving a fun, gelatinous bite. Their neutral taste pairs perfectly with desserts like bubur cha cha. Sago can also come in vibrant colors that boost the dish's visual appeal. Find sago at Asian groceries or online.)*
- *You can substitute granulated sugar for the palm sugar, but start with a smaller quantity and adjust the sweetness to taste.*
- *The thickness of the bubur cha cha depends on the ratio of coconut milk to water. For a thicker and creamier texture, use more coconut milk.*

tapioca starch; if it's too dry, add cold water, 1 tablespoon at a time. Roll the dough into a ½-inch (12 mm) log and cut or pinch the log into bite-sized pieces.

3. **Cook the jellies:** Bring a large pot of water to a boil (you can use the same pot with the water used to steam the sweet potatoes). Carefully drop in the tapioca jellies and stir to loosen them. When the jellies float to the top, after about 3 minutes, scoop them up with a strainer and rinse them under cold water. Keep them soaking in a bowl of cold water while you finish preparing the bubur cha cha.

4. **Cook the bubur cha cha:** Drain the pot and refill it with a generous 1 quart (1 L) water. Tear up a few more pandan leaves, breaking their fibers to release their flavor, and tie them into a knot. Place the pandan knot in the pot and bring the water to a boil. Add the palm sugar and whisk until it completely dissolves.

5. Transfer the sweet potatoes and taro cubes to the pot and cook them for 5 to 10 minutes over high heat until they absorb the sweetness of the liquid. Taste and adjust the sugar to your desired sweetness. Lower the heat to medium to prevent the coconut milk from separating or scalding. Add the salt, tapioca jellies (if using), and coconut milk to the pot and bring everything to a gentle boil.

6. **Serve:** Discard the pandan leaves and serve warm.

Orh Tau Kuih

(Savory Steamed Taro Cake)

For the batter:

2⅓ cups (330 g) rice flour

5 tablespoons (50 g) tapioca starch

3 tablespoons (20 g) wheat starch

1 teaspoon kosher salt

½ teaspoon mushroom seasoning

½ teaspoon five-spice powder

¼ teaspoon ground white pepper

For the shallots, taro, and mushrooms:

½ cup (110 ml) cooking oil

10 to 12 shallots (11 ounces / 310 g), thinly sliced

1 medium taro (16 ounces / 470 g), peeled and cut into ¾-inch (2 cm) cubes (see Note, page 323)

1 cup (28 g) dried shiitake mushrooms, rehydrated and cut into ¼-inch (6 mm) dice

For serving:

Thinly sliced scallions, white and green parts

Thinly sliced red chile

"Chicken" Rice Chili Sauce (page 35)

Sweet bean sauce or hoisin sauce

Makes one 9-inch (23 cm) cake (serves 4 to 6)

Taro cake is one of my all-time favorite snacks. In Teochew, orh tau, or taro, is prized for its subtle sweetness and earthy aroma, shining in savory kuih and sweets like Bubur Cha Cha (page 319). A good taro has white flesh speckled with purple, and when cooked, it becomes wonderfully fragrant, with a powdery texture that melts in each bite. To bring out its full flavor, I like to quickly sauté the taro before steaming it, similar to how you prepare a daikon radish cake (see page 163). This step partially cooks the taro, giving it a head start before you mix it into the batter for steaming.

For the best texture and flavor, make the cake the night before and gently reheat it the next morning for a quick and delightful breakfast. Inspired by one of the versions I had as a kid, I added warm, aromatic five-spice powder to the batter to complement the delicate taro. Serve orh tau kuih with a dollop of sweet bean paste sauce and pickled green chile slices for a tangy kick.

1. Make the batter: In a large bowl, whisk together the rice flour, tapioca starch, and wheat starch with 4¼ cups (1 L) water. Season with the salt, mushroom seasoning, five-spice powder, and white pepper. Set aside.

2. Fry the shallots and taro: In a wok or large saucepan over low heat, heat the oil and shallots until they start to bubble, about 2 minutes. Continue frying, stirring constantly, until the shallots color to a pale golden brown, about 20 minutes. Use a fine-mesh strainer to remove the shallots from the oil, then spread them out on a paper towel–lined plate to drain. (They will continue to cook out of the oil, so don't allow them to get too dark in the pan.)

3. Add the taro to the hot shallot oil and fry until the cubes become fragrant and golden brown on the

recipe continues

Note:

The elders in my family always advised wearing gloves when peeling taro, as its juices can irritate sensitive skin.

edges, 5 to 7 minutes. Transfer the taro to a plate. Pour the remaining oil from the pan into a clean bowl or jar for use in step 5, reserving 4 tablespoons (60 ml) in the wok.

4. **Cook the batter:** In the same pan over medium-low heat, sauté the mushrooms until they begin to brown and smell delicious. Stir the batter (as the starch may have settled) and pour it into the wok, quickly adding to the mushrooms and stirring to distribute the mushrooms in the batter. As the batter starts to thicken, in 2 to 3 minutes, fold in the taro cubes. Continue cooking until the mixture forms a thick paste, 2 to 3 minutes more. Remove the pan from the heat.

5. Grease a 9-inch (23 cm) round cake pan with tall sides with the reserved shallot oil. Transfer the hot, thick taro batter into the pan, pressing down with a spatula to form an even layer and eliminate air bubbles. Sprinkle half of the fried shallots evenly across the top.

6. **Steam the cake:** Prepare a large steamer rack over a pot of boiling water. Wrap the lid with a towel to prevent condensation from dripping onto the cake. Steam the taro cake for 45 to 50 minutes over medium-high, until it is firm throughout (use a toothpick to check that the cake is no longer soft in the center; it should come out clean). During steaming, replenish the water level in the pot as needed.

7. Allow the taro cake to cool completely before cutting it into squares or wedges.

8. **Garnish and serve:** Garnish the cake with the remaining fried shallots, the scallions, and chile. Serve with the chile sauce and a side of sweet bean sauce or hoisin sauce. Enjoy as a delicious breakfast or snack.

Suan Pan Zi

(Hakka Taro "Abacus Seeds")

Serves 2 or 3

These chewy dumplings, called suan pan zi (syun poon ji in Cantonese) and dubbed "abacus seeds" for their resemblance to the ancient counting tool, are a Hakka tradition. They often appear during festive seasons as symbols of wealth and prosperity, but outside of local Hakka restaurants they're a rare find. Shaping the dumplings is a simple, soothing process. After I boil them until tender, I like to stir-fry them in a savory sauce with mushrooms and any protein I have on hand. The slightly sweet earthiness of taro pairs beautifully with shiitake, and the soft, absorbent beads have an addictive QQ chewiness. Once you start eating them, it's easy to keep snacking on these little morsels one after another until the plate is clean.

For the "abacus seeds":

9 ounces (250 g) taro, peeled and cut into ½-inch (12 mm) slices (see Note, page 323)

¾ cup (120 g) tapioca starch, plus more as needed

Flour, for rolling

Kosher salt

Drizzle of cooking oil

For the sauce:

1 teaspoon soy sauce

2 teaspoons vegetarian oyster sauce

1 teaspoon Vegan Fish Sauce (page 49)

⅛ teaspoon dark caramel soy sauce

Dash of ground white pepper

2 tablespoons Shallot Oil (page 43) or cooking oil

3 medium dried shiitake mushrooms, rehydrated and thinly sliced

1 garlic clove, finely chopped

¼ ounce (7 g) dried wood ear mushrooms, rehydrated and thinly sliced

2 tablespoons textured vegetable protein (TVP), rehydrated and squeezed to drain

⅛ teaspoon kosher salt, plus more as needed

1. **Prepare the "abacus seed" dough:** Place the taro in a steamer basket over boiling water and steam for about 20 minutes, or until fork-tender.

2. Transfer the steamed taro to a large bowl and mash with a potato masher or fork. Gradually add the tapioca starch, stirring with a spatula until well combined. Once cool enough to handle, knead the mixture into a soft, smooth dough, breaking up any hard taro bits you find. Add more tapioca starch, 1 tablespoon at a time, until the dough is no longer sticky and has the firmness of an earlobe. The dough should be moldable and hold together well.

3. On a clean, floured surface, roll out the dough into a long rope about ¾ inch (2 cm) thick. Divide the rope into portions that are roughly the size of a gumball (approximately ¼ ounce / 7 to 8 g each). Roll each portion into a smooth ball, then gently pinch the middle with your index finger and thumb to create a circular dent in the center, without breaking through.

recipe and ingredients continue

For serving:

1 stalk fresh cilantro, finely chopped (both stems and leaves)

1 scallion, white and green parts, thinly sliced

Chile sauce (such as the "Chicken" Rice Chili Sauce, page 35)

It should resemble an abacus bead, a small disc with a dimpled center.

4. **Cook the "abacus seed" dumplings:** Prepare a large bowl of cold water. Bring a large pot of salted water to a rolling boil and add the oil. Carefully add the "abacus seed" dumplings to the pot and cook over medium-high heat until they float to the surface, 2 to 3 minutes. Once they float, continue cooking for another 30 seconds, until they are chewy and slightly translucent. Use a mesh strainer to transfer the dumplings to the bowl of cold water to stop the cooking process.

5. **Make the sauce:** In a small bowl, whisk the soy sauce, vegetarian oyster sauce, vegan fish sauce, dark caramel soy sauce, white pepper, and ¼ cup (60 ml) water. Set aside.

6. Heat the shallot oil in a large skillet or nonstick pan over medium-low. Sauté the shiitake mushrooms until fragrant and the edges start to brown, 2 to 3 minutes. Add the garlic and cook until aromatic, then add the wood ear mushrooms and cook for a few seconds, until they start to pop. Add the TVP and stir-fry until it starts to color, about 2 minutes.

7. Drain the dumplings and add them to the pan. Pour in the prepared sauce and increase the heat to medium-high. Toss and fold the mixture quickly until the dumplings absorb the sauce. Taste and season with the salt and white pepper as desired.

8. **Garnish and serve:** Fold in the cilantro and garnish with the scallion. Serve with the chile sauce.

Apam Balik aka Ban Jian Kuih

(Peanut-Filled Pancakes)

Makes two 10-inch (25 cm) pancakes

You know that moment when a whiff of something incredible stops you in your tracks? That's ban jian kuih for me—known as apam balik in Malay. At the market, the aroma of this crisp-edged, honeycomb-textured treat pulls me in every time. The vendor pours the batter onto the cast-iron griddle, swirling it with the back of a giant ladle for an even layer, then covers it with a stainless-steel lid. When the pancake sets, he scatters sugar and crushed peanuts all over it with a cupped hand, letting the sugar slip between his fingers. A flat pastry scraper loosens the edges, a wooden block slides underneath, and the massive pancake is folded in half and sliced into pieces. I'm right there, eyeing the crispiest edges. This is ban jian kuih in its classic form—the way it's been done since I was young. My vegan version skips the egg, keeping that subtle baking soda tang along with sweet sugar and roasted peanuts. A nonstick pan gets those edges just right, and don't skimp on the peanuts with sweet creamed corn—this pancake is crunchy, sweet, and nutty in one bite.

For the batter:

2 cups (240 g) all-purpose flour

2½ teaspoons baking powder

½ teaspoon baking soda

¼ teaspoon kosher salt

¼ cup (60 ml) aquafaba (see Note, page 329)

⅓ cup (65 g) sugar

2 tablespoons plant-based butter, melted

For the filling:

1½ cups (220 g) roasted shelled peanuts

1 tablespoon sugar, plus more as needed

4 tablespoons (60 g) cream-style sweet corn (from a can is fine), plus more as needed

2 tablespoons chilled plant-based butter, cut into thin slices, plus more as needed

1. Make the batter: In a large bowl, whisk together the flour, baking powder, baking soda, and salt. In a smaller bowl, beat the aquafaba with a hand blender until it's white, foamy, and doubled in volume. Add the sugar and continue beating until well combined. Pour this wet mixture into the dry mixture and gently fold together. Gradually add 1¼ cups (300 ml) water, stirring until no large lumps remain. Stir in the melted plant-based butter until the batter is thick and smooth. Cover the bowl and let the batter rest for at least 30 minutes.

2. Prepare the filling: Grind the peanuts in a food processor, pulsing several times until the nuts are the consistency of breadcrumbs. Use a spatula to loosen the peanuts from the blade between pulses, being careful not to overblend, as the heat from the blade

recipe continues

Note:

Aquafaba is the liquid from a can of chickpeas, which whips up to the consistency of egg whites. You can substitute unsweetened plant milk if preferred.

Crafting ban jian kuih the old-school way, with golden batter and nutty Malaysian charm.

can turn the nuts into peanut butter. (Alternatively, you can use a mortar and pestle to crush the peanuts.) Transfer the crushed peanuts to a bowl.

3. **Cook the pancakes:** Heat a dry 10-inch (25 cm) nonstick pan over medium-low heat. Divide the batter into two portions. Pour the first half of the batter into the pan and, using the base of a measuring cup, spread it in a circular motion from the center toward the edge, forming a thin rim around the pancake. Cover the pan with a lid and cook for 2 to 3 minutes, until small holes appear on the surface of the batter.

4. **Add the filling:** Uncover the pan and sprinkle about ½ tablespoon of the sugar evenly across the pancake. Cover and cook for 1 to 2 minutes, or until the center is fully cooked with no visible wet batter. Uncover and sprinkle half of the crushed peanuts over the pancake. On half of the peanut layer, spread 2 tablespoons of the sweet creamed corn and top with half of the butter slices.

5. Cover the pan and cook the pancake for another minute, until the butter has melted. Check if the bottom is golden brown by lifting up an edge with a spatula. Once ready, loosen the pancake and fold it in half to enclose the filling, forming a half-moon-shaped sandwich. Press gently and transfer the pancake from the pan to a cutting board. Repeat with the remaining batter and fillings to make the second pancake.

6. **Serve:** Slice into wedges and serve warm.

Ong Lai Peah

(Pineapple Tarts)

Makes 60 Ping-Pong ball–sized tarts

In Hokkien, ong lai means "pineapple," but it also doubles as a bit of wordplay, a homophone for "wealth is coming." In keeping with a charming tradition, my mama once rolled a pineapple into our new house to bring good fortune! Pineapple tarts are a hot commodity during Chinese New Year in Malaysia, and as the holidays approach, I like to bake this crowd-pleasing recipe in big batches and gift them to friends and family.

Making these tarts starts with fresh pineapple cooked down to a thick, sticky paste. My tip is to strain out the juice first so it reduces faster, giving you a concentrated flavor with minimal fuss. I also like to keep my filling a bit tart to balance the sweetness and complement the rich buttery pastry. Preparing the pastry is straightforward, just flour, plant-based butter, and sugar, mixed into a dough that's a dream to work with. You wrap it around the pineapple filling and pinch it into shape using your fingers. Once baked, the tarts are crumbly and tangy! Just pop one in your mouth and let it melt on your tongue.

For the pineapple filling:

2 large ripe pineapples (about 4 pounds / 2 kg flesh after peeling and paring)

½ cup (100 g) granulated sugar, or more depending on the sweetness of the pineapples

For the pastry:

2 sticks (1 cup / 225 g) unsalted plant-based butter, at room temperature

6 tablespoons (40 g) confectioners' sugar, sifted

3 cups (350 g) all-purpose flour, sifted, plus more as needed

Maple syrup, for brushing

1. Prepare the pineapples: Begin by cutting off the spiky crowns of the pineapples and slicing off the skin. Use a paring knife to take out all the eyes and cut the pineapple flesh and core into 2-inch (5 cm) chunks. Transfer these chunks to a high-speed blender and purée. Strain the purée through a fine-mesh sieve to extract the pulp (see Notes, page 332), reserving the juice to drink or for smoothies.

2. Cook the filling (see Notes, page 332): Transfer the pulp to a large skillet or nonstick pan (preferably with high sides to reduce splatter). Cook over medium-low heat, stirring occasionally, until most of the moisture has evaporated. After 30 to 45 minutes, the paste will start pulling away from the sides of the pan. Add the sugar and continue stirring until the mixture darkens

recipe continues

Notes:

- *Straining out the pineapple juice before cooking the pulp reduces cooking time and enhances flavor concentration.*
- *You can make the filling ahead of time and refrigerate it until ready to use.*
- *Adjust the dough-to-filling ratio to your preference. Using less pastry dough (I recommend a 1 to 2 g difference per tart) will result in a thinner crust, and vice versa.*

to a rich caramel color and achieves a moldable texture that's stickier than jam. Remove from the heat. Once cool enough to handle, divide the pineapple filling into gumball-sized balls (about ¼ ounce / 8 to 9 g each).

3. Make the dough: While the filling cools, prepare the dough. Preheat the oven to 350°F (175°C) and line a baking sheet with parchment paper. Using a mixer fitted with a paddle attachment, cream the plant-based butter and confectioners' sugar until the mixture is thick and pale yellow. Gradually add the sifted flour and knead into a soft dough. (You may need to adjust the amount of flour depending on the brand of butter used.) The dough should come together cleanly without sticking to the bowl. Transfer the dough to a clean surface and divide it into ⅓-ounce (10 to 11 g) balls slightly larger than the balls of filling (see Notes).

4. Flatten each ball of dough with your palm, then pinch the edges with your fingers to create a thin circular disc 2½ to 3 inches (6 to 7.5 cm) wide. Place a pineapple filling ball in the center and bring the sides of the dough up and around, sealing the dough with a pinch at the top. Roll gently into a ball. For a decorative touch, score a few crosshatch lines on the surface of the ball to resemble a pineapple.

5. Place the formed tarts on a baking pan, spacing them about a thumb's width apart, as they won't rise or expand much. Continue forming the tarts until all the dough and filling are used.

6. Bake: Lightly brush the tarts with maple syrup. Bake for 30 to 35 minutes, until the tops are slightly golden. Keep an eye on the time, as oven temperatures may vary: The filling is already cooked, so the goal here is just to bake the dough.

7. Serve: Enjoy warm or allow the tarts to cool completely before storing them in an airtight container in the fridge for up to 1 month.

Roti Empat Segi
(Roti Canai)

Makes 4 square roti

Buying a warm roti canai at the mamak stall near my house was how I often started my mornings before school as a young kid. Watching the mamak uncle flip, toss, and twirl the dough in the air before slamming it onto the stainless-steel table was mesmerizing, a skillful performance. Little did I know that this less-than-fifty-cent breakfast in Malaysia would become a five-dollar splurge in the States. But when you're craving a taste from home like I was when I first moved to the US, five dollars is a small price to pay.

Roti empat segi is simply standard roti canai folded into a neat square, its crispy, chewy layers perfect for tearing apart. While it is traditionally made with ghee, many places now offer vegan versions, and this homemade one with plant-based butter is just as delicious as the original. It's normally paired with warm, spiced dal, but I love serving it with my Kari Jap Choy (page 71) for a vibrant, hearty meal. Tear off a crispy layer, dip it into the creamy, spiced curry, and savor that first bite—the contrast of chewy-crisp roti against the lush sauce is pure magic. For those few moments at breakfast, it feels like the day is going exactly right.

¾ cup (180 ml) warm water

½ teaspoon kosher salt

2 teaspoons sugar, plus more for serving

3 tablespoons (45 ml) cooking oil, plus more (or more plant-based butter) for frying

2½ cups (300 g) all-purpose flour, plus more as needed

2 tablespoons plant-based butter, softened

Store-bought dal or Kari Jap Choy (page 71), for serving (optional)

1. Make the dough: In a large bowl, mix the warm water, salt, sugar, and 2 tablespoons of the oil until the sugar dissolves. Add the flour and stir with a spatula or chopsticks until shaggy flakes form. Brush off any remaining flour from the utensils. Knead the mixture in the bowl by hand until it forms a ball, adding more flour if the dough is too sticky. Cover the bowl with a lid and let the dough rest for 10 minutes. Knead again until the dough is smooth and elastic. Divide into four equal portions and shape into balls.

2. Rest the dough: Drizzle the remaining 1 tablespoon oil in a shallow dish or an 8-inch (20 cm) cake pan. Arrange the dough balls inside, ensuring they are

recipe continues

Note:

To freeze the roti, after step 4, place the uncooked square pancakes between sheets of parchment paper and freeze until solid, then store in a sealed freezer bag. When ready to eat, cook the roti as directed in step 5—it will just take a few extra minutes to cook the frozen roti.

Uncle's roti flips and twirls with skill, a sizzling spectacle on the griddle.

Golden roti empat segi glows, a flaky delight.

generously coated with oil to prevent sticking. Cover the dish and let the dough rest for at least 2 hours, or overnight in the fridge. (If refrigerating overnight, let the dough sit at room temperature for 30 minutes to 1 hour, until soft and pliable, before use.)

3. Assemble: Lightly grease your work surface and your hands with oil. Take one dough ball and flatten it into a circle using the heel of your palm. Gently stretch the dough into a paper-thin rectangle, about 16 by 12 inches (40.5 by 30.5 cm), aiming for it to be as large and thin as possible.

4. Spread ½ tablespoon of the butter across the stretched dough. Fold the short sides toward the middle, overlapping slightly, and pinch gently to seal. Fold the top and bottom edges toward the center to enclose the rectangle into a square packet. (To freeze the roti at this point, see Note.)

5. Cook the roti: Heat a thin layer of oil or plant-based butter in a large skillet or nonstick pan over medium-low heat. Place one roti in the hot pan, seam side down, and fry until golden brown, 3 to 4 minutes. If the roti browns too quickly, reduce the heat. Flip and cook the other side for another 3 to 4 minutes, adding more oil if needed. The roti will puff up as it cooks. Transfer the cooked roti to a plate and cover with a towel to keep warm. Repeat with the remaining roti.

6. Serve: Enjoy the roti warm, either on its own, torn and dipped into sugar, or with a savory side of dal or vegetable curry.

Thai Basil Zhua Bing

(Flaky Layered Pancakes)

Makes 4 pancakes

I grew up with roti canai and instantly fell in love with zhua bing's crispy, flaky layers when I first encountered it in Taiwan. Zhua bing, literally "grab pancake," is a street food favorite there, often made with scallions. You can't go wrong when you add fresh herbs to dough, and lately, I've been hooked on this Thai basil variation. It's a riff on my roti canai dough (page 333) and inspired by a zhua bing layered with fresh Thai basil that I tried near my mom's house.

Thin dough is brushed with oil, layered with chopped basil, then repeatedly folded and flattened to create the signature flakiness. Cooked on a hot griddle until golden and crisp, each bite delivers a satisfying crunch followed by a release of that peppery, basil-y flavor. Enjoy it on its own, fold it with a filling like a wrap, or pair it with a dipping sauce as a snack or part of a meal. These pancakes also freeze well (see Note, page 339). Be sure to allow time to let the dough rest at least thirty minutes or overnight before cooking.

For the dough:

2 cups (240 g) all-purpose flour, plus more for kneading

½ teaspoon kosher salt

1 teaspoon baking powder

1 tablespoon cooking oil, plus more as needed for rolling, shaping, and frying

For the basil paste:

2 cups (40 g) packed Thai basil leaves, washed thoroughly and patted dry

¼ cup (35 g) all-purpose flour

½ teaspoon five-spice powder

1 teaspoon sugar

½ teaspoon kosher salt

¼ cup (60 ml) cooking oil

For serving (optional):

Soy sauce

Chopped scallions

1. **Prepare the dough:** In the bowl of a stand mixer with the dough hook attachment, combine the flour, salt, and baking powder and mix on medium-low speed. With the mixer running, slowly pour in ⅔ cup (150 ml) water. Continue mixing until a soft, elastic dough forms, adding more water, 1 tablespoon at a time, if needed to incorporate any dry spots.

2. Transfer the dough to a floured work surface and knead until smooth. Divide the dough into four equal portions, knead each portion to remove air bubbles, and shape into balls.

3. Drizzle the cooking oil into an 8-inch (20 cm) cake pan or similar-sized dish. Place the dough balls in the pan, rolling to coat each one generously with the oil. Cover and let rest for at least 30 minutes or refrigerate overnight.

recipe continues

4. Make the basil paste: While the dough is resting, coarsely chop the basil and place it in a heatproof bowl with the flour, five-spice powder, sugar, and salt. Heat the oil in a small saucepan until it reaches 350°F (175°C) or the wooden tip of a chopstick sizzles upon contact with the oil. Carefully pour the hot oil into the bowl with the basil mixture. Stir quickly with a spatula until well combined. The basil will darken and release moisture as it cools.

5. Shape the dough: If the dough was refrigerated, let it sit at room temperature for 30 minutes to 1 hour, until soft and pliable, before proceeding. Uncover the dough balls and pour any excess oil from the pan (or more as needed) onto your work surface. Working with one ball at a time, flatten the dough with your palm. Using greased fingers or a rolling pin, stretch the dough into a thin rectangle (about 12 by 7 inches / 30.5 by 17 cm), nearly translucent and as thin as possible, sticking to the board. Spread a quarter of the basil paste evenly over the dough (to ensure flaky layers), pressing lightly to adhere.

6. Starting from one long edge of the dough, fanfold into 1½-inch (4 cm) pleats, leaving a 1- to 2-inch (2.5 to 5 cm) flap at the end, to create a belt. Fold this flap down like an envelope, press gently, and stretch the belt by slapping it onto the surface. Coil the dough into a cinnamon roll shape, tucking the end underneath. Repeat with the remaining dough and let the coils rest for at least 15 minutes.

7. Gently press or roll each coil into a disc about ¼ inch (6 mm) thick and 5 to 6 inches (12 to 15 cm) in diameter, using greased fingers or a greased rolling pin. (To freeze the pancakes at this point, see Note.)

Note:

If freezing, after step 7, place the shaped but uncooked pancakes between sheets of parchment paper and freeze until solid, then store in a sealed freezer bag. When ready to eat, fry as directed in step 8. They will just take a few extra minutes to cook.

8. **Fry the pancakes:** Heat a cast-iron or nonstick pan with a thin layer of oil over medium-low heat. Place one disc of dough in the pan, cover, and cook until the bottom is golden brown, 2 to 3 minutes. Peek occasionally and adjust the heat if needed. Brush a layer of oil on the top of the pancake. Flip the pancake, cover, and cook for another 2 to 3 minutes, until both sides are crispy.

9. **Fluff and serve:** Place the cooked pancake on a cutting board. While still warm, clap your palms on opposite sides of the pancake to fluff up the layers. Cool your palms down by pressing them on the cutting board. Clap the pancake again until fluffy and loose. Serve warm, as is or with a side of soy sauce with chopped scallions. Fry, fluff, and serve the three remaining pancakes.

Mama's Jian Mi Hoon Kuih

(Coconut Milk Crepes)

Makes six 8-inch (20 cm) crepes

Usually I'm all about savory breakfasts, but I can't resist these delicate sweet "crepes," or mi hoon kuih, which translates to "flour cake" in Hokkien. Imagine the thin layers with a chewy center and crispy edges, fragrant with coconut and lightly sweetened. My mama loves to whip them up in the morning, and I picked up the recipe from her during visits home. When she serves them spread with kaya (page 315), I can't help but tear off a warm piece, dip it into the sweet custardy jam, and devour it before going back for more. Full-fat coconut milk is the magical ingredient here. It infuses the batter with fragrance and a hint of sweetness. Complete the meal with a strong, hot cup of teh tarik (pulled tea, frothy from pouring between jugs) or a bowl of Red Bean Soup with Glutinous Rice Balls (page 303) for a satisfying breakfast fix.

1 cup (120 g) all-purpose flour

7 tablespoons (100 ml) full-fat coconut milk

1½ tablespoons salted plant-based butter, melted

¼ cup (60 ml) plant-based egg liquid

2 tablespoons sugar

Pinch of kosher salt

Cooking oil, for frying

Pumpkin Kaya (page 315), for serving

1. Make the batter: In a large bowl, whisk together the flour, coconut milk, melted plant-based butter, plant-based egg liquid, sugar, salt, and ½ cup (120 ml) water until a thick, smooth batter forms. Let the batter rest for 5 to 10 minutes.

2. Cook: Lightly grease an 8-inch (20 cm) nonstick pan with a thin layer of oil and heat it over low heat. Pour ⅓ cup (80 ml) of the batter into the heated pan, swirling it to spread the batter evenly across the base and up the sides. Cook over low heat until the bottom is golden brown and the edges begin to lift, about 2 minutes. Flip the crepe and cook for another 2 minutes, until it is dry to the touch and golden brown. Repeat with the remaining batter.

3. Serve: Serve the crepes warm, paired with pumpkin kaya.

ACKNOWLEDGMENTS

I never imagined sharing my recipes with friends worldwide, let alone writing a cookbook. Acknowledgments are the last chapter, but they come first in my heart. Without my family, friends, community, and readers, these pages would remain blank. Many of you who've tried my online recipes have showered me with love and support. Your comments and shared dishes with loved ones truly brighten my day. They're the greatest gift I carry to bed each night. I'm grateful for this chance to share my humble homemade food and my hope to inspire a meatless meal daily. May this book be our kitchen companion, fostering shared meals and learning with friends and family.

My anticipatory, feast-ready grin at a family wedding dinner banquet.

My family is my foundation; without them, I couldn't share online or write this book. My beloved husband, Shein Loong Yap, you're the talent behind the scenes—capturing stunning photos for this book and videos for my blog. You're my rock, never doubting my ability. It's remarkable that we share this mission to inspire meatless meals. You're my forever love.

Jie, my cherished daughter, Tiffany, Mama adores you deeply. You're steadfastly supportive, and though younger, your wisdom and discipline inspire me. I'm immensely proud of you and I admire you, Jie. Your nudge to record my recipes sparked this book, leading to my social media journey. Didi, my precious son, Justin, Mama cherishes you. Your support, checking on me daily and being my champion, touches my heart. Your passion for cooking and curiosity about recipes shaped this book. You and Jie are my finest tasters.

My Chia family—Ah Ma, Mummy, Papa, Kang Pheng, Sui Goh, and all the members—holds a special place. Mummy, your healthy cooking inspired many recipes here. Thank you for creating a cozy nest for me and Kang Pheng on weekends, sharing mushroom soups and Western breakfasts. I share your passion for simple food with readers worldwide. Papa, I hope you're proud of my lifelong commitment to this diet, now shared through this cookbook. Kang Pheng, my dear brother, your "Seventeen Dimes" nickname and egg fried rice adventures fueled my stories. May this book be a storybook for your children, showcasing your vibrant spirit. Sui Goh, your financial support for my

US education paved the way for this book. I'm deeply grateful.

The Yap family, whom I can never thank enough, is my extended haven. Mama, you're a superstar, cooking tirelessly for our large family with love in every dish. Mama, ni hen bang, wo ai ni. I weave your wisdom into this book, hoping to honor you. Thank you for entrusting me with your incredible son. Papa, you're a phenomenal father-in-law, fretting over my workload and aiding in the kitchen. You suggest takeout to ease my efforts, yet savor every dish I make with a warm smile. To my brother, sisters, cousins, nieces, and nephews, your embrace of vegetarian meals during our Malaysia visits and cleaning off the plates of the food I made for you warms my soul. You've welcomed me with open hearts. My four vibrant Yap sisters are the truest friends I could wish for. Your boundless love humbles me.

This journey began with your email, Lucia Watson of Avery. I still can't believe I'm writing a book, Lucia, recalling my stunned gaze at your message. Thank you for this opportunity and your flexibility during tough times. To Isabel, Ashley, and Avery's copyediting and design team, your expertise crafted a stunning book. I treasure your guidance.

Charlie Brotherstone, my trusted literary agent, your steady counsel is invaluable. Thank you for being my anchor.

Hannah Che, my Instagram sister, you eagerly became my recipe tester. Your meticulous feedback, advice, and polishing of headnotes and intros enriched this book. Your support is a true gift.

This cookbook traces my path from novice cook to mother, shaped by Food Network and hands-on learning at the Fo Guang Shan temple in Dallas (IBPS). To the Venerables, thank you for letting me volunteer in your kitchen and teaching me to transform simple ingredients into delightful meals. I'm forever thankful.

To my online community, friends near and far, and readers—you're my light. Every recipe you've cooked and story you've shared has made this cookbook possible. Your incredible support has given me the best platform I could have asked for. I've met inspiring friends online who always offer support, even though we haven't met in person. Kim-Julie Hansen of Best of Vegan, your wise advice and endless encouragement mean the world. Seiran, my dearest friend, thank you for being there whenever I need you, whether for a sponsorship contract review or just listening. To my wonderful friends who support me online: Nisha Melvani, Nisha Vora, Michaela Vais, Seonkyoung Longest, Tina Choi, Joanne Molinaro, Zuliya Khawaja, Sara Tercero, Mark Dacascos, Christine Wong, Jon Kung, Jeeca Uy, Joe Yonan, David Yeung, Timothy Pakron, and the whole social media family. Thank you, Food52, *VegNews*, *Thrive Magazine*, The Feedfeed, and *South China Morning Post*, for sharing my recipes effortlessly.

Finally, I'm immensely grateful to all of you—terima kasih, xie xie, doh jeh, gam sia.

INDEX

N

O

P

R

S

U

V

W

X

Y

Z